BLOOD
TRAILS

BLOOD TRAILS

The Combat Diary of a Foot Soldier in Vietnam

Christopher Ronnau

BALLANTINE BOOKS • NEW YORK

A Presidio Press Mass Market Original

Published in the United States by Presidio Press, an imprint of The Random House Publishing Group, a division of Random House, Inc., New York.

PRESIDIO PRESS and colophon are trademarks of Random House, Inc.

ISBN 0-89141-883-0

Printed in the United States of America

Presidio Press website address: www.presidiopress.com

OPM 9 8 7 6 5 4 3 2 1

To my mom and dad, of course. Also, to the gold-star moms and dads of America who had it worse off than any dough-boy, dogface, or grunt could even imagine.

Me, I'm the one,
I'm the one of all the rest won't die.
I'll live through it.
I'll go home.
The band will play.
And I'll be there to hear it.

—RAY BRADBURY, *The Drummer Boy of Shiloh*

Author's Note

My military service in Vietnam is a source of great pride for me. I am very thankful for the diary I kept while in Indochina. It has turned out to be one of my most cherished possessions.

The diary helps me keep my memories of Vietnam based in reality. At every Black Lion reunion I've attended, there seems to be a significant display of faulty-memory syndrome. The decades have corroded all our memories, including mine, to the point that we disagree on so much that if you listened to our conversations you would wonder if we were talking about the same war. Without the written contemporaneous account of my activities in the diary, I am sure that I would no longer remember many of the events of 1967 and would have erroneous memories of others.

Unfortunately, the diary is jammed with numerous derogatory terms for various racial groups as well as some negative comments about gays. Mea culpa. They are the product of my incomplete social development at the time. That's the way eighteen- to twenty-one-year-old infantrymen spoke back then. Fortunately, I have grown and now live beyond those thoughts and comments. I would be mortified if my children ever heard me speak that way. They never have.

The negative comments have not been expurgated from this text because it would not be historically accurate to do so. To anyone who is offended, which is not my intent, please accept my apologies.

Some of the names in this book have been changed.

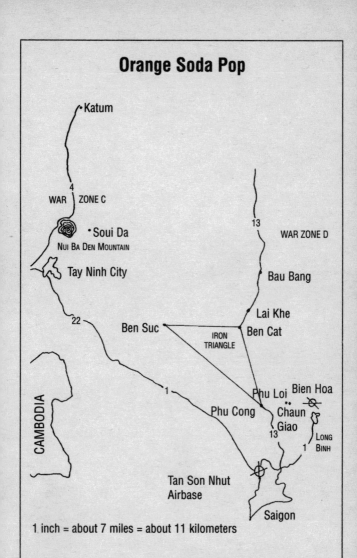

Orange Soda Pop

Katum

4

WAR ZONE C

Soui Da
NUI BA DEN MOUNTAIN

Tay Ninh City

13

WAR ZONE D

Bau Bang

22

Lai Khe

Ben Suc

Ben Cat

IRON
TRIANGLE

CAMBODIA

1

Phu Loi   Bien Hoa

Phu Cong

Chaun
Giao

13

1   LONG
BINH

Tan Son Nhut
Airbase

Saigon

1 inch = about 7 miles = about 11 kilometers

JANUARY

For me, Vietnam was better than a poke in the face with a sharp stick. I got a lot out of it. I grew there. However, not knowing this ahead of time dampened my enthusiasm so that when it came time to go, I didn't, at least not right away. Earlier there had been more eagerness in my effort. I didn't like the giant global monolith that was communism and, like the hawks in our government, I believed in former president Eisenhower's domino theory. If one small country in Southeast Asia fell to the Red Menace, the others would soon follow suit, falling like a row of dominos and then everyone involved would be miserable.

Wanting to do my share, I volunteered for the army. In what can only be described as a monumental attack of nearly terminal stupidity, I enlisted only after being guaranteed an assignment to an infantry unit. My misguided fear was that the few Cs and Ds that I had managed to earn in classes at Long Beach City College might get me a clerical job or some other behind-the-scenes position. That wouldn't do. I wanted to see some action.

In *Gone With the Wind*, a bunch of ignorant and naïve southern boys rode off from Ashley Wilkes's plantation, Twelve Oaks, to join the Confederate States Army when war is declared between the states. As they ride off they are all hollering rebel yells in excitement and anticipation of the glories of combat that will surely soon follow. Like them, I didn't want to miss the war, to let it pass me by. I had joined the infantry so that I would see combat. Such was the state of my adolescent mind. It was not a well thought-out plan.

After four months of basic training and advanced infantry training, the army was beginning to seem more real. My departure date for assignment to a combat unit interfered with my earlier sophomoric brain patterns and made me slightly less enthusiastic about leaving exactly on time. As it turned out, the impending proceedings were temporarily interrupted by my sister. She had acquired student tickets to the Rose Bowl, which was on my departure date, New Year's Day 1967. There we saw Purdue defeat Southern California.

Southern Cal in the Rose Bowl was worth going AWOL for; that couldn't be missed. My thinking was that the army was so desperate for fresh troops that they wouldn't dare lock me up. The worst they could do was send me to Vietnam and that was already happening. When my bus arrived at the Oakland Alameda Naval Air Station no one even mentioned the fact that I was three days late.

There were thousands of GIs stationed there awaiting transportation. For a few days we were housed in giant warehouses with nothing but rows of metal bunks and chairs. It was frightfully boring. Most of the stay was an exercise in the time-honored military tradition of "hurry up and wait."

We did, however, get our immunizations updated while walking a medical gauntlet between two rows of army medics carrying air-powered vaccination guns. They simultaneously blasted us numerous times in both arms as we passed by. When it was over my shot card showed that I was then up to date for typhus, influenza, bubonic plague, smallpox, cholera, typhoid, tetanus, and yellow fever. How could people live in a country with this much sickness? Who would want to?

The vaccination guns made a loud hissing noise when fired and left a visible welt that felt like a jellyfish sting. The experience was slightly unnerving. One guy flinched so wildly that he got one injection in the armpit. We all howled with laughter.

After processing we were sent to Travis Air Force Base outside Oakland, California. So many planes swooped in and out of there in those days that soon, like the dingy gray sea-

gulls that were everywhere, you just didn't notice them anymore. Like most servicemen headed for Vietnam we traveled
by commercial airliner. My flight was a Continental Airlines
seven something seven, complete with stewardesses and a
meal. There were no civilian passengers and there was no
movie. The flight was so boring and so long, more than twenty
hours, that a single movie would not have saved us. That
would have taken at least the entire Cannes Film Festival.

After a number of hours of flying we landed to refuel in
Honolulu, where we were allowed off the plane for forty
minutes to stretch out legs and walk around in a restricted
section of the airport. It was sad to be in paradise without
being allowed to experience it. I didn't see any of the tourist
spots, sample their seafood, or even have a drink. It was pathetic. The highlight of my trip to Hawaii was shooting down
a fly in the urinal of an airport restroom. However, from then
on I could answer in the affirmative if anyone asked me had
I ever been to Hawaii. Just don't ask to see my snapshots of
the trip.

Halfway between Hawaii and Vietnam, the pilot came on
the intercom to give us the cheery news that the local Viet
Cong, in celebration of our arrival, had blown up the runway
at Pleiku, our destination, with mortar fire. Accordingly, our
flight was being temporarily diverted to the Philippine Islands. We were going to Clark Air Force Base near Manila to
wait until the runway was repaired.

As soon as we landed, two sourpuss MPs came on board to
tell us that we could sit on the plane or get off and stand in a
hangar. "There's no smoking," the taller of the two barked
loudly, "and no goddamn wandering off because we don't
want to have to come and look for you." Descending the
metal stairs, it was impossible not to see the sleek, majestic
A-12 Blackbird spy plane parked next to us. About this time,
the taller MP added, almost as an afterthought, "And no picture taking, because that plane doesn't exist, so we don't
want any goddamned photographs of it." This was immediately followed by a chorus of clicking cameras so numerous
that it sounded as if the crickets had come out.

Four hours later, we took off for Tan Son Nhut Airbase. They had not been able to make the Pleiku airstrip service-able for commercial jets in such a short time. We were headed for III Corps in the Saigon area instead of II Corps in the central highlands. This was disappointing. I had hoped to be in the 1st Cavalry and II Corps was their area. The 1st Cavalry got all the glory. They were always on the news and in the newspaper. It was not to be. Just like that, a few VC (Viet Cong) with a mortar tube and nothing better to do on a Friday night had changed our fates and futures forever, in ways we could not even begin to fathom. It was possible that those among us who had been destined to be killed or wounded or see very little combat had all been changed be-cause of this night that we would all soon forget. It was fit-ting to start off with such a whimsical event, a harbinger of the capricious nature of the year to come.

It was almost dawn when we landed in Vietnam. Air that was too wet and too hot met us at the exit, forcing me to hold my breath for a second and wonder if I could actually breathe this atmosphere. This place was going to be about as com-fortable as a steel mill. The people on the ground acted as if it was normal and they were quite used to it. Thoughts of no air-conditioning for a long time, unless General Westmore-land invited me over for dinner, crossed my mind.

At the bottom of the ramp, the stewardess with her shoulder-length blond hair encouraged us on, "Hurry up, boys, hurry off to war." Her comment seemed slightly flip-pant. She was old for a stewardess, maybe thirty, but she was also friendly, cute, and really stacked. She should have been given combat pay for all the antics and comments she put up with during the flight without smacking anyone's face. I al-ready had a crush on her and secretly wished that she was coming with me.

Tan Son Nhut was the busiest airport in the world in 1967, with more flights per day than anywhere else. Activity was visible everywhere, with commercial airlines and military transports hauling in fresh loads of cannon fodder and taking home the old. Sleek air force jets zipped in and out, which was exciting to watch. It was also surprising to see an F-100 Super Saber take off right next to us with a ten-foot cone of fire coming out of its rear that was so close you could have roasted marshmallows as it passed. I thought we had stopped using the F-100 after the Korean War. I had read in a magazine that the war was costing a million dollars an hour. The sight of all those jets and jet fuel flames made me think that maybe that amount was correct. The rest of the airport that wasn't claimed outright by fixed-wing craft was peppered with helicopters. They seemed to behave like butterflies and land wherever they pleased.

From the tarmac we were herded onto faded yellow buses that were dustier than a frontier stagecoach. Our driver sat so motionless, giving his steering wheel such a blank stare, that it appeared as if he had died before our arrival or was bored literally out of his mind. He would not have noticed if the Radio City Rockettes had danced onto his bus. He said nothing. Such was his year in the combat zone. I didn't realize it yet, but over half of the military men involved in the war had behind-the-scenes jobs that would put an insomniac to sleep.

The air inside the bus was ancient. Thick chicken wire fencing over the windows didn't help. In theory, this was to keep locals from throwing anything into the vehicle that might hurt us before we could get signed in as official participants in the hostilities.

Suddenly, a figure wearing black pajamas emerged out of the darkness and raced up the dirt embankment toward me and the bus. The person's head was covered by one of those white cone-shaped hats that I knew all too well from the news on television. The situation alarmed me. Near panic set in. The hair on the back of my neck stood at full attention and my heart raced. Before I could cry out a warning, the attacker reached the tarmac just outside my window. There, I could see that she was carrying a double load of laundry balanced on a pole over her shoulder.

Furtively, I glanced around to see if anyone had noticed my reaction. They hadn't. I tried my best to look tough. It's hard to look tough while sitting on a bus. My first brush with death, an old laundry lady on her way to work nearly had me crapping in my pants. Even if she had tried to bean me with her bundle of laundry the wire mesh over the windows would have saved me. Now it seems silly, but it was unnerving at the time.

A bumpy bus ride delivered us to Long Binh, a massive military complex about fifteen miles northeast of Saigon that was our largest base in Vietnam. We were told that every inch of the road we traveled was secure, that there was no enemy threat in the area. It made me wonder why we were escorted front and rear by jeeps with mounted machine guns.

The first order of business once we became temporary members of the 90th Replacement Battalion at Camp Alpha was, of course, paperwork. There were clothing forms, meal forms, vaccination forms, and change-of-address forms. We were all given a color postcard depicting a burly GI standing with a bayoneted rifle next to a globe of the world and preparing to stamp out a fire that covered Southeast Asia. We were ordered to write our mothers with the encouraging news that we had arrived safely and all was well, as if the plane flight had been the most hazardous part of our tour, and it was all downhill from there.

As soon as the cheerful postcards were collected, we turned our attention to the casualty-reporting forms. Those were the who-do-we-notify-when-you-get-your-balls-blown-off forms.

To my surprise, I was the only one in the group who checked the box indicating that no one was to be informed if I were wounded. In my mind's eye, there were visions of my poor mom receiving a notice saying that her baby had been injured but not indicating the nature or severity of the injury or even where I was recuperating. She, of course, would then call the Pentagon and deal to the point of exasperation with no-name clerks who would say they had never heard of me, or if they had that they weren't authorized to release any information without a release of information form that I had to sign if they could find me. I couldn't put her through such an ordeal.

The sergeant in charge tried to dish me up a plate of grief

over my decision not to panic and notify the entire world the minute I got shot in the butt with a peashooter. "Come on now, you need to put somebody down there," he remonstrated. He couldn't grasp my point of view, which I tried to carefully explain, and scolded me with a warning, "Well if you end up in a coma or dead or something we're going to tell your next of kin whether you like it or not." The sergeant had not made me change my mind but had given me a headache. It was a relief to be finished with this guy and his paperwork palace.

They also took away our American money, and replaced it with paper currency that we called Monopoly money. They were two-by-four-inch multicolor bills that felt like real dollars but were labeled as military payment certificates, or MPC.

All denominations featured the same anonymous female face with short blond hair and pearl earrings striking a pose like Queen Elizabeth on a Canadian dollar. No one recognized her. She was probably just a local Washington, D.C. chick who happened to be screwing someone at the Bureau of Engraving. The twenty-five-cent MPC was an unusually gaudy red, white, and blue piece of work that looked like a ticket to a circus or a rodeo. They didn't seem right but we got used to it. They also took away our American coins. Now we couldn't even lag for pennies or quarters when we were bored.

Besides greenbacks, I had a bunch of American Express traveler's checks. They made me cash those in also. In retrospect, it seemed kind of stupid to take traveler's checks to a war, just the type of goofy thing that an American would do. We had also been given the option of trading in some of our cash for local currency. Their monetary unit was the dong. That's what was printed on their bills, but everyone called them piasters. I never figured that one out. At the time, there were 118 piasters to the dollar.

Most of us took half and half. Our military stores accepted only MPC. Vietnamese merchants wanted piasters. However, most would accept MPC after feeling it carefully, holding it up to the light, and wondering what it would be worth if the U.S. military ever skipped town.

After the paperwork came three positively brutal days, brutal, as in boring with a capital B. We lined up in formation four times a day so that the names of those assigned to various units could be announced. Those people would then depart for their new duty assignments.

Other than that, we just sat and waited. Sitting in a tent for three days of waiting is no picnic. I wouldn't wait that long for the second coming of Christ.

There were a few work details and some guard duty but I couldn't seem to get an assignment to save my life. Three in the morning of my second day in limbo found me outside pacing back and forth in the gravel next to the tent. One of the sergeants was a perceptive fellow who noticed that I didn't appear to be sleeping well and offered me sentry duty, which I gladly accepted. Another guy, named Vincent, and I were each given an M-14 with sixty rounds of ammo apiece and sent to occupy a sandbag bunker at the main gate from 0400 to 0800 hours.

Highway 1, also known as the Street Without Joy, ran right in front of our position only a few feet away. There was an intermittent flow of pedicabs, motorcycles, and small trucks, which zipped by at any speed desired. Between vehicles, all was quiet.

It was really quiet just before 0600 when Vincent went to the mess hall for breakfast and left me alone. That was dangerous. I had no instructions or idea of how to cope with any of the innumerable situations that might arise. I was by myself and the place got creepy in a hurry. The shadows began to move and there were more noises out there than I had noticed before. The selector switch on my rifle went on full automatic before Vincent had buttered his toast.

A little before 0700 hours, a rapidly approaching school bus blew a rear tire and skidded sideways toward my bunker. It kicked up a storm of little stones and pebbles. The driver slowed down only briefly. He then redirected the bus toward the road, stepped on the gas, and disappeared, never knowing how agitated I was or how close I'd come to shooting up his dirty bus.

At 0800 I was relieved of guard duty and returned to the unemployment line. A little finagling got me onto a construction crew that checked out enough shovels and wheelbarrows to build another Boulder Dam. We then marched to the construction site, where we were promptly given the day off because the load of cement that we were going to pour into a foundation had not arrived.

That afternoon I discovered some on-base juke joints the army operated for fun and profit. There was music, beer, and slot machines. I never liked the slots but enjoyed anesthetizing myself with Hamm's beer while watching others lose their money to the one-armed bandits.

A few hours after dark, I was quite pickled. When the mortar shells started falling, I went outside to watch. What a show! It was an awesome display of firepower, with round after round crashing into the base about half a mile away. There were bright flashes and delayed dull roars. It didn't seem like any of them were going to land near me. At this stage of the game, I was still taking my cues from strangers. No one around me made a mad dash to the nearest bomb shelter, with women and children first and all that sort of thing. So neither did I. When it was over I went to bed.

The next day, inside one of the many nondescript Quonset huts, an unseen clerk struggled to cope with the relentless mound of paperwork that slowly grew, like a fungus, on top of his old wooden desk. Between sips of instant coffee and drags on a Marlboro, he divided the big pile into several smaller piles and placed these into several metal trays. Voilà! I was now in the 1st Infantry Division.

It was time to get on any of the trucks that were loading up for a convoy down Route 1 to division headquarters at Di An (pronounced zee-on). The trip was brisk, about 50 mph, with lots of erratic jerking to dodge slower-moving oxcarts and bicycles on both sides of the road. No such courtesy was extended to the three-wheeled pedicabs that seemed to be driven exclusively by morons with a death wish. They darted in and out of the caravans, between the trucks, passing on the right and left, oblivious as to what their fate would be if they miscalculated in the slightest. Our driver didn't even tap his brakes lightly when they came up on one side, crossed in front of us, then passed the truck ahead of us on the other side. It was crazy.

The trip also gave us a protracted view of povertyville. That's what you get when thousands of farm families are relocated to neo-urban enclaves without farmland or employment. There were rows of beat-up cinder-block houses without doors. Pigeons perched in windows without glass. Unattended children played perilously close to the traffic zooming by. Laundry flapped in the breeze over too much domestic animal shit, which was everywhere. The yards were small, barren, and unattended without any flowers to be seen. You can't eat a flower. Pigs and chickens were everywhere. There were more dogs in some yards than there were children and often the dogs were cleaner. It appeared as if what we were fighting for was a giant Oriental Tijuana.

We entered Di An driving past a sign that proudly proclaimed the division's motto. No Mission Too Difficult. No Sacrifice Too Great. Duty First. Soon, we were once again subjected to heavy doses of waiting, only there we often did it in line as if something was about to happen. By sundown I was in what we all hoped would be the last line of the day when something did occur.

A thin wisp of a man with a corporal's stripes and a clipboard of official-looking papers walked up and spoke with the noncom in charge. The noncom slowly shook his head and gave the corporal a grim look, as if to say that this wasn't right. The corporal then stepped to the front of the line, tried to stand taller than he actually was, and shouted, "Are there any 91-Bravos here?" Collectively we froze. No one moved or spoke. You could have heard a bullet drop. "Are any of you guys medics?" he shouted. Again, no one answered. "One, two, three, four," he said as he walked down the line, pointing his finger in the faces of the first nine guys. "Good, you guys are now medics," he announced. Then he explained that some unit had gotten the shit kicked out of it and lost a lot of their medics. They had to have replacements, now. The nine guys—who were now cursing, swearing, and protesting to the heavens—were ordered onto a nearby truck.

"Bullshit," stammered one of the nine, "I ain't no god-damned medic," but he got on the truck anyway. I had been number twelve in line and was decidedly glad about that.

This was the most wild and reckless action the army had taken in my presence, ever. I was incredulous. It would have been less of a shock if the corporal had pinned stars on my epaulets and announced that I was a general. It was hard to imagine getting shot in the throat and then receiving your care from a medic who was really trained as a jeep mechanic. This had to be some kind of prank. It wasn't. It was the army way. It makes truck drivers into cooks and cooks into truck drivers and then looks perplexed when the food is always late and tastes bad when it gets there.

Another GI, without a clipboard, approached and spoke with the noncom in charge. He then turned and asked, "Is there a Private Ronnau here?" Fortunately, this guy turned out to be Bob Reeves, one of my best friends from high school. He was a coder-decoder with the 121st Signal Battalion and had been in country for several months. It was a relief to find out it was Bob. When he had called my name, I was afraid they were going to tell me that I was now a helicopter pilot or a tank commander. Bob laughed when I told him the story of the medics but didn't seem too surprised.

Bob had the best setup that I had seen so far. He lived in a forty-man tent with five other GIs. They had lights, electricity, plenty of mosquito netting, and a small refrigerator. They even had a pet dog, named Travis.

Bob was a ladies' man in high school, tall and handsome with brown hair and eyes. He always had a girl. In Vietnam it was no different. With a borrowed jeep, he regularly visited a nearby village where he was dating the third daughter of a local peasant woman. Apparently he couldn't pronounce her name and she grew weary of trying to teach him. Anyway, they compromised and he just called her Tres. Bob was banging number three.

He had recently received a care package of cookies and things from my mom, for which he seemed very grateful. Like most GIs, he was lonely there and missed being back in the world.

"I'd rather get mail than eat," he told me.

We toured Bob's part of the camp on foot just so I could see it. On the way back to his tent, we passed a GI walking in the opposite direction. After a few steps Bob started whispering. He told me that the guy that had just passed us was the one who had the incurable clap. He had been quarantined and wasn't being allowed to go home because of it, to keep it from being spread around the United States. It was called black gonorrhea.

I was awestruck and looked back over my shoulder to sneak a glimpse. This guy was a legend. Every VD lecture in the States made reference to his incurable clap and the perils of not using rubbers. Seeing him was like seeing Casper the ghost and discovering that he was real.

We had also been told that the secretions leaking out of this guy's pecker weren't the standard purulent yellow normally associated with gonorrhea. Rather, they were thick and dark black like used motor oil. Also, for this guy taking a leak felt like trying to piss out ground-up razor blades. The hoped-for lesson had been, let the screwer beware, use a condom or else. If you wanted to ride bareback you did so at your own risk.

That night we drank beer and laughed until it was very late. It was more fun than anything else I had done so far in Vietnam.

The next day, eight of us were assigned to ride shotgun on a convoy of trucks from Di An to Ben Hoa and back. First, we were sent to an armory for weapons. The clerk gave us each an M-14. They were heavy blunderbusses and not very sophisticated compared to the M-16s we were expecting now that we were actually members of the division.

The clerk was a jocular southern fellow who insisted on

guessing where each of us came from before handing over the rifles. It was his hobby. He pegged me as being a New Englander because I didn't have a hint of a tan. It was narrowed down to Vermont because I was tall. Go figure. All of his other guesses were also wrong. He said he was from Jawja, as he pronounced it, and gave me a blank stare when I asked if that was anywhere near Atlanta.

We each got one empty clip but no bullets. The clip would make it look like the weapons were fully loaded, but we weren't to be issued any live ammo. Those were his instructions.

Behind the counter, in the center of the floor was a disheveled mound of explosives about four feet high. It contained mines, grenades, mortars, and even an antitank rocket sticking out of the top of the pile like a giant candle on a birthday cake. The whole mess seemed out of place amid the orderly rows of rifles and neatly stacked boxes of cartridges. The clerk told us that this was contraband that had been taken away from GIs who were processing out at Di An to go back to the world. God only knows what they were going to do with this stuff back on the streets of America. I doubted that they knew or had even given it much rational thought.

Half an hour after we picked up the rifles, our convoy headed out toward Bien Hoa. Riding through the countryside was a welcome change of pace. Our deuce-and-a-half trucks were empty except for two of us in the back of each one. We really didn't need ammo to not guard the cargo that we didn't really have. The situation was starting to make sense.

Most of the trip was on dirt roads through flat countryside. There weren't many structures until we reached the outskirts of Saigon. There we passed a sugarcane refinery that made the road smell like a dead horse for about a mile. The sight of a Chase Manhattan Bank made me nostalgic for a moment. The sight of two ARVN (Army of Republic of Vietnam) soldiers holding hands as they walked down the street killed the nostalgia and made me stare like a shocked child. The other shotgun rider unleashed a torrent of queer this and faggot that remarks that made us laugh out loud. I can't remember his exact remarks—they were the usual stuff and seemed quite funny. The driver laughed and said that guys sometimes held hands over here or sometimes walked along with their arms around each other even if they weren't queers. It made me wonder if VC or North Vietnamese soldiers held hands. Maybe they did, but somehow I couldn't picture it.

At Bien Hoa, the lead driver stopped his truck in front of an army Quonset hut and went inside carrying a clipboard. Soon he reemerged on the front steps with a lieutenant. They spoke for a few moments and leafed through the clipboard papers. The driver then half skipped back to his truck while holding his right index finger aloft and swirling it in a circular motion as a signal to us to turn our vehicle around. We were leaving. He gunned his engine and we followed him back to Di An. Our mission, whatever it was, was over.

That evening, as usual, I went over to see Bob and have a cold beer. Unlike the other evenings, there was an organized activity available. The Red Cross was going to show a movie on a big outdoor screen. We hauled our beer to the viewing area and drank our way through *Nevada Smith*, starring Steve McQueen.

The only other thing I did at Di An was to periodically stand in the dirt courtyard in front of our tents where several times a day a sergeant with a booming voice would read off a list of who was going to which company and battalion within the division. If your name was read, you were sent to join your new unit.

The center of the courtyard was marked by a two-foot-square cement pillar firmly embedded in the dirt. At each list reading, one lucky GI used it as a stool and was able to sit down during the proceedings. Invariably, the GI would eventually find the metal plaque that was attached to one side of the pillar. It was in memory of Private James Ray Griffey from Harvey, Illinois, who was shot dead in January 1966 on that very spot by a sniper. Griffey was just nineteen at the time, had only been in Vietnam a few days, and had not even been assigned to a permanent unit. Without fail, when the plaque was discovered, the squatter would stand up and move away slowly, staring at the pillar. I'd done it myself the first day. It didn't seem right to plant your cheeks on someone else's memorial. Further, it gave me the willies to sit where I knew a guy had been nailed.

Private Griffey must have been one of America's earliest fatalities, killed at a time when it was practical to put up memorials honoring the fallen. Later on, if you erected a metal plaque for every guy put in a body bag and sent home to a marble orchard, the southern half of Vietnam would look like it was wrapped in tinfoil.

Eventually I was told that my unit was to be C Company in the 2/28 Battalion, also known as the Black Lions. Their permanent base camp was at Lai Khe on Highway 13, just north of Saigon in the III Corps area.

The trip from Di An to Lai Khe was fun. About two dozen of us piled inside the back of a twin-engine, propeller-driven, Caribou cargo plane. There were no seats. We sat on the floor and hung on for dear life so that we didn't get vibrated right out the back. The crew hadn't closed the rear cargo doors. They were wide open. I was sure that this violated some FAA regulation and jokingly mentioned it to an older guy who appeared to be the crew chief.

"Kid, this is Vietnam, there aren't any rules," was his response. Then he chuckled a bit. Soon we got used to the doors being open and enjoyed the view, which was spectacular. The visibility was so good that we could see for what seemed like a hundred miles. Verdant jungle spread out below us as far as the eye could see. Occasionally the land below was dissected by curling rivers. I assumed that the largest one was the Saigon. Not infrequently we saw vast tracks of farmland and rice paddies that had been carved into numerous squares and rectangles like farms in the United States. In the distance a fire sent a column of coal-black smoke several hundred feet in the air. As it turned out, almost every time that I would ride in a helicopter or an airplane with a view smoke was on the horizon. My guess was that this was normal. In a war zone something was probably always on fire somewhere.

The first order of business at Lai Khe was five days of combat indoctrination school, which everyone called jungle school. It was mandatory for those of us with an MOS (military occupational specialty) that might involve combat. My MOS was 11-Bravo, which meant infantry. Most of us at the school were infantry. There were other MOS designations, each consisting of a number and a letter. The armored cavalry were 11-Echo, the military police were 66-Alpha, and some of the medics were 92-Bravo. A bunch of others I didn't recognize. That's how you knew what a guy did in Vietnam, by asking what his MOS was.

A sign over the gate to the jungle school proclaimed

This training will provide the enemy soldier with a maximum opportunity to give his life for his country

On the dirt path up to the school I found Herbert Beck, a friend from infantry training at Fort Gordon, Georgia. He was going to Alpha Company. Herb didn't have much of a military appearance. He was a little overweight, with pronounced baby-fat jowls, and could never manage to stand up straight and tall no matter how much starch was ironed into his fatigues.

We greeted each other happily, as familiar faces did in this place. For a few moments we traded disparaging remarks about the heat, the mosquitoes, and the country in general. Soon we got down to the nitty-gritty and began reassuring each other that we would both almost certainly make it home without even minor injuries. Both of us were sure that this was almost an obvious fact.

Once we were seated on the rows of wooden benches, instruction got under way almost immediately. Several dozen of us neophytes watched various captured Russian and Chinese weapons being assembled and disassembled. We saw mines and booby traps. There were lots of commonsense do's and don'ts. There was much hyperbole from the instructors about existing in the III Corps area along with personal accounts of harrowing experiences, many of which seemed apocryphal at the time.

Sergeant Fuentes was an affable fellow but sometimes hard to understand. My high school Spanish was marginal at best. He was, however, eminently more believable then Sergeant LaGuardia, whom we called Sergeant Lasagna. Lasagna was a swarthy man, gave all of his talks shirtless and had *sweet* and *sour* tattooed over his nipples. Somehow I couldn't picture him ever lecturing at Harvard or even Long Beach State.

That same day, we were all issued a ton of gear including a backpack, canteens, poncho, ammo pouches, and a helmet, but no live ammo or explosives. After signing on the dotted line, I was given my very own M-16 and told to memorize the serial number, 179619. It rhymed a little, which was good, but lacked other special significance. I would have liked one that was similar to my phone number or street address back home. That would have been a really nice psychological boost because, despite having already bumped into a couple of stateside friends, I was more than a smidgen homesick.

At night, we slept on cots in a large forty-man tent. It wasn't fancy but was comfortable enough. Although the formal instruction for the day was over, we got a couple of practical lessons on life in the Nam that first night. About midnight, a battery of 155-mm howitzers, not far from the tent, suddenly opened up. With all six of the cannons firing at once, the roar was incredibly loud. The collective muzzle flash was so bright that it came right through the canvas tent and lit up the area well enough for us to read a book. The forty of us sat up in unison, jerking our heads in all directions to see if the big attack had started. By the second or third night, few of us even woke up for the barrages anymore. Lesson number one, if you wanted your Z's in the combat zone you had to adapt. This place wouldn't be nap time with mommy.

At dawn our education continued when we discovered that two pistols and a knife were missing from our tent. Lesson number two, some low-life GIs would steal a cold turd if it wasn't nailed down. I needed to watch my stuff and guard my belongings.

Lai Khe had at one time been a viable, French-operated rubber tree plantation and still contained many acres of neatly rowed trees. They were thin, without branches on the trunk, but with a rich plumage of wide dark-green leaves at the top that fanned out like a giant umbrella. The leaf edges of one reached out and touched the next, forming a giant canopy about forty to fifty feet off the ground. This blocked out much of the sunlight and left huge cool spaces below without much ground-level vegetation. Often breezes trapped by the canopy created a refreshing wind-tunnel effect down at ground level.

Dozens of old French colonial homes stood adjacent to the abandoned rubber trees. They were inhabited mostly by Vietnamese and were part of the Lai Khe village. The other part of the village consisted of numerous shanty-type dwellings made out of sheet metal, plywood, rubber tree leaves, corrugated iron, and other odds and ends. All around the village were varying amounts of Cyclone fencing and barbed wire. A nighttime curfew was in effect for the villagers. By the time the sun went down, they had to be back inside their village and stay there until dawn.

The village was encircled on all sides by a thick layer of 1st Division units. There was an airport with helicopter squadrons as well as an ammo dump. The base medical aid station, PX (Post Exchange), and administration HQ were closer to the center of the camp with armored units, motor pool, and artillery batteries a little farther out. Infantry companies formed the most external layer, the perimeter. A thin ring of foxholes and bunkers rimmed the periphery for 360 degrees, separating the base on the inside from no-man's-land on the outside. The no-man's-land on the eastern and southern parts of the perimeter consisted of dense jungle that grew to within a few meters of the bunkers on the picket line. The area just outside the bunkers was heavily laced in some areas with barbed wire, trip flares, and mines. The commotion of monkeys cavorting there made the sentries nervous and trigger-happy. Trip flares sent the monkeys off screaming and scurrying. Mines sent them to the big zoo in the sky.

No-man's-land on the northern and western parts of the perimeter was less anxiety inducing. It sloped gently down and away from the bunkers about a hundred meters to the Muy Thinh River, which skirted the camp on that side. The river was as narrow as five meters in some places and as wide as twenty-five meters in only a few spots. As such it wouldn't have been much of a military obstacle in preventing a ground assault. However, there was not much vegetation between it down below and our bunker line higher up. We didn't need flares or mines. The area was one vast, open shooting gallery. The jungle on the other side of the river was as thick as a pile of cinder blocks.

A patch of no-man's-land at the western edge of the base, known as the shooting range, was used for gunnery practice by the jungle school. We spent most of one day there pummeling this beaten-up wooden area with antitank rockets and grenades. We splintered trees and snapped vines with long bursts of .50-caliber fire. Tracer bullets started small fires here and there. A good time was had by all. Just when I thought my ears were going to fall off, Lasagna signaled for us to cease fire and take a break. Of course, none of us had been smart enough to bring earplugs. We didn't think much about going deaf.

POP, POP, POP! AK-47 shots were coming back at us from the shooting range and raising little clouds of dust as they thudded into the ground around our feet. Everyone scattered. This was one hell of a welcome wagon to the neighborhood. Being shot at was a first for me.

"Sniper, sniper, sniper," Fuentes yelled as he dove behind a bunker. He then shouted orders to everyone, speaking as fast as was humanly possible. Unfortunately, he was speaking Spanish and sounded like Ricky Ricardo having a temper tantrum on *I Love Lucy*. By now we were all prone in the dirt, waiting to see how our instructors would handle this impromptu lesson. We still had a vision of ourselves as third-party observers rather than participants in the conflict and so we just lay there as if we were watching a war movie on television.

Shooting Range Charlie was well known in the area. He frequently popped up from his hiding place just after one of the firing groups had finished practicing and tried to pick off somebody. A few months earlier he had fired from a position a little farther east and killed a guy from C Company during mail call near the company street. From the way the event was described to me, the distance from the sniper to the victim was about three hundred meters. My hat was off to the sniper, he was either a very good shot or a very lucky shot. I couldn't hit anything smaller than a dump truck from that distance. It would have been nice if somebody could have gone out and nailed him, but there was so much unexploded ordnance out there that only a lunatic would send out a foot patrol after him. We did, however, make an attempt to return the fire.

Today's efforts were led by Lasagna, who, after calming down Fuentes, fired off an M-60. Another teacher from the jungle school used an M-16. Soon a jeep arrived with an M-60 on a mount and the longest belt of machine-gun bullets that I had ever seen. It lay on the floor of the jeep in a pile the size of a five-gallon bucket. He used it all. My contribution to our national defense that day consisted of firing a few shots with my Kodak Instamatic camera. Before leaving California, I had used some of the green and brown colors from my model airplane paint kit to camouflage the camera. I got some good pictures of the episode.

The next day we practiced setting up and exploding claymore mines. At one point, Sergeant Wilson, two other GIs, and myself were behind a small mound connecting a detonator to a wire that went out forty feet or so to a claymore. Wilson sort of nodded when I asked if he wanted me to blow it yet, so I blew it.

"You fucking idiot! I didn't tell you to do that!" he screamed in my face. He bellowed that the other guys were still out there setting it up and that I had probably killed them. Then he raced off.

That moment seemed to last forever. Despair engulfed me. My heart sank, my body sank. Blackness surrounded me. I couldn't move to look over the mound. Light-years passed as I sat there until Wilson and the others returned. They had left the mine before the detonation and no one was injured. I wanted to throw up. From the start I had been concerned about the possibility of accidentally killing or injuring some of our own troops. With so many kids carrying so many weapons, it was bound to happen to someone. I didn't want it to be me and was more worried about hurting someone with friendly fire than I was about getting nailed myself by enemy fire. Why, I don't know.

Later in the day, once again, we got shot at by Shooting Range Charlie. It was nearly time to go, so basically we just left. For the sake of appearances we made a cursory attempt to fire a few rounds in his direction before leaving. It was pure show.

Back in the States, college professors agonized over failing grades. It might mean the loss of a student draft deferment and land that student in some far-off jungle, perhaps to die. At this school the opposite was true. Everyone was passed so that they could go into the jungle, perhaps to die. Nobody failed, not even me with my stupid, premature claymore detonation incident. The graduation ceremony was quite brief, in fact, only a handshake. We didn't even get a certificate of any type. One noncom who happened to be hanging around shook our hands and wished us success as we left. I'm not completely sure which one it was, probably Fuentes, but I'm certain that it wasn't Wilson. Most of the other instructors were already back in their tents drinking beer when we walked off.

Charlie Company was toward the northwestern part of the perimeter, close to the shooting gallery, about the distance of a city block from the school. During the walk over to my new company's area, a Huey helicopter gunship appeared on my left, out over the jungle. When first spotted, it was at an altitude of about two hundred feet. Rushing toward the Lai Khe airstrip, it was down to about one hundred feet as it passed over me. Heavy smoke trailed out behind it and little flames at the base of the main rotor shaft licked upward. The starboard side windows had been shot out. The copilot stared right at me as they went by but didn't move a muscle in his face or change his expression in any way. The chopper disappeared from sight behind the tall trees of the Michelin plantation. There was no loud crash or great fireball, which probably indicated a safe landing and happy ending to the flight.

At the company headquarters there was surprisingly little paperwork. A clerk put a check by my name, then told me to pick up my gear in the building next door. He pointed it out for me. After that I was supposed to report to Staff Sergeant Sharp. My next stop was the armory, a cinder-block structure with an iron door, a concrete floor, and no windows. Inside was a long counter. Moving down it, the clerk passed me a bayonet, a claymore mine, dozens of boxes of M-16 bullets, and an equal number of magazines. We were told that each rifleman had to carry at least three hundred rounds of ammunition. Moving down the counter was like the mess hall except that instead of food to keep you alive you were given things you could use to kill people.

My last stop was the grenade section. The clerk told me to pick what I wanted. I had to carry at least four, one of which had to be a smoke grenade. It could be any color available except red. The other three could be anything I wanted. He pointed with pride to a tastefully arranged rack that displayed numerous types of grenades, among which were white phosphorous, tear gas, smoke, thermite, World War II–era pineapples, and the newer avant-garde Mark 26 fragmentation grenades. The new frag grenade was smooth on the outside and looked like what it was called, an egg. Instead of the big square chunky pieces of shrapnel the pineapple had, it contained a coiled serrated wire that broke into shards when it went off. In theory it was more deadly. The armory experience was like a shopping trip at Bloomingdale's, only cheaper. I chose a smoke because I had to, a pair of pineapples so that I would look like John Wayne in *Sands of Iwo Jima,* and a tear gas because I thought it was cool. Only the police had those. Shortly after leaving the armory I was given two more pineapples as a gift from one of the guys in the platoon. He told me that you were considered to be traveling light if you didn't carry, besides the smoke grenade, at least four frag-type grenades, either pineapples or eggs.

Now, to my way of thinking, when the people around you are passing out hand grenades either you have a really shitty job or you're in a really bad neighborhood. For me it was both. The reality of this place and the not-so-fun times ahead were at some point going to have to sink in, but they hadn't yet. For me it was all still just a big camping trip.

Sergeant Al Sharp, who would be my immediate superior in the Nam, met me in the company area. He ran 3rd Squad of the 1st Platoon, C Company, 2nd Battalion, 28th Regiment, 3rd Brigade, 1st Infantry Division, my permanent group. Sharp was from one of the Appalachian Mountain states or somewhere else in the South. He came across as laid-back and laconic, rarely initiated nonessential conversations, but was friendly and polite when you spoke to him. His only distinguishing features were a small face, a frequent trace of a smile, and a distinct southern drawl. He was a career military man, and I'm not sure that he made it out of high school, but he had a PhD in common sense. The squad liked him because he didn't play favorites. He dispensed unsavory tasks like sentry duty and shit burning in equal doses to all. Sentry duty was self-explanatory. Shit burning wasn't, but I was afraid to ask. Later on I'd get a firsthand lesson on the subject.

Sergeant First Class Fairman was the platoon leader. Sharp pointed him out to me as he stood over by the company HQ about fifty feet away. He was slightly short with a mildly ruddy complexion, didn't smile much, and seemed kind of gruff to me. My guess was that he was twice my age and maybe the oldest soldier in the company.

There was no lieutenant assigned to the 1st Platoon because there weren't enough of them to go around at the moment, and there sure didn't seem to be any hurry to find one

to fill the position. Fairman was viewed by the CO and everyone else as being able to run his own platoon without need-
ing an officer. This view never changed much and most of
my tour of duty in 1st Platoon was spent with no assigned officer. Fairman had been in the Korean War and had fought on
Pork Chop Hill. His first name was Mancil, and you can believe me that I didn't make any comments about it. I'd rather
carry the heaviest guy in the company piggyback through a
minefield than make fun of Fairman's name and wait around
to see what happened. I would have ended up with my ass in
a sling.

Overhearing our conversation, Fairman looked up and
stared at me hard for a few seconds without speaking or even
nodding his head. It appeared to me that he didn't really care
much about knowing who I was, but did want to memorize
my face so that he would be able to identify my body in case
he was ever asked to do so. That was probably because he
knew that if he couldn't identify the body there was going to
be a hell of a lot of paperwork, and he didn't want that.

A row of rectangular barracks lined the company street. Each
structure housed two squads, about twenty men, and was
made of old ammo boxes on a flat cement slab. The floor was
wood, as were the walls up to a height of about four feet.
From there to the sheet-metal roof, which was held up by a
series of two-by-fours, there were only screens. The screens
fended off the barbarian hordes of insects that visited us
every night. As such, the screens were treated by the men
like fine Rembrandt paintings. They were not to be bumped
into, leaned upon, or disturbed in any way. The sheet-metal
roof above would help keep us dry many times and as such
had to be appreciated immensely, even if being under it during a good rainstorm sounded like sleeping next to a snare
drum being played with enthusiasm by an intoxicated teenager.

Each man had a cot with metal springs and a footlocker.
There was no other furniture, no electricity, no running water,
and no common space except the center aisle. A couple of

the guys had a dirty mattress about three inches thick on
their cots. I never found out where they got them. The rest of
us just slept on bare springs, which was slightly better than
the floor. The accommodations, then, could be described as
spartan at best. As luck would have it, I got a bunk at the very
end of the hootch. This was a wonderful break, which in-
stilled an ever-so-slightly increased level of privacy to my
existence there. It meant having a snoring, farting GI on only
one side of my bunk instead of a performance in stereo. I decided against asking what happened to the guy that owned
the bunk before me.

My new domicile was at the end of the row farthest from
company headquarters and the base perimeter. It was built
to look just like all the other barracks. The army thrives on
uniformity. However, it was distinguished by a large wooden
propeller bolted over the front door. This souvenir came from
a trip into Injun country that the squad made to rescue the
crew of a Cessna spotter plane, the type that was sometimes
referred to as a Birddog. It had been either shot down or
brought down by mechanical failure not far from the base
with the crew escaping unscathed. The plane was irreparable
and had to be torched after the prop was removed as a trophy
of sorts.

My reception by members of the squad was more polite
than enthusiastic. Introductions produced quiet nods and an
occasional tepid handshake as if I was being welcomed to
some unsavory place like hell or a prison. Lopez the RTO
(radio telephone operator) summed it up best by saying,
"We're glad to have you with us but sorry to see you here."

I was introduced to Jerry Height and Stanley Gilbert, the
machine gunner and assistant gunner, respectively. Height,
always openly respectful of everyone, stood up as we approached his bunk. After wiping a drop of saliva from his
lower lip, he dried his hand on his hip pocket and then held it
out for me to shake. A broad grin creased his face. He was,
though, something of a nonentity, doing his job from day to
day without drawing much notice. No one seemed to really
like or dislike him, he was simply there. He smiled and

grinned a lot and always managed to have a little patch of stubble somewhere on his chin that he had missed while shaving.

Having already served nine or ten months in the country, he was closer to going home in one piece than any man in the platoon. The previous gunner, Jim Jolly, had gone home a few weeks earlier resembling a dartboard after the VC blew a claymore on the gun crew during Operation Attleboro. Height then inherited the job of machine gunner.

Gilbert was new. A well-fed, almost muscular kid from Dexter, Minnesota, with light-brown, wheat-colored hair, he grew up on a farm that had been owned by his family for generations. At twenty-one, he was a year older than I but had only been in Vietnam for a week longer than I had. On arrival he became the assistant gunner. He was polite but taciturn and didn't like to talk about himself a lot. It was like pulling teeth to get him to tell me about his family farm. In fact, he was so quiet and reserved that not many of our conversations blossomed beyond the necessary. Accordingly, we never became close. Certainly not anywhere near as close as two guys on the same machine-gun crew sharing the same foxhole in an actual shooting war should have become. It was unfortunate.

His family sold a lot of ingredients for powdered eggs and powdered milk to the government. I liked to needle him about selling that shit we had to eat in the mess hall. He didn't like it and tried to ignore me. Poor Gilbert, his assignment overseas meant that he had been doomed to a year of squinting. The military had given him a new pair of army glasses and frames just before he came to Vietnam. Unfortunately, the prescription was slightly off-kilter but he couldn't get it corrected before going overseas. It seems that it was Christmastime in the States just before he left and the base opticians were on holiday leave. The glasses were, however, free of charge. Gilbert's squinting was exaggerated and could be unnerving to those who didn't know him. The first time he looked at me, his face contorted so that it appeared as if he was either going to have a seizure or attack me.

After the introductions, I set up house in my footlocker, then found a couple of loose nails that I pounded into the wall to serve as a rifle rack. It was curious to me that no one else had done this. Rifles were either leaned against something or put on the floor. It was odd.

The place was stark. There were no pictures or photos from home anywhere. A few guys had DEROS calendars pinned up. Everyone knew his DEROS date. The word stood for something like date eligible to return from overseas. It was exactly one year from the day you arrived in the Nam. The calendars were mimeograph drawings of nude, well-built females with their bodies divided into 365 numbered spaces. Each day you filled in a space with a pen or a colored pencil. Most of the calendars had the nipples as days three and two left to go. I don't need to say where number one was.

Later I went outside to smoke. The last of my Winstons from home were long gone and I was reduced to smoking whatever was left for sale at the PX. Filtered cigarettes sold out fast so I was blowing Lucky Strikes. Yesterday's Camels had been like smoking a piece of tree bark, but smoke them I did.

Wandering around outside, I came upon a large tent about fifty meters south of our hootch. Inside all the bunks were empty except one. It was occupied by a conversation-starved guy from New York with a thick Brooklyn accent. His arms and hands were bandaged. He stood to greet me, groaning as he rose, and explained that his platoon, the mortar platoon, was off doing something but he was being allowed to stay behind because his wounds were still painful. He had recently received multiple superficial shrapnel injuries in a mortar attack. He showed me Polaroids from the emergency room and pointed out the red blood on the bandages. Now the blood looked like dry brown dirt. There were stray mortar rounds lying on the floor by his bunk. Sensing from my expression that I was a FNG (Fucking New Guy) and not used to such a sight, he kicked one with his boot sending it skidding across the floor where it crashed into a footlocker with a thud.

"See, they won't go off," he laughed.

Next he showed me his Purple Heart certificate. Two more of these and he was exempt from going out in the field. "It's a rule," he explained, "three Purple Hearts and you don't have to go out in the jungle anymore, you get permanent rear echelon duty. If you're lucky, you'll get some wounds like mine."

He seemed so cheery about the whole process that I was beginning to suspect some type of unseen head injury, but eventually decided that's just the way he was. It was getting dark so I left.

As usual, the next day we arose at 0530. The spring bed had been tolerably comfortable and I was thankful that my fears about getting a punctured lung or some other injury had been unfounded. Charlie Company was on stand down. Operation Cedar Falls was still progressing in the Iron Triangle area so it was necessary to have some forces behind the scenes in ready reserve. If any of our units got into hot shit, as they called it, we would be their emergency assistance. The 11th Armored Cavalry Regiment and the 173rd Airborne Brigade were under the operational control of the Big Red One for this mission so we had to be ready to help them out if necessary. Most of the men would lounge around all day while we waited for any emergency calls for help. A few squads would have guard duty on the perimeter. One lucky squad, mine, would go on patrol that morning just outside the camp. This was a routine practice to keep the VC from setting up anything near our base.

I was eager to go. It would be interesting to see the jungle up close, plus a real patrol under my belt would help me fit in and feel more like one of the guys. It would make it easier for me to believe that I actually belonged there. In addition to my own gear, I was carrying two 100-round belts of machine-gun ammo, one slung over each shoulder, which created a brass X on my chest. It helped me feel tough, like a real soldier, and I wished that my folks or Bob Reeves or somebody I knew was there to see me. I didn't mention this, of course, but tried to stand up straight while acting nonchalant so everyone could see that this was nothing new for me.

On the way to the patrol we stopped at the mess hall which was also made out of used, wooden ammunition boxes. A kid named Dan Huish told me to park my rifle outside in a long wooden gun rack with slots for nearly a hundred rifles. Most of the slots were empty because the 3rd Squad was the only armed group at the moment. The others who weren't slated for patrol were allowed the luxury of not lugging their weapons to breakfast, or if desired not lugging themselves to breakfast.

Outside it was dark and chilly. A light dew settled over everything, creating a layer of moisture that would disappear within moments of the sun's arrival. Inside the air was steamy. Naked lightbulbs hanging from the ceiling added to the heat and harshness of the place. Huish told me, without being queried, where to get a tray and where to get in line. Huish was from Utah but he wasn't a Mormon. If he was he would almost certainly have been one of those so-called Jack Mormons, the type that follow only about half of the rules at best. Most of the time he was in a good mood, seemed glibber than the others, didn't mind being the center of attention, liked to stir things up, and seemed to believe that FNGs like me needed some verbal direction. He was right.

At least Huish was reasonably cordial about the situation and didn't try to make me feel unwelcome, like a leper or Typhoid Mary. Some guys reacted to the FNGs with utter disdain. FNGs were looked down on because they did dumb things and got themselves killed. They were also feared because they sometimes got others killed in the process. Their propensity for self-inflicted carnage was born of ignorance and inexperience. In jungle school we had been told that more than half of our casualties were suffered by guys who had been in Vietnam for three months or less. In the weeks to come, I would be regaled over and over again with stories of unintentional FNG suicides, each more stupid than the previous one. The tales were, I suppose, meant to be instructional.

The most memorable of the FNG stories, which had occurred recently, was that of a new staff sergeant in C Company, the ill-fated Sergeant Morgan, who had only been in country about ten days. He was made a squad leader in the 1st Platoon. As he led a patrol across the river because of his rank, not his experience, they encountered a complex booby trap of two grenades hung in a tree at different heights. Risky or dangerous booby traps were blown up in place with explosives rather than being dismantled. This one was going to be destroyed by firing a claymore mine at it. Seconds before he set off the claymore, the upright sergeant was yelled at and warned by several different grunts that he needed to get down, get prone, and hide behind something. He was warned that even though the claymore was aimed away from him, parts of it could still sail back in his direction.

Ignoring their advice, Morgan detonated the claymore while still standing. A piece of the outer plastic cover of the mine blew back and struck him in the throat. It severed his carotid artery or some other large blood pumper and the poor sergeant bled to death before he could be carried back across the river. He was married and had children. The story was sad.

Behind the mess hall counter a company cook, Specialist Four Jones, was working hard and sweating furiously. Small rivulets of moisture crept down his face, glistened momentarily in the light, then dived off his chin. Several rebellious drops made it to the grill and sizzled to death. Some landed perilously close to the piles of scrambled eggs and fried potatoes being prepared.

Jones, the most flamboyant of the company cooks, was quite a character. He was always sweaty even when it was cool. Some thought that he sweated in the shower. His white T-shirt was like a running menu. One could look at the outermost layer of spots and see what had been served at the previous meal. He fretted and stewed about his contribution to the war effort, trying his damnedest to keep the company well fed. Sometimes while cooking he packed a .45 on his waist, just in case. I couldn't imagine the VC attacking the chow hall, but if they did he was ready for them. Nobody was going to fuck with his waffle irons. My fear was that he would stand too close to the gas stove, heat up his pistol, and end up blowing off one of his feet.

Everyone liked Jones and appreciated his efforts. Accordingly, despite the fact that this was the army and bitching was a birthright protected by the Constitution, there wasn't much grumbling about the cuisine within earshot of Jones. Besides, common sense dictated that when subjected to institution food, be it in boarding school, prison, or the military, you don't want to piss off the cook. Do that and you'll end up with chow lousier than the slop being served to our POWs at the Hanoi Hilton.

The best thing about the mess hall was that there wasn't any KP (kitchen patrol) duty for us grunts. Local Vietnamese were hired to do it for what was slave's wages to us but a small fortune for them, a dollar or two a day. This system worked well despite the belief, widely held by many older sergeants, that if the GIs didn't have to pull KP duty the earth might spin off of its axis and crash into the sun. As it turned out, the food was more than acceptable. I mean, how badly can you screw up breakfast? Bacon will always taste like bacon. The biscuits were especially good despite the fact that the little black dots weren't poppy seeds but small gnats that had flown into the dough mixer. This happened all the time but didn't bother me. I just put on extra jam, which seemed to be the proper antidote. Reconstituted eggs could never be served sunny-side up but at least they tasted somewhat like what they were supposed to be. The reconstituted milk, however, was a different story and a major disappointment for a lifelong milkaholic. It tasted like rubber tree sap and should have been outlawed by the Geneva Convention. I never drank it again.

Fortunately though, aside from the milk, any noxious qualities the reconstituted or powdered substances might have had were outweighed by my fuel requirements. Most of the time I seemed to be in a negative caloric balance. It was a struggle to keep my weight up. Accordingly, I would have eaten powdered cantaloupe if they had tried to serve it.

Between meals the mess hall didn't serve food. If you missed chow time because of some duty you either went hungry or ate C rations out of your footlocker. You could, however, get a cool drink from the mess hall between meals. This was necessary to ward off dehydration and heatstroke. There was usually a pair of chrome-colored, seven-gallon metal jugs full of ice and a sweet mysterious liquid sitting on a table in one corner of the dining area. The available flavors were always green and purple. Not lemon-lime and grape. Green and purple. It was worse than Kool-Aid. Nobody knew exactly what it was, not even the Pentagon. We called it jungle juice. It was too sweet, too tart, and had an aftertaste like heartburn. I always rinsed my mouth out with water afterward because I was afraid that it would eat the enamel off my teeth. Nonetheless, I drank gallons of the stuff over time when I was near death from dehydration and I was grateful to have it.

After breakfast, we headed toward the edge of the camp and the start of my first combat patrol. A narrow path from the company area to the bunker line passed through a maze of shrubbery. Overgrown roots and branches poked out at our ankles trying to trip us. With the first hints of daylight, black masses became gray shadows in front of us. Our pace was purposefully slow. At times we came to a complete halt and waited for more light. Like the star of a new play opening on Broadway who wouldn't go onstage until the curtain was fully opened, we waited. Sharp wouldn't take us across no-man's-land until the sun was completely up and we could see what was on the other side.

"Goddamn, it's a cannonball," I said, picking up one of several dirty eighteen-pounders next to the path. No one feigned a modicum of interest. They'd seen them many times before. Gilbert, the other FNG, couldn't care less. He squinted at me once, then ignored the situation completely. I wondered about the history of those useless weapons. They looked like rusty dinosaur eggs. Before us, the Vietnamese had fought the French, the Japanese, and the Chinese. We hadn't been taught much about the history of Vietnam so I couldn't think of any others that they fought, but I knew there were others. A metal fuse on top stared back at me like an eye on a potato. Could this thing go off if I fooled around with it enough or dropped it? All right, playtime was over. Gently, I put it back and moved on. I thought they were cool.

Just before we left the perimeter, Sharp had us line up so that he could check a certain piece of equipment we were all supposed to be carrying. That day it was smoke grenades. Everybody had one. These surprise quizzes were pulled on the squad or platoon every once in a while. The next time he might check to see that everyone had a claymore mine or the required number of fragmentation grenades or bullets. The idea behind these unannounced inspections was to ensure that there were no scofflaws among us and that everyone was carrying the required amount of gear.

While checking out everyone's gear, I noticed that the guy next to me, Golambiski, nicknamed Sleepy, had a white phosphorus grenade on his belt. Everyone referred to those as willie-peter grenades and I didn't want to walk next to anyone that was carrying one. We had all heard stories about those things getting hit by a bullet and going off, incinerating half the squad. Also, whereas a regular grenade weighed about a pound, the willie-peters were around four pounds apiece. Golambiski was skinnier than I. Throwing one of those grenades would be tantamount to heaving a shot-put ball. It would have taken King Kong to hurl it far enough away so that you didn't get incinerated when it went off. Quietly, I slipped a little farther down the line, away from Golambiski.

The same thing was true for those who carried the flamethrower. It didn't take a brain surgeon with a large imagination to see how big a weenie roast would ensue if bullets or hot shrapnel punctured one of those black tanks full of jellied gasoline. Hell, I'd already seen it happen a couple times in the movies. How could anyone in their right mind not be jumpy about being next to that guy? Fortunately, the patrol was only a squad-sized affair, so I didn't have to worry about the flamethrower. They went out only on platoon- or company-sized missions and were not going to be with us for this patrol.

The river was chest-deep and colder than a witch's tit, which woke up any stragglers from the previous night's sleep. Starting the hike with wet, chaffing underwear was unpleasant. Then, the patrol itself was hard. The ground was wet from a heavy rain the previous night that had created a thick layer of mud that tried to slow us down and suck our boots off. We encountered a lot of thick vegetation that we had to hack our way through. It took five hours to travel a scant three kilometers out and three kilometers back. That was a distance of a little less than four miles.

We crossed several more streams that were chin-deep for some of the shorter guys. Unlike the early morning river crossing that was so uncomfortably cold, these were refreshing. Because we had become sweaty and overheated they served nicely to cool us off. Sharp thought that one of the streams was too deep to ford on foot. Instead, he opted to chop down a nearby dead tree trunk so that it fell across the stream. His plan worked perfectly and we used it to walk across. For me, the machete chopping noise had been way too loud and made me nervous. I was afraid that the enemy would hear us and was greatly relieved when the tree finally toppled over and we were able to leave the area.

Aside from the noise caused by hacking at the tree, I wasn't very nervous about being in the jungle. That was probably because all of the other grunts were so laid back about the patrol. I was beginning to absorb their attitude. As I would eventually figure out, a lot of patrols didn't amount to a hill of beans because we wouldn't actually encounter the enemy or other forms of danger.

On the return leg of the patrol back to base camp, Lopez tangled his foot in the trip wire of one of the crudest booby traps ever devised by man. It was set up to send a four-foot strand of barbed wire whipping across his path at eye level, like the branch of a tree that has been pulled back, then let go. Lopez was ahead of me when he got tangled up. Huish, behind me, spotted the gizmo and shouted for Lopez to stop walking, which he did. Then Huish unwrapped the wire from around Lopez's boots while Lopez stood first on one foot and then on the other. I had no idea what was going on. Afterward, we all joked about it.

A hundred meters ahead, the little depression that held the river came into view. Behind it were the tan- and olive-colored bunkers that guarded the approaches to Lai Khe. It had been an all right day. There was more swagger and less crouch in everyone's gait the closer we got to safety. Sharp, who had been leading the way, stopped and leaned against a tree. As we passed, he watched calmly, like Caesar reviewing a parade of his victorious legions. My impression was that he was counting heads to ensure that no one had been left behind.

This tranquil scene proved to be more than Huish could endure. Quietly he began collecting an armful of unexploded mortar shells from the riverbank. The mortar batteries at Lai Khe routinely hammered the jungle area around the base at night with random shells to keep anyone from sneaking up on us. There were always duds lying around just outside the base perimeter. Huish's action was a thinly veiled attempt to rattle a few cages, which worked quite well. A couple of guys began to swear at him. I couldn't understand what Lopez was saying to him in Spanish but it didn't sound friendly. Everyone moved away except Sharp, who stood his ground as unflappable as ever. "Negative, Huish, leave those things alone," Sharp ordered. Huish then explained that if he didn't police up these live rounds the VC would find them, turn them into booby traps, and blow up somebody. Sharp dismissed that military logic with a farmer's simplicity: "Well, we don't want them to blow us up now, do we, so get rid of them." Huish complied and we all moved on.

When we got back, we found out that there had been VC out there with us, a squad of them. They had been spotted by air recon. It was unclear to me how close they had been to us or if the information had been radioed to Sergeant Sharp while we were still out there.

Herb Beck came by on his way to get a haircut, so I joined

him. Fairman wanted everybody's hair to look like they were undergoing chemotherapy. He had already groused once that I was beginning to look like a goddamned hippie. He said it with a passion, with no space between words as if the whole phrase was actually just one long word. Beck informed me that at Lai Khe you got haircuts from Chang and Tits. He hadn't been at Lai Khe any longer than I but somehow he knew things I didn't yet. The barbershop was located in one room of a white stucco building with blue shutters in a central area of Lai Khe known as the Crossroads. There was even a large wooden sign out front with Crossroads in blue letters on a white background. Most of the stucco building was occupied by the Post Exchange.

Chang and Tits ran the barbershop and gave haircuts. Those weren't their real names but that's what we called them. Chang was in his late thirties and slightly stoop-necked from years of barbering. He was also a trifle pudgy. Being even a little overweight was unusual and made me think that he got more to eat on a regular basis than the other Vietnamese that I had seen. As for Tits, holy mother of the pyramids, her breasts were enormous by Vietnamese standards. She really stood out in a nation of flatter-than-pancake women. She was younger than Chang and sexier than sin. Unfortunately, like lots of locals, her blouses had no buttons in front and a closed collar so there was no chance of catching a glimpse. We didn't know what her relationship with Chang was.

The haircuts were satisfactory. A blind person couldn't botch a military haircut. No one really much cared as long as it was sufficiently short. They cut my hair a couple of more times until Chang was killed in a firefight at Bau Bang. He turned out to be a Viet Cong and had been found dead in a trench after a shoot-out. Tits never returned to the shop. Understandably, the haircuts had to continue. Chang and Tits were replaced by two guys that were skinnier, didn't have nicknames, and were too old to be active members of any military group.

The names Chang and Tits were pretty mild compared to the other slurs that were commonly used. The people we were fighting for were slopes, slants, squints, dinks, and some-times even zipperheads. This last one seemed more born of actual hate and malice than the others. All of them made rice-eaters seem almost polite. Gook was the clear-cut win-ner among the GIs and was used more than all the others combined. The slurs were purely racial, not military or polit-ical. Racially, all Orientals were gooks. Politically, gook was ambiguous, like the word *bogey* from World War II. It was an unknown. If you said that a gook was coming down the trail that meant simply an Oriental and didn't specify if he was a friend or foe. If the Oriental had an AK-47, so that you knew he was an enemy, you wouldn't say that a gook was coming but rather that a VC was. It was, however, socially acceptable to refer to the VC as gooks if you were in an unambiguous situation where everyone in the conversation was aware that the gooks in question were VC, such as in a firefight.

Maybe the Vietnamese were more cultured than we were because they didn't seem to have degrading racial terms for us. If they did have such words I never heard them. On the other hand, we Americans had managed to come up with ugly names for practically every opponent we had ever fought.

Guard duty on the perimeter bunker line was peaceful, restful, and sometimes entertaining. Several dozen species of orchids grew wild in Vietnam but only occasional flowers were to be seen in Charlie Company's section. Some were exotic compared to the flowers my dad grew at home, but I had no idea what qualified a flowering plant as an orchid. Al-though there weren't a lot of flowers in our area we did have more than our share of reptile creatures. We were overrun with nervous little lizards that scampered off at high speed if they caught sight of their own shadow. Once safe, they would shriek out a high-pitched noise that sounded just like they were yelling, "Fuck you." Most of the time they said it twice in quick succession. "Fuck you, fuck you." Logically, we re-ferred to them as fuck-you lizards.

On this day there was also entertainment. It came in the form of an A-1 Skyraider, a large, single-engine, propeller-driven attack bomber, flying at low altitude over the jungle adjacent to our bunker line. These vintage planes could carry so much ordnance that they were nicknamed flying dump trucks. As it moved slowly by, about half a kilometer out, a bright red tracer flew up at it. American tracers were red. In theory, communist-country tracers were green. It didn't matter. This shot came from one of the enemy, probably using a captured American rifle and ammunition.

The Skyraider turned back, went into a slow, lazy dive and dropped a wagonload of bombs on the tracer's origin. We all cheered. The plane then circled the area several times as a jagged pillar of smoke grew skyward. When the pilot grew weary of this and started to fly off, another tracer was shot at it, which resulted in another load of bombs being dropped and another round of cheers. The cycle was repeated once more before the tracers stopped and the Skyraider left. The American taxpayers had just spent a ton of money trying to kill that one guy. It was great fun to watch.

Later in the evening one of the squad leaders, Sergeant Jim Conklin, became delirious. He had been sick for a day or two with a fever, sweats, and muscle aches. So far that hadn't bought him much sympathy. In Vietnam, you had to be really sick to get pulled off duty for medical attention. Minor conditions like fits, farts, and freckles didn't count. However, now that Conklin was non compos mentis and talking out of his head like an imbecile, he had to be sent back to the aid station. We couldn't have someone who was supposed to quietly pull night guard duty be babbling out loud because he thought that he was at a barbershop in Omaha, chewing the fat with neighbors. Conklin was gone only a couple of days. When he returned, he didn't seem to have the foggiest idea what had been wrong with him in the first place. As I would discover, guys with high fevers that became delirious weren't all that uncommon in the Nam.

Our next mission was inside Lai Khe and got under way at 0400 hours. We were awakened early and told to gear up and go to breakfast. This was kind of a double whammy for me because the night before we had been short of men on perimeter guard duty and some of us only got two or three hours' sleep. The good news was that the mess hall was serving creamed chipped beef on toast, the most notorious menu offering in army history. It had been called SOS, or shit on a shingle, since long before World War II and a lot of GIs wouldn't go near it. As for me, I loved the stuff. They couldn't serve it often enough for my lower-class taste buds.

Unfortunately, three minutes after we got to the mess hall a line of trucks and jeeps pulled up outside. Lieutenant Judson, our executive officer, ambled in and announced that breakfast was over and we should all go outside and get in the vehicles. This precipitated a lot of grumbling because most of us hadn't finished eating. Some hadn't even started. The grumbling wasn't lost on Judson, but didn't do much good. He wasn't noted for being overly friendly or sympathetic with the troops. He matter-of-factly grumbled back that if any of us was still hungry we would be allowed the luxury of finishing our food as we walked our trays over to the dirty tray rack. This was provided, of course, that we didn't walk too slowly. He further suggested that an alternative approach to getting fed was to simply wait for the next meal. Apparently, eating was being added to sleeping on the list of frivolous, nonessential activities for grunts.

We motored to Lai Khe village and encircled it while others went inside for a massive shakedown operation, not unlike those inside prisons back home to look for shanks, drugs, and other contraband. This was done on a periodic basis to prevent the buildup of weapons or explosives in the village. The brass didn't want to ignore the possibilities and end up with a fort inside a fort. Most of the time, all they came away with was hungover GIs sleeping off the previous night's drinking and whoring. The village was, in theory, off-limits after curfew.

Fairman stationed me by a section of the chain-link fence with a gaping hole in it and walked off.

"What'll I do if a bunch of GIs try to get out this way?" I yelled. He was no help.

"Stop 'em," he said over his shoulder without looking back. I wondered what that meant. Ask them to stop, wrestle with

them, shoot them? I had nasty visions of some bulky black
kid who grew up in the Cabrini-Green projects of Chicago
emerging. He wasn't going to stop for a skinny white private
waving his arms and screaming halt. He'd trample me. I didn't
have good instructions and didn't want to be there. After six
hours, Fairman returned and said the raid was over. He didn't
ask or care if I'd seen anyone, which I hadn't. I took this as
meaning that if I had seen the kid from Chicago I should
have let him go.

Back at the company, I learned that a female with $2,700
had been arrested as a presumed VC tax collector. She was
probably a hooker. Also, one M-16 had been found and a few
unidentified GIs had made the usual escape over the fence
topped with barbed wire on the west side of the village.

Beck showed up for another visit. We talked for a while,
then walked over to the company club for soda pop. We
couldn't get beer. They didn't sell it before evening because
they didn't want the troops sloshed all day. We smoked some
cigarettes, then Beck asked if I wanted to go to Disneyland.
Once again he knew about something that I didn't. Disneyland was the local red-light district, a brothel full of prostitutes in the Vietnamese section of Lai Khe. It was right in the
center of our base camp. The army really managed it. They
made up all the rules for the place, like when it was open or
closed, when the enlisted men or officers could or couldn't
go there. They even had the women checked for venereal dis-
eases by our doctors. This place was my tax dollars at work.

His idea seemed reasonable at the moment, so I agreed.
Whispering as if my guardian angel might be listening, I told
Beck that I was Catholic so he couldn't tell anyone about our
little escapade. After attending Catholic grammar school and
high school, I possessed an infinite capacity for guilt beaten
into me at the knuckles with a wooden ruler by Sister Mary
Godzilla. This was going to be a mortal sin, not just a venial
sin, so I would have to find a priest for confession or one of
those general absolution deals before getting shot at again.
According to the Baltimore catechism, if I died before con-

fessing this sin I would go straight to hell, probably on a rocket sled.

Beck knew how to get there and led the way. The place was far from fancy, though it did have electric ceiling lights and a working jukebox playing rock-and-roll tunes. It wasn't uncomfortably loud. There was an odd collection of tables and chairs scattered about with lots of GIs and working girls drinking and talking. They served beer there.

Milliseconds after we sat down, two girls joined us.

"You buy me Saigon tea?" they said together. Thimble-sized cups of tea with no alcohol, which sold for a few dollars each, helped keep the place profitable when customers wanted to drink and talk for a while before making their selection of women. Not many guys wanted to walk in the door, drop their pants, and start balling for dollars right off the bat. It was a type of foreplay, I suppose. For me, the conversation was as awkward as awkward could be. It was certainly worse than any clumsy, stumbling attempt to ask a girl for a date that I had ever experienced back home. Further, I wasn't asking this girl for a date, I was asking for sex: "Hi there, I realize you don't know me but do you mind if I bang you?"

It was also awkward because she was Asian. In California I didn't even know any girls that weren't whiter than Wonder Bread. Now I'm facing a chick who's so exotic I couldn't figure out if she was older or younger than me. Then she asked if I wanted to get really good *boom-boom* from her.

Fortunately or unfortunately, I was saved by the long arm of the law. Before we could consummate the negotiations by agreeing on a price, a couple of 66-Alphas—military police— arrived to evict us. It was evening change of shift time. From now until the close of business, the place was exclusively officers' country. All of us enlisted men had to vacate the premises so that the brass could have their whores in private. If the West Point wives' club ever figured out this routine they would have collectively blown a gasket. Oh well, maybe I hadn't gotten laid, but at least I'd found the place. It was a start.

Beck and I split up and returned to our respective units.

Back at my hootch, I learned that some soldier that I hadn't even met yet had finished his year overseas and shipped out that day to return home. Now, two other guys were arguing over who had dibs on the skinny little mattress that he had left behind.

One of the two, John Sievering, was thick as well as solid, built like a linebacker. He had sandy-colored hair and a face that was more friendly than frightening. The other, Clarence Ortiz, was shorter, darker, and Hawaiian. Although smaller, he seemed more menacing to me. This was probably because his gene pool put his appearance closer to Viet Cong than any of the rest of us. Ortiz spoke a pidgin-Hawaiian dialect that was at times difficult for me to understand. Some words were incomprehensible and he didn't seem to enunciate. It was like listening to a Navajo code talker.

Sievering started to remove the mattress from the now-abandoned bunk. "Who dat you take dat?" Ortiz asked, in more of an accusation than a question.

"What?" said Sievering, "He left it to me."

"No!" Ortiz said, grasping the mattress from his side. "He said it mine."

The tugging on the mattress from both sides lasted maybe a half a minute before the situation suddenly deteriorated as the two grunts simultaneously began pounding each other with knuckle sandwiches. The punches looked hard, at least hard enough to break some facial bones or knock a hole in a plaster wall. The fight quickly ended with both of them on the floor, worn out and panting for air. It was a tie. I can't remember which of them got the trophy.

My first overnight trip into the boondocks came the next day. The company was being sent back out to rejoin Operation Cedar Falls. So, in the dawn's early light, trucks carted us over to the Lai Khe airstrip where about two dozen helicopters from the 1st Aviation Battalion were lined up in rows with their motors whining and propellers fluttering.

I was learning army lingo. These troop movers were called slicks. They had two door gunners and could accommodate about ten of us crammed inside with all of our gear. Sometimes one of these GI taxis would also have attached rocket pods. Hogs or gunships were helicopters with racks of forward-facing machine guns and rockets. They didn't ferry GIs but were filled with ammo and were used as flying gun platforms. Dust-offs were the medical evacuation helicopters that we sometimes called medevacs. They had a large red cross on a white square painted on the front and sides. The crosses looked like targets to me, which wasn't a good thing. The VC and NVA (North Vietnamese Army) had already demonstrated many times that shooting down a medical helicopter full of defenseless wounded and even unconscious people was well within their moral parameters. It didn't bother them at all, but not much did.

The noise on the strip was deafening. On a hand signal from Sharp, we all ran out among the choppers with 3rd Squad piling into one up front. We ran in a bent-over position so we wouldn't get our heads chopped off, even though the main rotor blade was about fifteen feet off the ground. There was so much dirt swirling around that it was impossible to keep your eyes clear and see well. I never heard of anyone actually being struck by the main blade while I was there, but I'm sure it happened somewhere. When the choppers lifted off they sometimes wobbled a bit, which brought one side of the blades' arc lower to the ground, often down to legitimate decapitation height. Later on during my tour of duty in Vietnam, I saw a Black Lion walk into a tail rotor, which is a lot closer to the ground than the main rotor. It was an alarming sight that quickly became funny when we realized that there was no serious damage. The impact put a big dent in the GI's helmet and knocked him stupid for a few minutes. Fortunately, he wasn't badly hurt and his mental status quickly returned to baseline, which probably wasn't all that great to begin with, given that he was in the infantry.

Inside the helicopters, space was tight. With eight on board the chopper was actually full. With the entire ten-man squad, it was quite cramped. At this close range, I noticed that Sharp had a rifle slug stuck in one of the grenades on his belt. Likewise, Golambiski had a slug stuck in the right side of his helmet. This group had been around a bit. Unfortunately, I didn't ask either of them how the bullets got there and lost a couple of stories that were probably worth hearing.

There was a fair amount of helmet graffiti as well. Lopez had "Cast My Fate to the Wind," someone else had "Born to Lose." Another guy had the months of the year written down on the side of his helmet and was crossing them off one by one. More than one Catholic in the company had inked on the initials "J.M.J." for Jesus, Mary, and Joseph. It was interesting that the army allowed this attempt at individuality when it worked so hard to stamp it out everywhere else. Helmet graffiti had become a combat zone tradition. Still, there weren't any peace signs or drawings of marijuana plants to be seen in Charlie Company during my time there. I ended up putting "Conlan Abu" on mine. This was Gaelic for victorious forever and came from the coat of arms of the Irish side of my mother's family, the Moore Clan.

A lot more guys individualized their helmets by carrying things stuck inside their headbands. The most common item was a little, clear, plastic bottle of insect repellent. Then came matches, cigarettes, spare grenade pins, M-16 magazines, and—of course—the ace of spades. This stuff all looked to me like a target to facilitate a good head shot so I didn't carry anything this way. If a sniper was going to tag one of us, I wanted it to be somebody else, not me.

Lopez had unscrewed his radio antenna before boarding so that he wouldn't skewer anyone in the eyeball. We all carried more gear for an overnight trip, including community property. This stuff included, among other things, machetes, shovels, heavy radio batteries the size of a carton of cigarettes, and blocks of plastic explosives. I'd been given a LAW (light antitank weapon) rocket as part of my share of community property to lug around in addition to my two belts of machine-gun ammo. We didn't carry a LAW on every patrol. Sharp decided when to do so, and that was mainly when we were going into an area he thought might contain bunkers. They were used as bunker busters. Thank God, the other side didn't have tanks for us to use them on. The LAW rocket was just over two feet long, weighed about ten pounds, and fortunately came with a shoulder sling.

Still being a follower at this point, I was the last one inside the helicopter and ended up by the door, which remained open. Despite never having ridden in one of these flying egg-beaters, I wasn't worried. It had to be safe because everyone else was doing it.

We cruised along at about five thousand feet. The consensus was that at a mile up we would be safe from rifle potshots fired at us from below. Also, because we were so high, they wouldn't waste much ammo on us, hoping for a one in a million shot to bring us down. We could relax for the next few minutes. As it turned out, the ride was quite comfortable. The rotor pulsed like a mother's heartbeat, causing almost everyone except me to doze off into short catnaps. I didn't fall asleep because the sights below were new and interesting. The view of the jungle was much better from the lower-flying helicopter than it had been from the higher-flying Caribou cargo planes that I had traveled in before this. The jungle that we flew over appeared to have already been worked over quite a bit by artillery and the air force. There were craters everywhere. Particularly well-hit areas looked like uninhabitable moonscapes. Some holes were sixty feet wide and thirty feet deep. Many were half full of water which had seeped up from below. Forests of trees with no leaves leaned outward, pointing away from the blast sites. Thousands of severed branches lay in jumbled heaps around the craters. From the air, they looked like a pile of giant Pick-Up Sticks. How could anyone survive in such a place?

A gradual descent brought everyone back to reality and fully awake. Each rifleman pulled out his clip, checked to see that it really was full of bullets, then replaced it. This was done over and over, nervously, too many times. I started doing it. The last part of the descent, over the actual LZ (landing zone), was about as subtle as falling down an elevator shaft. Some of us were standing outside of the helicopter on the skids at this point, staring down at a rather soggy-looking rice paddy surrounded by jungle.

At about three feet or so, I jumped and sank in up to my hips. Heavier guys went in deeper. Mike Soja, the overweight flamethrower guy from Chicago, just plain disappeared. Soja was a nice enough guy but he was large and rough. I was sure that he had big felt dice hanging on the rearview mirror of his car back home and considered bar fights a legitimate form of recreational activity. After he sank, his helmet bobbed on the surface. Half a second later he reemerged, unleashing a scathing verbal attack, at whom I'm not sure. It was so garbled I couldn't tell if it was Polish or English with heavy choking sounds. But the message was clear, he was pissed.

We waded out of the water and up to the top of the embankment, where we found level ground leading into the jungle. After we had taken just a couple of steps, a five-hundred-pound bomb exploded in front of me. My guess was that it was only about seventy-five meters away and that we would have been killed by the blast and shrapnel had it not been for the thick vegetation between us and the bomb. For me, this was giving a whole new meaning to the phrase *close air support*. The concussion knocked me off balance. Only clutching a nearby tree kept me from going completely over as three more bombs went off in quick succession. The air in front of us was becoming palpably hotter than the air behind us. Lethal shrapnel that we could hear but not see whizzed by. We dove on our stomachs for cover. Each of us managed to find the base of a thick tree trunk or a mound of dirt or something else to position between us and the blasts for protection. We were following President Johnson's political advice that sometimes, when things are out of your control, the best strategy is to "hunker down like a jackass in a hailstorm and wait for things to blow over."

Occasionally chunks of shrapnel would slam into trees or bushes, causing them to rattle and quake, giving off large clouds of dust that had been covering them. Sometimes this made the trees and bushes look almost as if they were exploding. It was neat, I thought at the time. The bombing continued for almost an hour. It would be calm for a few minutes, then we would see flashes of F-4 Phantoms passing from right to left in front of us through the treetops, then more explosions and whizzing sounds. Fortunately, on most bombing runs, the loud, screeching noise made by the jet engines was audible five to ten seconds before the bombs were dropped. This warning noise gave us time, if we moved quickly, to jump for cover. Still, it was hard to believe that none of us got hurt.

Certainly being this close made the bombs appear more menacing and larger than they really were. One sortie came in so low that I could read the small numbers painted on the fuselage and see the pilot's face. That plane was dropping bombs the size of Volkswagens. Radios crackled everywhere. Smoke grenades of various colors were going off all around us as signals to the bomb jockeys where they should or should not drop their ordnance. I wanted to throw one in the worst way and eagerly searched the faces of nearby squad leaders and platoon sergeants for one that looked like he was about to ask someone to pop a smoke grenade. It didn't work. My assistance in this matter was not needed or requested.

That day, Charlie Company used every color available except red to mark our position. In the 1st Division's TAO (tactical area of operations) our commander, General DePuy, had ordained that this color be designated as a marker only for the enemy. Forward observers in single-engine Cessnas and spotters in helicopters used red smoke grenades and rockets on enemy positions. From the air, red smoke meant drop your bombs here. From the ground, it meant run for your fucking life, bombs are about to be dropped here. In theory, ground troops would only use this color if they were being overrun and had to call in bombs or artillery on themselves from what was known as an FDP (final defensive position). I guess we didn't think in those terms because not a soul in Charlie Company carried red smoke.

General DePuy sounded like an interesting character and I was sorry that I never got to meet him in person. Napalm seemed to be one of his favorite words. More than once I was told that it had been his terse reply when asked by his subordinates how to handle some thorny tactical problem presented by a battle or engagement already in progress. He was considered a soldier's soldier and was well known by us low-men-on-the-totem-pole for his quote that went, "If one GI is attacked, he becomes the division commander because he then has all of the resources of the division at his disposal." Now that was sticking up for the little guy.

Every division in Vietnam, including ours before DePuy arrived, had subdued shoulder patches made using only olive drab, black, and various shades of gray. All other colors had been eliminated for camouflage purposes. DePuy overturned that plan and brought back our original division patch on which the number one was colored fire-engine red. That was fine with me. I was in the Big Red One, not the Big Gray One. The high regard in which DePuy was held was pretty much universal within the division. The same thing couldn't be said for a lot of other division commanders.

Who knew why the air force was bombing? I didn't. This was to become a reoccurring theme, the ignorance theme, not knowing in the present what was happening or why and not being able to find out afterward what had happened. For me it was painful. Maybe scout planes spotted something before we landed. Maybe we had been shot at during the approach. Maybe it was precautionary. I was told that the CO preferred some type of preliminary bombardment when possible. About two months earlier, on Operation Attleboro, a landing without prior bombardment was met by a solitary VC who shot our point man, Garcia, between the eyes, then disappeared. The shot blew out the back of his head and nearly blinded the second guy in line with a blast of hot brains to the face at supersonic speed. I don't know if he got a Purple Heart for being hit by human shrapnel.

As suddenly as it had begun, it ended. The air strikes were over. Charlie Company moved off into the jungle on a search-and-destroy mission. The object of Cedar Falls was to clear out a fifty-square-mile area known as the Iron Triangle that lay a little northwest of Saigon. This area didn't have many roads, hadn't been given proper attention by U.S. forces for some time, and was now a large supply and storage area for the enemy. On day one of the operation our forces seized the major village, Ben Suc, brought in Chinook helicopters, and relocated the people, all their possessions and even their livestock. The village was then bulldozed flat. This was done so that after our departure the area could be declared a free-fire zone and periodically pummeled with artillery fire to keep the enemy from returning. Anyway, that was the theory.

Army commanders on the ground at Ben Suc displayed uncommon wisdom and compassion that day when villagers requested a delay in the proceedings to retrieve personal items of value that had been buried or hidden around the village. This was a common practice to safeguard valuables from VC tax collectors, looters, and plain old neighborhood thieves. In atypical fashion, the military timetable was temporarily abandoned so the people could collect their treasures. Despite this short stay of execution, the relocation was carried out expeditiously. Nobody in the 1st Division would want to hear what was being said about them around the campfire in the new village that night, wherever it was.

The rest of the Iron Triangle was now being searched by us as well as the 173rd Airborne and the 11th Armored Cavalry Regiment. No large ARVN units were involved. They had not even been told about the Cedar Falls plan until it was obviously in progress. The prevailing rumor was that the brass in Saigon were afraid that if the ARVN knew about the operation ahead of time they would tip off the Viet Cong.

About midday, we found a rice cache. Five tons of the stuff in bags stacked on a wooden floor, which was two feet off the ground, on stilts, to keep it dry. Thick bamboo poles supported a corrugated metal roof to keep the rain away. The structure, which was about the size of a one-car garage, didn't have walls. The bags were in good shape. It was hard to believe that there wasn't some species of critter out there that would chew through the bags to get at the rice. We approached the cache with great caution, wondering whose unseen eyes were watching us and wondering if they would fight us for their rice. As luck would have it, the stash was unguarded, but it was booby-trapped. An American egg grenade with its pin removed lay between two of the bags. Captain Paone, the company commander, removed it and replaced the pin with an extra one he was carrying. Everyone carried spare grenade pins for just that purpose.

While the cache was inspected by those in charge, we stood our ground in positions on all sides. Most of us sat down to get off our feet while waiting. I leaned back against a tree, closed my eyes, and asked Tynes, one of the grenadiers in the squad, to wake me if they left. Calmly and methodically he chewed me out, up one side and down the other, with biting sarcasm. No, I wasn't going to nod off like some dimwit. My job was to remain alert, watch my section of jungle for any signs of danger, and be ready to deal with it. This was a team sport with everyone participating. It wasn't nap time. Obviously he was correct, so I complied without so much as a whimper of protest.

Ken Tynes, from Los Angeles, was the only black in the squad. He was slightly darker than average, perhaps because he went without a shirt much of the time back in base camp. He frequently wore his helmet tilted to one side, which made him look cavalier, even cocky, when in reality he was cautious and contemplative. I listened when he spoke. So did the others. The other distinct minority in the squad, Ortiz the Hawaiian, seemed to be Tynes's best friend in the company. They were both grenadiers, carrying the M-79, which fired a 40-mm grenade. Oddly, the weapon didn't have a safety. In order to keep it from accidentally discharging most grenadiers kept the breech open while on patrol.

The army had experimented for a while with a giant, 40-mm shotgun shell designed to be used in the M-79. Each shell fired twenty-seven .32-caliber lead balls. They were actually in use when they were recalled for unknown reasons. Tynes had quietly kept some and always had one in the chamber, ready to go. Anyone that tried to fuck with Tynes on patrol was going to find that his first shot back was going to be a real bitch.

After further inspection of the rice shed for hidden weapons or documents, the center of the pile of bags was packed with blocks of C-4, a plastic explosive. We lit the fuse and ran for our lives. As we hunkered down and waited, I was a trifle nervous, having visions of fifty-pound bags of rice raining down on us. I could see one landing on my spine. Seconds later the hootch was gone. There wasn't much of a crater but the earth oozed steam and smoke. How many finds like this would it take to make them hungry? We moved on.

After a couple more hours of looking for rice, we stopped for the night. That morning I had forgotten to fill my canteens and was beginning to feel as dried out as a raisin. During the day I had been too embarrassed to ask anyone for some of their water because I didn't want them to think of me as a stupid asswipe. We didn't have running water at Lai Khe. We got our drinking water out of a thousand-gallon metal tank on wheels parked in the dirt yard adjacent to the mess hall. It was kept there as a matter of convenience. In theory, when we saw it after breakfast on the morning of a new operation, it would jog our memories and remind us to top off our canteens. Unfortunately, that morning I hadn't been smart enough to connect the dots and figure out that I should load up on water before we left on patrol.

Finding a crater with some gray water at the bottom was easy. I slid the ten feet down its mucky side to the bottom and drank like a mad dog. The water had a strong metallic taste, like licking aluminum siding, but was still refreshing. I gulped away until my stomach was stretched and uncomfortable. In my mind, it was doubtful that I'd ever make the empty canteen mistake again.

At each NDP (night defensive position) as the sun went down the shovels came out. We dug so much that we should have been in the United Mine Workers' Union. If the first shovel swings produced only laborious groans, that meant tillable soil. Strings of curse words meant earth that was as hard as rock or thick roots. Nonetheless, we dug in every night. We slept next to our foxholes, not in them. For bedding, we used a plastic poncho. It wasn't intended to be soft padding, just a partial barrier against wet ground and crawling insects. Because they produced a little bit of noise they were only used when we were in the relative safety of a large NDP. Ponchos weren't used on night ambush or LP (listening post) duty where we were small in numbers as well as isolated and noise abatement was even more of an imperative. My backpack worked well as a pillow.

Fairman paired me with Jack Alvarez, a Mexican from California. He was smart, seasoned, and an all-around good soldier. Accordingly, he was on the verge of being given his own squad to run and would soon be promoted to sergeant. If Fairman wanted him to teach me the ropes he would have to rely on nonverbal communications because Alvarez hardly said anything.

When the holes were done, we made an attempt at chopping back some of the vegetation out front. This was to help us spot the enemy before they could sneak right up next to us. We also set up two claymores. This was done every night at every hole. Some of the more uptight guys would remove the grenades from their web gear for easier access and place them in a neat little row next to the poncho they slept on. This part of the ceremony wasn't compulsory. I didn't do it at the time because I didn't know about it yet. Later, when I did know, I still didn't do it. My thinking was that the grenades should remain attached to my gear in case there was ever any urgent need for me to quickly collect my stuff and rapidly change positions or make a run for it.

As the saying goes, there is "the right way, the wrong way, and the army way" of doing things. We, of course, used the army way—dividing night watch into an hour on and an hour off. At about 1930 hours it was pitch-black. Alvarez went to sleep and I took first watch with my legs dangling in the foxhole. A few minutes later I got out a cigarette and lit up my Zippo, instantly realizing that this was a dumb thing to do. Sliding forward into the foxhole I crouched down and waited for all the VC that had seen my flood lamp signal to start shooting at me. It didn't happen.

In the morning nobody said anything, but I did get the

FNG stare from one or two guys. Fairman didn't know. If he did, he probably would have skipped the tongue-lashing and gone right to a pistol-whipping. It was another one of those little mistakes that you make early in your tour. Eventually they diminish with time and disappear. Either that or you eventually disappear.

The next day brought two pleasant surprises. First, when we were out in the field we didn't get up at 0500 or 0-dark hundred, we slept until the sun came up. There was no purpose in arising before it was light enough to do anything. Second, Jones the cook showed up in a helicopter loaded to the gunnels with scrambled eggs, bacon, and hot coffee. "This is wonderful," I said to Alvarez. He mumbled something back to me in Spanish. My immediate impression was that we were going to eat breakfast like this in the jungle every day. My later impression was that it had been a special treat organized by the division brass because Operation Cedar Falls was almost over and had gone so well. Hot breakfast in the field was never sent out to us again while I was there.

After breakfast we took off on another six-hour sweep. My rifle and I were both walking wounded that day. The left side of my neck had a large abrasion surrounded by painful little blisters. During yesterday's march, the back-and-forth motion of the LAW rocket as I walked had caused the carrying strap to slowly dig a hole in my skin. If I wore it on the same side today it would eventually erode down deeper and slice through my jugular vein.

Another medical problem was my left hand, which was infected. I had snagged it on one of those thorny, wait-a-minute vines, giving myself several shallow cuts. Overnight it had developed a patch of vesicles. Some were leaking yellow pus and others oozed a blood-tinged fluid. It looked nasty and felt about as good as it looked. My immediate course of action was to show it to Doc Baldwin, the platoon medic. I liked Doc, he was humorous and entertaining. Often animated, he was always smiling. Inside him was a mischievous streak a mile wide. He came up with more sarcastic comments and funny lines than anyone else in Charlie Company.

In any event, Doc told me that my condition was yaws, and gave me some penicillin pills from a large bottle. He didn't have a container to dispense them in so they went in my pocket like loose change. Doc also said that the bacteria that caused yaws was closely related to the syphilis bacteria. Therefore, I might get a false positive result for syphilis if I ever had to take that test to get a marriage license back home in California. I needed to be ready to explain that one away pronto. Vietnam was continuing to be one pleasant surprise after another.

My rifle, old 179619, was also in sad shape that day. In just one night, the bolt had corroded shut. Again, it was my mistake. The problem was either not enough oil or inadequate cleaning. The bolt wouldn't budge despite my repeated beating and pounding on it with various pieces of my gear. Not to worry, there was a live round in the chamber. I consoled myself with the thought, perhaps delusional, that if I fired this round, it would jar the system loose and spring my weapon back to life. Fortunately, I didn't have to test the theory. My embarrassment over this situation was so great that I didn't mention it or ask for help. It was somewhat comforting that I also had a pistol. My dad bought me a government-model .45 automatic before I left California. Lots of guys carried a pistol in addition to their rifle, though most got their weapons from the army rather than bringing them from home. The more weapons you carried over, the more you were appreciated. Some positions, like medic and assistant machine gunner, were normally only issued a .45 and not obliged to carry a rifle. They were encouraged to request a rifle as well, however, and most of them did. Then they carried both weapons.

The day's patrol was not very fruitful. We wandered around for several hours but didn't find much of anything. Eventually all of the companies in the battalion linked up on a preselected flat space several acres in size. Gaggles of helicopters began arriving to lift us out and take us home. Because this was a battalion-sized lift, maybe six hundred men, the entire process took about an hour and a half. My squad was one of the last to leave. Being among the last out was a bit worrisome but had its advantages. By the time we got back to the company area, it was too dark to be sent out on ambush patrol.

Fortunately, we made it back in time for dinner. The evening mess hall meals were pretty darn good, sometimes even scrumptious, and always beat eating out of a can. They served entrees like baked ham, beef stew, roasted chicken, and meat loaf with gravy. There were side dishes of mashed potatoes, rice, pasta, canned fruit, and lots of different cooked vegetables. The biggest surprise was the bread, which they made fresh daily in the mess hall. It was delicious and as a bonus didn't seem to have as many protein bugs as the breakfast biscuits.

The next day, we spent most of our time hacking away at the exuberant growth of foliage in the company area which threatened to devour our hootches. Weeds had sprouted in the cracks between the wallboards. Vines crept up the sides, tugging at the screens, scouting for a place to enter. The dead space between the dwellings had become a mini-forest. Maybe they thought it was a fire hazard. Maybe they just wanted the place to look tidy like an army camp. Or it might have been their attempt at giving us a de facto day off without telling us. They couldn't actually tell us to take the day off. That would go against the military image. Anyway, we enjoyed the task. It was a lazy man's paradise. The Cokes and cigarettes we consumed outnumbered the plants we uprooted.

Around noon, we broke for lunch. Instead of heading directly to the chow hall, I walked over to division HQ to view the spoils of war. The division had captured beaucoup weapons and explosives during Cedar Falls and a lot of them had been put on display in an open courtyard. There were hundreds and hundreds of rifles, machine guns, and mortar tubes along with rows of mines and rockets and carefully sculpted piles of enemy hand grenades. It was an impressive haul. A lot of the captured weapons were American products that they had previously taken from us either in battle or by deceit. Those included two recoilless rifles, fifteen Bangalore torpedoes, and about a dozen PRC-25 radios, which we all called a prick twenty-five. There weren't any pistols to be seen, they had all been swiped by the officers. Numerous civilian photographers that were invited had arrived to take pictures. Obviously, the higher-ups were hoping to get some favorable press coverage for the division. There was a letter from General William DePuy, the division commander, being passed out. It stated that although we hadn't killed as many VC as on similar large operations, we had captured much more booty than expected and we should all be very proud of ourselves.

In the afternoon, we were sent to guard Bravo Company's line. They had been sent elsewhere. This job was an even lazier man's paradise. There were four or five of us at each bunker. Half a case of warm Korean beer lay in the dirt at our position. Of course, we quickly drank it and to our surprise it was real good for a foreign beer. Hooray for the Koreans! I had already tried Vietnamese beer. It tasted like mule piss.

None of us had ever actually seen any Korean soldiers at Lai Khe. However, we knew that there were some in Vietnam just like there were some soldiers from Australia helping us out. President Johnson had jawboned their leaders into sending them so that he could make it look as if we weren't acting alone in Vietnam but were actually part of some grand alliance of nations trying to fend off Ho Chi Minh.

During the afternoon, one guy listened to music on the radio and stood guard while the rest of us slept. Nothing bad ever happened on the perimeter during daylight so it was acceptable for us to take naps as long as at least one guy was semi-awake and reasonably alert. In reality, a trained seal would suffice if you could teach it to wear a helmet and bark "halt" every once in a while.

Early in the evening, 3rd Squad got tagged for ambush. As a matter of routine, C Company sent out at least one ten-man squad for ambush duty on most nights we were out in the jungle as well as on some when we were back at base camp. Because there were only a dozen rifle squads in the company, it was pretty obvious that night ambush patrol was going to be fairly common in my immediate future. After waiting for our relief to arrive and then hoofing it back across the camp, we were late. The river was crossed at 1940 hours. Leaving the perimeter in total darkness was as rare as it was foolish.

There wasn't enough residual daytime warmth to dry our clothes. Unseen sticks and vines made us stumble or even fall. There was way too much noise. Our fear of the unknown kept us from going more than a hundred meters past the river. I'm not sure how far out we had been told to go, but we weren't doing it. No one discussed this or made a big deal of it so there was no complicity on anyone's part that could be referred to the next day if questions were asked. Everyone knew what was going on and condoned it. This was a small piece of silent rebellion dictated by common sense. It had happened before and it would happen again.

Unfortunately, when we decided to stop moving we couldn't seem to find our way out of an area that was full of thorns sharp enough to turn back Texas longhorns. It was comparable to spending the night sleeping on a pile of old barbed wire. That was the good news. The bad news was that the dope leading the patrol, Sergeant Conklin, had us set up on both sides of a narrow trail. If we were to ambush a target from that situation, we would be shooting across the trail at each other like a Polish firing squad. Stupid.

None of us was managing to get much quality sleep, so we left at the first hint of daylight. The situation would have been described in World War II as a snafu—situation normal, all fucked up. For us, a more popular term was *fubar*—fucked up beyond all reason. The previous night, as we headed out into this misery, I cursed the powers that were. It was their fault that everything was so fubar. Now that it was over, I wondered if maybe it was our own fault for downing all that Korean beer, moving slowly like fat slugs, and arriving late at our ambush sight. I concluded that it didn't really matter anymore.

The company was a beehive of activity. Everyone was in full gear, including thick, heavy flak jackets, which I hadn't seen before. They were loading up a convoy of troop trucks headed for Di An. We had to step on it if we were going to change into dry clothes before departure.

The most important part of changing your attire was finding dry footwear. Each of us had three or four pairs of boots. Some were the older style, made entirely of leather. Others were the newer, so-called jungle boots, made partly of leather and partly of olive-colored canvas, which was supposed to help your feet dry out more quickly after you got them wet. A pair of little metal drains about half the size of a dime in the instep were designed to let moisture escape. It was my impression that these boots had been created specifically for the Vietnam War.

I had two pairs of canvas boots and two pairs of leather. Most boots not being worn were left outdoors on the sunny side of the hootch they could air out and bake dry. Some boots weren't under contract. Their owners had died, been evacuated, or rotated back to the world. Rightful ownership was determined by names and serial numbers inked on the inside. If these were illegible or it was dark, ownership was determined by location. You remembered about where among the rows of boots that yours were supposed to be. If these methods failed, the tiebreaker was size. If there was confusion but they fit well, they were yours; if not, you tried on another set. I always claimed a distinct area, the northern edge of the back row, to leave my boots. However, I wasn't too picky because I had owned only two pairs of boots when I had first arrived in Vietnam.

After changing clothes and boots, it was time to change my community property load. So far, it had consisted of two belts of machine-gun ammo and a LAW rocket. The rocket had to be ditched. It was too unwieldy and the sling cut into my neck. My carefully calculated plan was to hide the rocket in my footlocker under some dirty underwear. Then I'd show up for the day's mission wearing four belts of M-60 ammo and act like that was what I normally carried. My hope was that if Sharp still wanted someone to carry a rocket he would pick somebody who wasn't carrying as much as I was. It worked. I never carried a rocket again, and no one ever asked me what happened to the one I had been carrying.

At the supply shed, we were loaned flak jackets, which I referred to as heatstroke blazers. They were over an inch thick and weighed in at about seven or eight pounds. As such, they caused so much heat retention that it wasn't practical to wear them while humping on patrols out in the jungle. We used them only for motor convoys, during which the cooling effect of the fast air in the back of the open trucks would keep us from overheating. The flak jackets were useful for blocking low-velocity shrapnel or rifle shots fired from a distance but couldn't stop an AK-47 bullet fired from close range.

The convoy that day was going to be on Highway 13. This was the main road in our area connecting us to Di An and Saigon, which was about fifteen miles due south. If you traveled north about thirty-five miles, the road disappeared into Cambodia. It was not comforting to learn that the high frequency of adverse events—which included snipers, mines, and ambushes—had earned it the monikers Thunder Road and Bloody 13. Whenever I was on Thunder Road, the fear that some mine up ahead might be lurking just beneath the surface to get me was never far from the back of my mind. It was sort of like the eerie feeling that I sometimes got while swimming in deep water of the Pacific Ocean, that something lurking below the surface might be about to come up and bite me.

In my mind's eye, the mine shrapnel coming up at me would always somehow strike my groin area. It was as if I feared that the enemy had magic shrapnel that could penetrate the truck from any angle and still end up ripping into my private parts. Trepidation at this prospect was a common phobia among GIs. Eventually, if the anxiety was talked about enough, I would feel real discomfort down there until something else a little farther down the road would distract me.

While waiting to leave we discussed the well-known story, perhaps jungle legend, that to harm our morale, the enemy would try to blow up the beer truck in supply convoys to Lai Khe as often as possible. Who knows if it was true? Much of the road was actually paved with asphalt in both directions. However, there were some sections of gravel and some of only dirt. Those sections boasted potholes the size of bathtubs. That made for a rough ride.

Hurry up and wait. After being badgered to move more quickly, we finished our business with alacrity, piled into the trucks and then sat for three hours while the sun beat us like a drum. A layer of sandbags covered the truck bed to absorb the blast and shrapnel from any mines. Months, perhaps years, of alternating between soaking rains and baking sunshine had turned them into veritable bricks. We were supposed to kneel on them and face outward with our rifles. Kneeling on a cobblestone street would have been more comfortable. I felt like a pussy forever whining to the nuns about kneeling too long inside St. Bartholomew's Church.

During our wait, we were made to practice what we were going to do in the event of an ambush. We actually had various plans worked out in case we were presented with this or that scenario. If we were attacked but our truck was still moving, each of us was supposed to throw one hand grenade over the side, then start shooting rapidly at anything and everything. If our truck was damaged and had to stop, we were to each throw one grenade, dismount after it exploded, and line up in the dirt on both sides of the truck. We practiced this several times, trying to end up with the machine gun in the center, one grenade launcher on each side of the gun, and at least one M-16 between each of those positions as well as on both ends of the line. This was pretty much the way we were supposed to be lined up when on squad patrol.

Jumping out of the truck and running to our battle position in full gear and flak jackets was hard work in the heat. We practiced it several times. Afterward no one bitched about being left alone in the truck to bake like a pie. That might have been the reason for the ambush practice in the first place, to shut us up. The heat of the day was worse inside the driver's cab. Our driver complained loudly and frequently.

Eventually, just as a jeep passed by, he lost his composure and opened the door suddenly to jump out. The impact mangled the door and broke the hapless driver's leg. We simply gawked. Graciously, the jeep driver stopped so that the injured man could be loaded and driven to the aid station. Out of nowhere, it seemed, a new driver appeared for our vehicle.

Once we got rolling, there was no lollygagging. We motored fast. Clouds of beige dust trailed each of our two dozen vehicles. The dust stuck to our sweaty faces and arms, turning us into a bunch of floured lamb chops. The blacks looked as if they had been worked on by color-blind makeup artists.

Along the way, we saw houses, stores, and filling stations with names we recognized, like Gulf and Texaco. Civilian traffic was heavy, including many American cars from the 1940s and 1950s with very bald tires. There were plenty of beautiful young ladies wearing the traditional Ao Dai gowns, which were made with bright colors and flowed freely as they walked. Many pedestrians wore sandals with tire-tread soles which everyone called Ho Chi Minh sandals. The adults ignored us, which I found disconcerting. They didn't seem to recognize us as soldiers who had come to help defend their country and were risking our lives to do so. They didn't wave or smile or even look up very often. They seemed apathetic and unconcerned. This struck me as ominous.

The kids were a different story and lots of fun. They ran to the roadside shouting "chop-chop." That was their way of asking for food. We threw them cans of C rations, which they wrestled for like people at a baseball game going after a foul ball.

The craziest part of the trip came every time we passed a grammar school. We would fire a dozen or so cans of food into the playground. The entire school, hundreds of children, would then immediately emerge, screaming at the top of their lungs, running in all directions to get at the cans. The skirmishes that ensued were hysterical to watch. The kids were followed by red-faced teachers, steam coming out of their ears as they yelled, waved their arms, and tried to restore order.

Trading food for laughs like this wasn't very common, though. Most of our unwanted food was given away one can at a time to individuals we encountered on farms or footpaths. I was touched by how many guys in the platoon, instead of throwing away an unwanted can of white bread or beans, would lug it around for two or three weeks just to give it to the next emaciated old lady who clearly needed the calories. Doc Baldwin was always collecting discarded Cs for this purpose. Sometimes he had dozens of cans inside empty sandbags hanging from his backpack.

One reason that some rations weren't eaten was the limited variety. There were only about a half-dozen different main courses: ham and eggs, pork slices with gravy, beef slices with gravy, beans and franks, beans and meatballs, and—my personal favorite—ham with lima beans. Out in the field you ended up eating each one three to four times a week. It got repetitious. Most GIs had some meals that they just couldn't stomach anymore and would no longer eat under most circumstances. A lot of guys had taken to doctoring their meals with Tabasco sauce or other nonperishable condiments and spices from home.

At mealtime on most days, I was so hungry that I could eat the ass off a mule. This was especially true if things were hectic and I had missed a meal or two. Ham and lima beans had more grease than the other entrees, which is why I liked them. There were more calories per can in this stuff than anything else. Most of the time it wasn't possible to stop or to cook the meal and the grease remained congealed in a layer on top. Not wanting to discard the calories, I stirred the grease into the ham and beans below and wolfed the whole thing down cold.

Besides the main courses, there were side dishes inside each box of C rations. There were varying combinations of smaller cans of fruitcake, pound cake, pecan rolls, peaches, fruit cocktail, and pears. Those were some of the more sought-after items. There were also a larger number of C ration meals that contained less expensive, less tasty side items such as white bread or crackers. These, however, were accompanied by a smaller tin of yellow cheese spread, peanut butter, or jam to make them more palatable. These items provided some variety to mealtime but weren't enough to keep most GIs from getting tired of eating them over and over again. Eventually a lot of GIs began calling them, contemptuously, C rats.

Incredibly, some of the cans had dates on them going back to World War II. Most of the peanut butter was from 1942. I could hardly believe it. Quarter-century-old food. It was older than I was, but edible. Nobody got sick from it. Some of the guys thought that some of the old rations had an odd metallic taste, especially the yellow cheese spread. You couldn't prove it by me. I thought the stuff was great. I liked cheese in any form under any circumstances, so much so that I would have eaten gravel if it had a little melted cheddar on it.

Our convoy took us to Di An, which was an enormous, well-secured base. Infantry, armor, artillery, and thousands of support troops occupied several dozen square miles. There were hundreds of Quonset huts, wooden billets, and cinder block buildings. Charlie Company was going to camp out overnight on a softball field inside the camp. It was surrounded by hootches full of REMF (Rear Echelon Motherfucker) troops and had to have been one of the safest places in all of Vietnam.

The Big Red One conducted itself like a STRAC unit. That's an acronym for something like "straight trooper ready around the clock." It meant that we were anally retentive in our overall approach and tried hard to always be prepared for anything. It was sort of a better-safe-than-sorry approach. In the long run, this is a good thing. It meant that fewer people would go home in flag-draped, reusable metal boxes. That night the concept was being stretched a little too far. Despite our location, we set up a perimeter, dug foxholes in their softball field, set up claymores, and pulled our normal 50 percent guard duty all night. Our activity made us the center of attention and produced guffaws when the onlookers realized what we were doing. My claymore was aimed at three

GIs sitting on a porch in lawn chairs, drinking beer, and laughing at us. They thought we were a bunch of deranged paranoids.

After getting all dug in we sat around and laughed at ourselves. We were tired but secure. Someone brought up the story that the Viet Cong had a fifty-dollar bounty on Black Lions because they were always so well prepared, like that night, that it was hard to get the jump on them and kill them off in large numbers. I wanted that story to be true. It was an ego boost to have an image of myself as so bad that there was a bounty on my head. However, it may have been just another unstoppable jungle legend. Eventually, at one time or another, I would hear the same bounty claim made by just about every group in Vietnam, from Special Forces Green Berets to lifeguards at the Ben Hoa swimming pool. Everybody wanted to be perceived as a badass tough guy.

Early the next day we moved a few miles down the road to Long Binh. Our campsite was just outside the base in no-man's-land. Long Binh was enormous. It dwarfed Di An. Camping on its periphery was like being on the outskirts of Chicago. Inside was all the usual military stuff I'd seen at other bases, plus some unusual amenities such as a golf course, a bowling alley, several Olympic-sized swimming pools, and restaurants. The PX there had as much for sale as the ones back in the States. This place was a dream assignment for the REMF troops.

The site the company camped at was geographically odd. Flat spaces alternated with areas of depressions and small hills. Some areas were parched, with no vegetation. These alternated with thickets of thirty-foot trees. It was strange, as if God had had difficulty making firm decisions the day this portion of the earth was created.

Specialist E-4 Tom Jamison and I were sent farther out, about a hundred meters past some small, nearby hills to be an OP (observation post). If the company was stationary during the day, we sometimes sent out two guys to observe the situation in front of the company. This was an observation post. We did the same thing religiously at night. However, because the two guys couldn't see much in the dark and were listening to what was going on in front of the company it was called a listening post at night, not an observation post. We were supposed to be a cheap early-warning system. However, to warn anyone on this day we would have to shout out loud or fire our weapons in the air because we hadn't been given a radio, which was unusual for an OP.

Along the way to our OP position, I found a lustrous chrome cylinder the size of a flashlight. It had a screw cap. Another rookie mistake on my part occurred when impulsively, I picked it up. How stupid. I didn't even know what it was. It could have been anything, even a mine or a booby trap. I thought about that right after grabbing it. Not having the foggiest idea of what it could be, I showed it to Jamison.

"Oh, don't fool with it," he said, tossing it over a nearby knoll. He didn't know what it was either. I'd been excited about finding a military toy and he had wrecked my fun. He was obnoxious and wasn't very merry when he wasn't drinking.

Jamison selected a site on the crest of a little knoll and we tried to dig in. Our instructions were to produce a foxhole at our OP site. A thousand years of sun had baked the earth in the area to stone. Using the shovel like a pickax, we spent hours flailing away. Each swing chipped up a scrap of ground that was about the size of a fifty-cent piece. We were plunging toward the center of the earth at an inch an hour. My thoughts were that we should admit defeat and give up. Jamison insisted that we follow orders. He did outrank me. Everyone did. He would later make sergeant before accidentally doing himself in and being sent home on a stretcher.

It was hot, there was no shade, and the sun was hard upon us and bright. My head throbbed and my sweat glands stopped working. Sauntering over to a nearby stream, I collapsed to the ground for a short break and promptly drank three quarts of water. Returning to our excavation site, I drank two more quarts and didn't even have to pee. Five quarts of water in twenty minutes without pissing, it was astounding.

More excavation made the shovels duller, our tempers

shorter, and the hole not much deeper. Mercifully, a messenger arrived saying that the CO had changed his mind and didn't want an OP out there. It was as if the governor had called and commuted my sentence. This was wonderful, now I could stop digging and leave. Plus, I didn't have to spend any more time with Jamison. He was seriously dreary.

The following day, a patrol of two squads went out sixty-three hundred meters from the Long Binh perimeter. Sharp made me the point man for our squad. As usual, the point man was given the option of carrying a sawed-off shotgun. It was an army-issue Winchester 12-gauge called a trench gun, a relic left over from the Great War. Its barrel had been cut back a bit to fit the circumstances. The logic seemed to be that it was a little shorter than an M-16 so it didn't get in the way of your machete swings so much. Also it would be easier to hit someone with a left-handed shot if you were chopping with your right hand when you ran into the enemy.

A soldier named Fred Kirkpatrick seemed to walk point more often than anyone else. He was pleasant, well spoken, and a little too swarthy for a pure Irishman. Maybe the ancestors in his family tree included some of the fabled black Irish. Kirkpatrick took the shotgun approach a step further than anyone else. Normally only riflemen walked point, not machine gunners, grenadiers, or RTOs. Fred was a rifleman. However, when he was on point he sometimes swapped weapons with one of the grenadiers and carried a grenade launcher loaded with one of those 40-mm, beehive-round shotgun shells.

Part of my decision-making process should have been to find out what type of ammo was in the shotgun that they were offering me. Was it birdshot or buckshot? It could have been rock salt for all I knew. What would be best for hunting humans? Unfortunately, I was still too much of a military drone and didn't think to inquire about the ammunition. In any event, my choice that day was to stick with my rifle.

Some guys taped two clips together in a block so that they could reload quickly without digging into their canvas ammo pouches. They did this routinely, even when they weren't walking point. My worry was that the extra clip would fill with debris over time and jam my weapon unless the clips were cleaned regularly. Not having time to do this every night, I went with the one-clip approach most of the time. However, walking point was double-clip time for me, so I taped a couple together for the patrol.

The army told us that we could put twenty rounds in each clip. Coincidentally or not, that happened to be the number that came in one box of bullets. However, a widely accepted jungle legend dictated that a clip filled to capacity would put too much pressure on the spring mechanism inside. This could cause the clip to malfunction at some critical juncture, like when you really, really, really needed your rifle to fire. Accordingly, most of the riflemen in Charlie Company, me included, put only eighteen bullets in each clip. No one knew exactly why it was that number and not, say, seventeen or nineteen, but that's what we did. All of our clips were straight. None of us had any of the curved type, the banana clip that held thirty rounds. They weren't yet available.

The first half hour of my stint as the point man was absolutely draining, it sapped my strength. There were unexploded mortar rounds everywhere from years of random harassment fire. That's the way it was just outside all of our bases. As the point man, it was my duty to spot the rounds first and alert the guy behind me. If they were partially buried or hidden, it was also my job to drop a sheet of toilet paper on them as a marker. Trying to chop the jungle right in front of me, watch for trouble up ahead, and spot explosives on the ground was more than stressful. The stress was compounded in my own mind by the hacking noise of the machete, which made me feel about as inconspicuous as the leadoff batter in the World Series. Fortunately, reading the map wasn't the point man's job. Another guy in line, often the squad leader, did the navigating and told the lead man which way to go. Often the second in line didn't read the map either, because he was supposed to concentrate on being immediate firepower support for the point man if we walked into VC or NVA.

As much as possible I tried to cut through the vegetation with my left arm because it was much more comforting to carry my weapon on the right. This approach proved to be of only marginal utility. My spirit was willing but my flesh was weak. Multiple swings with the left arm were required to do the work of one good, right-handed swing. One feeble south-paw attempt glanced off a bamboo pole of only modest pro-portions and slammed into my left knee with the dull edge. The pain was alarming. For a second I thought that when I looked down my kneecap would be lying in the dirt between my boots. How inglorious, injured and sent back to the States because of a self-inflicted spastic attack.

Fortunately, it didn't even draw blood, for which I was grateful. Being overly self-conscious, I fretted about what others thought of me. The lack of blood would help me con-ceal the mishap and avoid the verbal slings and arrows of my current peer group. Later that day, my knee turned blue.

The patrol had begun with two columns of one squad each, moving parallel to each other but about twenty-five meters apart. One of our goals was to try to find the opening to any tunnels going into Long Binh that could be used for sabo-tage. Hacking out two paths simultaneously proved to be too loud and too slow. Part of the way through the patrol, Sharp realigned us into one column, with the other squad in front.

It was a thrill to get out of walking the point position until I was relocated as a caboose, the very last guy in the column. That was unbelievably creepy. Half of the movies that I'd ever seen about World War II in Asia or the Pacific had at least one guy that got picked off from the end of the column by having his throat slit from behind. As we walked, I could feel the eyes moving up and down my back. Chills went up my spine and made the hair on the nape of my neck stand up. Several times, I heard a noise behind me and damn near sprained my neck by jerking my head around quickly to spot my opponent. Frequently I moved up to the guy ahead of me in line, McClosky, then turned around and sank to one knee to stare back at the jungle, looking for any type of move-ment. Just before the column was about to lose me, I would get up and trot back to join them. The day went on and I never got used to the situation. When the patrol ended, the caboose position was just as creepy as it had been in the beginning.

Most of my nights were spent outdoors at nameless locations where we had stopped walking for the day and dug in. Sometimes sites were chosen because of their strategic value or easy defensibility. Other times they were chosen simply because that was where we happened to be when the sun went down. In general, there were two men at each foxhole. Sometimes, after everyone was assigned to a two-man position, there was one guy left over. His stock soared. Everyone wanted him. Whichever hole he was assigned to became a three-man position. This meant two hours of sleep for each hour of staying awake on guard duty instead of the usual one to one ratio. Occasionally they would deal with an odd number of guys by keeping the three-man machine-gun crew together at one hole. This didn't happen often enough as far as I was concerned.

Being awakened every other hour was torture for the circadian rhythm of life. It was distinctly unpleasant but survivable. The on-guard hours were a nightmare of boredom spent sitting on the edge of the foxhole listening and trying to go as long as humanly possible between peeks at your wristwatch. You couldn't sleep, smoke, read, talk, or anything. You could eat if it was quiet food. No opened-mouth lip smacking was advisable. I ate for recreational purposes, just for something to do. Unfortunately, my gut wasn't large enough to eat every other hour. In the dark, I played with my fingers ad infinitum, bending and contorting them in every conceivable way. Some sessions were spent making silhouettes of imaginary faces or animal heads and then wondering what the hand shadows would look like if I had a flood lamp and a blank wall. All the while, I was trying to follow the advice of a drill instructor from basic training to "be as quiet as a mouse pissing on cotton."

During my first few nights in the jungle, much of my thinking revolved around fear. Each falling leaf or passing insect sounded just like a platoon of Viet Cong headed for my position specifically to cut off my testicles. After a few nights, the leaves and insects began to sound like leaves and insects. This decrease in the fear factor helped push the boredom level to almost unbearable heights. Being forced to sit in the dark for hours with nothing to do and not fall asleep was worse than the Chinese water torture.

One night, when my fingers were worn out and my belly was full, I got out my stationery and started keeping a diary. Now there was something to do on guard duty in the jungle. By the light of the moon or sometimes just the stars I wrote away the time. As I would discover, some nights were too dark to see what I was writing but that tended not to stop me. Legible script was possible if you wrote slowly and deliberately using "The Palmer Method" of penmanship that the nuns had taught me in grammar school.

There were descriptions of what had transpired that day, who had said what, and even diagrams of weapons or small crude maps. Often the writing caused my mind to wander as I searched for just the right phrase or word. This made the time pass even more quickly. It was a miracle. The simple concept of a journal had changed the most mundane, tedious, and painful aspect of my Vietnam existence, night guard duty, into an entertaining and relaxing avocation. Of course, basic ground rules still applied, so that the paper had to be quiet, none of that crackling, crunchy parchment type stuff. On my return to Lai Khe, I bought enough notebooks to write the sequel to *War and Peace*.

We spent most of the next two days on guard duty at our campsite on the outskirts of Long Binh. This was tantamount to getting a weekend off. Coincidentally it happened to be Saturday and Sunday. Ironically, this was the only period in my life during which the days of the week did not need names. It didn't matter if the months had names, it only mattered that they passed.

More standard ailments of this Oriental paradise visited me, namely crotch rot and trench foot. Most soldiers simply referred to all skin problems as jungle rot. I wasn't sure if in my case they were the same pathological problem in different anatomical locations or distinct maladies. The working theory was that trench foot was a breakdown of the skin caused by its being wet for too long. The rot problem was breakdown caused by fungus. They looked similar, with the skin becoming red and irritated then sloughing off. It itched like hell and looked ghastly. There was leprosy in Vietnam and because I was more of a worrier than a warrior at heart this bothered me a little until the others reassured me that no GIs ever got leprosy.

The Medical Corps had little square tins of what they believed to be a miraculous white powder. It cured the skin, it was said, no matter what the problem. However, it wasn't working for me. A doctor that I bumped into at one of the bases told me that the trick was to dry things out at night. He suggested that I open my fly, let the wind in, and even let my privates hang out. The open-fly part was acceptable to me but not the rest. I couldn't accept looking like a pervert dangling his dork for bait in some type of bizarre mosquito trap. As it turned out, the rot would come and go of its own volition. When you left the Nam, it would leave you.

A more pressing problem for me at the moment was my grossly swollen trigger finger. It was thicker than my thumb and it throbbed. Everyone in the squad agreed that it was a classic case of bamboo poisoning, an infection started by a bamboo splinter. If I was lucky, my whole arm would swell up like an inner tube, necessitating a respite in the hospital to get antibiotics. Fortunately Doc saved me from that fate with penicillin pills. The jungle was a constant challenge to your immune system. If the VC didn't get you, the germs would.

FEBRUARY

On the Sunday of that weekend that we spent on the edge of Long Binh, I was included in the half of our squad that was sent to guard four engineers from a demolition unit. It seems that the overabundance of mortars spotted on the previous patrol had come in part from an ammo dump that had been blown up by saboteurs. The demo team was to retrieve the still-functional shells. We escorted them out and stood guard as they worked, at what we assumed was a safe distance. They must have known what they were doing because they collected mortars all over the place without one detonation. They acted as if they were immortal. They didn't even carry weapons for protection. At 1600 hours sharp, their workday ended and we returned them to the base.

Two other grunts and I were then sent back out to do LP duty. We sneaked out about seventy-five meters with a radio just as the sun went down. We tried to time our departure so that there was just enough light left that we could see where we were going and what was in front of us. We wanted to arrive at our LP site just as it became too dark for anyone to see us, which was tricky timing. There would be many chances for me to practice in the future because as a rule each rifle platoon sent out one LP every night that we were in the boondocks. Happily, we didn't send out LPs when we were at Lai Khe.

Being on LP was more dangerous than staying back at the night lager with the others. On LP there would be no safety in numbers at our location, and if we got into trouble no one was going to march out to save our butts before sunrise. We would be on our own. Despite the risks, I still subscribed to the Alfred E. Newman school of thought, "What, me worry?" I hadn't given the situation the serious consideration that it deserved and wasn't overly concerned. I just zoned out and let the others do the worrying.

Trying to be as quiet as possible meant no foxhole. Although we would sometimes dig a hole during daylight at an OP, we never dug one at an LP. Three men on LP was a treat, because LP was typically a two-man position. That was it. We just listened to see if anyone was coming. At five minutes after each hour the one who was awake would put on the radio headphones. The platoon RTO would call to check on us.

"Lima Papa one, this is one-six, sitrep, over."

Sitrep was army talk for situation report.

We didn't speak back. If everything was cool, you were to press the speaker button on the radio's handset twice, slowly. The command post would hear two clicks. All was copasetic. If there were problems or VC around, the response was a single click. This would trigger a series of terse questions that were to be answered, one click for yes or two clicks for no. That night our situation remained two clicks every hour.

We stayed there at the LP site most of the next day functioning as an observation post. The sun was roasting the place when we rejoined the company. The perimeter line was fairly flat and defoliated, probably the work of bulldozers. Our foxholes were at least thirty meters apart, twice the usual distance, because the area was wide open with good visibility between all the positions. There was also good visibility out in front of our line for a ways until thick vegetation started.

Considering the open spaces and clear lines of vision, I was more than a little dismayed to find a booby-trap hand grenade in the bottom of my foxhole. At first it appeared to be just a grenade that had fallen off someone's belt, nothing more. No one was missing a grenade, however, and the others, including Fairman, insisted that it was serious business. Our hole had been left empty overnight and apparently the guys guarding the holes on either side had been a little too casual in their efforts. The grenade was almost completely buried with its spoon down. We couldn't tell if there was another one under it or if something else was under the dirt where you would have to stand to reach the grenade we could see. For a moment we stood there pondering the situation. Gilbert squinted and Fairman bitched. Then we got down to the basic problem at hand and began discussing various angles and approaches to disarming or removing the device. They all approximated a crapshoot. In my mind, I weighed the merits of risking everything to save my hole versus the chances of having a heart attack or heatstroke while digging a new hole. Discretion prevailed. Huish, who secretly wanted to be a demolition man, gave me one of the blocks of C-4 he carried. It destroyed the grenade and the hole, turning that into a wide but shallow pit.

All things considered, the episode was clearly headache material. If they could sneak in with impunity and do this type of thing, then why hadn't they already killed me in the middle of the night? What was there to stop them from trying it sometime in the near future? The situation should have alarmed me more than it did. However, like a juvenile dunce, I was still more concerned about having to dig a new foxhole than about someone planting a lethal device in the area that might blow off my legs.

Fairman hung around after the C-4 explosion to give me some hints on how deep to dig my new hole and how much effort to put into the project. Then he reversed course and decided that because I didn't have a hole I could join Will Smithers on LP. This was a scary proposition. Smithers had been in the country half as long as I. We were both ignorant FNGs. We were to go out into Injun country, alone, at night, and I'm the guy in charge. Something was seriously wrong with this scenario. Wouldn't it be simpler to just shoot me?

Smithers was a new replacement, a nice guy from Tennessee with brown hair that always seemed to be in place even though I never saw him use a comb. It was even like that after he wore his helmet all day. He often had his mouth slightly open, like a fish, or James Dean in the movies.

The night was uneventful except for my nerves. It wasn't anything like the previous night's LP. Because I was the guy in charge of the patrol, I couldn't quite just follow along blindly. I had to think about things like which way to walk, where a good place to stop might be, whether we might be making too much noise, and what to do if we saw enemy or—worse—they saw us. The situation definitely had me worried.

We stumbled our way out but not the requested hundred meters. After about seventy meters, it appeared to me that while the distance wasn't all that far, there was so much thick vegetation between us and the NDP that we were really cut off from the others. Feeling isolated and vulnerable, I made a command decision that because seventy meters was almost a hundred, we would stop and set up our LP right there. Smithers didn't seem concerned at having me for a leader, which made me pretend even harder that I knew what I was doing. For me it was a scary night, even though our sitreps were always two clicks. When it was finally over and we got to rejoin the company I was greatly relieved. Admittedly, I also felt a little pride at having pulled off the patrol. It occurred to me that I had done all right. Some of these tasks, like point man and LP, required only a little common sense, grit, and determination, not specific learned skills like map reading.

One of my secret fears was that Fairman would make me the map reader–navigator on a patrol. We'd end up in Malaysia. Rand McNally, I was not. I hadn't been able to read maps well back at infantry training in the States and the maps in the Nam were worse, they were absolutely inscrutable! If it didn't have a large dot with an arrow and the phrase "You Are Here," it was beyond my skills. Fortunately, they never handed me a map.

There was a new guy in the company, Sergeant Rodarte, a career military man. He had just transferred to the army from the navy because he believed that there would be more opportunities for promotion in the army. It wasn't clear to me if he realized that positions were opening up because the people in the army were getting killed.

Rodarte was a really fun guy, a friendly person with a wide range of interests who enjoyed a good discussion. Maybe being a good conversationalist was something he had developed while floating around at sea for long periods without much else to do. He was a tad portly and early on seemed to get worn out by long marches, carrying all the gear we had to carry. With these things in mind, Doc Baldwin gave him the nickname of The Dart. It was the antithesis of his appearance. We all thought it was funny and The Dart didn't seem to mind.

It was intriguing that The Dart, like me, couldn't read a map very well. But whereas I had been trained in map reading but just didn't get it, he simply hadn't had much map training in the navy. He might have been great at reading sonar reports or depth charts, but that wasn't going to help him much in the infantry. Given that he was a squad leader, this was a significant problem. Fortunately, he was smart enough to realize it and solved the problem by admitting it up front and getting help from riflemen in his squad like Cordova, who had already been in Vietnam for several months and was a good map reader.

With each passing day, I felt and became a bit more of a vagabond, resigned to my current role, doomed to wander around this little area of Southeast Asia without meaningful connection to the outside world until they told me that I could go home. Sometimes I would carry my wallet with me as a money pouch when we were going to be away from Lai Khe for any length of time. However, a lot of the time it sat in my footlocker. It no longer went with me on the short one-day patrols or night ambush duty across the river outside of the Lai Khe perimeter.

I never carried my keys anymore. At first the key ring had been comforting. It held one of those inch-long license plates that the DAV (Disabled American Veterans) mailed to your house for a donation. It matched the California plates on my mom's VW bug and in theory would get lost keys returned to you if the finder dropped them in any mailbox. Initially, having the key ring in my pocket connected me to home and helped keep me safe. Now I was feeling more secure and really didn't want to lose it. So it stayed in my footlocker as well.

The same went for my driver's license and other identification. Losing any of those in Vietnam would be a major mistake. One of the most indefatigable jungle legends was that, if the VC discovered your stateside address, they would mail a bomb or exploding package to your family. This story was told at basic training in California, at advanced infantry training in Georgia, at the jungle school in Nam, and at every airport USO in between. Better yet, half of the raconteurs claimed to have actually known one of the victims. The story was just unstoppable. Of course, I had relayed the warning to my parents, who then stayed on the lookout for suspicious packages the entire time I was overseas.

Our next patrol was another search-and-destroy mission. The full company went out, but didn't find much. To be honest, we didn't find anything. To be really honest, after a while our platoon couldn't even find the rest of the company. I think that Lieutenant Judson was plotting our course. Sometimes he stayed in the rear as our XO (executive officer) and sometimes he was out in the field with the 1st Platoon. Unfortunately, today he was with us and must have been reading the map with his left eye.

Our platoon was hundreds of meters away from the rest of the company, maybe even as far as a kilometer. The gravity of the situation became more obvious as the shadows lengthened, and we quickened our pace to link up. Radio chatter was incessant. Smoke grenades were thrown often to signal to each other where we were at as we tried to bull our way through the thickness that stood between us and the rest of the company.

As we rushed, my Instamatic and my gas mask were ripped from my gear. Huish found the camera and later returned it to me.

"You gave the VC a gas mask?" Lieutenant Judson bellowed. "Goddamn it!"

It was clear to me that the course of the war in Southeast

Asia might hinge on this one lost item of equipment. What a bonehead! This guy loses an entire company, marches us halfway to Burma by mistake, then blisters me over a lousy gas mask. I gave him a flat stare. It had been a difficult and draining day. Most of us were in the grips of the fuck-'em syndrome, including myself. My stare said it plainly. "Fuck you." He walked away shaking his head. Fortunately, he hadn't noticed that I had slipped while he was cursing me and jammed my gun barrel into the ground, clogging it with soil.

On ambush that night, Tynes, Smithers, and I manned the end position of our line, which was in the weeds and shrubs a few feet off a dirt road, just the nearside of a bend in the road. After an uneventful night we began to pack up. A thick morning fog covered everything, making us all slightly damp. My claymore was ten or twelve meters down the road, pointing up the dogleg. I tiptoed over to retrieve it. As I knelt down to unscrew the blasting cap, a glance up the road revealed that the cloud of fog had suddenly parted like the Red Sea. A platoon of Viet Cong were on the road and headed in my direction, shoulder to shoulder, four abreast, and six or seven rows deep. They weren't spread out like a patrol but marched in formation as if it was the May Day parade in Moscow. Dressed in black or khaki, most had floppy canvas hats, but some were bareheaded. Some, but not all, carried rifles. I think one guy was carrying an axe. They were a motley group but distinctly fearsome in appearance. I didn't have time to notice much else. I quickly decided to get my ass out of there as fast as possible.

Scared shitless was the best way to describe me. Leaving the mine, I raced back, trying to strike a careful balance between moving quickly and being quiet. To my mind, I accomplished neither. I told Tynes that there was a whole bunch of them coming down the road. He stared at me real hard for two full seconds, looking for a better explanation in the depths of my eyes. Saying nothing, he crawled back to the road and almost dislocated his neck trying to see what might be around the bend. Returning, he waved me to stop standing there like an idiot and get down before shouting a whispered warning to the next position.

We all faced the road, motionless, and waited with our weapons pointing out for about half a minute. Each of us glanced from face-to-face searching for the one who knew where they were. They didn't materialize. Tynes rose to put on his backpack.

"Let's go, let's get out of here," he said. We all followed suit without comment, including Sergeant Conklin, the ambush leader.

Not wanting to go back toward my claymore, I yanked the wire hard and reeled it in like a fish. Thank God it didn't get hung up on anything. We didn't exactly run back but we were certainly moving a hell of a lot faster than our normal walking speed. The captain seemed mildly interested but not overly concerned. As far as I know, our plans for the day were not changed in any way to deal with the VC I'd seen.

As it turned out, our plan for the day was a fifty-eight hundred-meter sweep, during which we didn't find so much as a cigarette butt. The real fun came when the hike was over. There weren't any flat spaces or rice paddies nearby but the brass wanted us to get some supplies via helicopter. Maybe it was something semi-urgent such as batteries for the radios or new maps. Anyway, we had to chop out a fifty-meter-square landing zone. Half the company stood guard and the rest of us cut down everything using axes and machetes.

After an hour of landscaping like deranged gardeners, we had the area sufficiently denuded of vegetation. Only one obstacle to a helicopter landing remained. Looming like one of the great pyramids of Egypt in the center of our proposed new landing zone was an anthill six feet high and three feet thick at the base. This stalagmite was made out of some secret cement-like substance, the formula for which only the ants knew. It was as hard and heavy as concrete, and could have stopped a tank. We took turns pummeling at it with axes and shovels until we were blue in the face. The results were negligible at best. The ants were going in and out of a hole on the tip of the anthill and their activity by this point was quite frenzied. We widened the hole using a shovel, then packed two claymores and a few blocks of C-4 inside. Huish cut a fuse thirty seconds in length so that there would be plenty of time to run and hide. I was laughing as I ran, remembering putting firecrackers in ant holes back home as a child and thinking, now this time I'm really going to win.

To my amazement, after a thunderous explosion, the smoke cleared to reveal the anthill still standing. It had been cracked in half vertically with the two sides spread apart at the top creating a big V sticking out of the ground. All the ants were gone, turned into a fine mist. It took several of us to wrestle it down, one side at a time. Voilà, a landing zone.

That night we had ambush patrol with Mr. Blind Leadership, Tom Jamison, leading the charge. It was a good thing that we had finished the LZ, I thought: We were going to need to use it to have ourselves flown out on a medevac helicopter before the patrol was over. It was truly a nightmare.

Leaving the NDP, we went out about a thousand meters over hilly terrain covered with six-foot elephant grass and arrived at where we thought we were supposed to be. The distance was unusually long. We didn't normally get a full kilometer away from the rest of the company on ambushes. As usual, before going out, the squad leader, Jamison, showed the weapons platoon our anticipated ambush site on the map. They, in turn, marked several sites on the map that we could call mortar or artillery fire onto to help us locate our true position or guide bombardment of the enemy if we got into trouble. That night's checkpoints had all been given female names.

As we set up our ambush, Jamison radioed for one artillery shell to be fired at Mabel, three hundred meters due south of us. BOOM! The shell landed five hundred meters to the east. Jamison studied the map, pirouetted 360 degrees, turned the map upside down, turned another 360 degrees and then called for a shot at Sally, three hundred meters to the east. BOOM! This one landed off to the north. We were lost. By now, the sun was down and the moon was so dull it would have been easier to read the map using the Braille method.

Furthermore, it wasn't wise to continue jabbering on the radio. It was clearly time to circle the wagons. We moved to the top of a nearby knoll and set up a three-position triangle defense in the tall elephant grass.

This wasn't an ambush anymore. We were hiding. Being lost meant no artillery support if we got attacked, no mede-vac helicopters if we had wounded, and not being able to call the company out to help us if we were getting picked apart. This was serious stuff.

The gravity of the situation wasn't completely lost on me, but it didn't strike fear into my heart and leave me trembling at the prospects, at least not during the first half of the night. When on guard, I sat with my legs crossed, writing in my journal, unconcerned, like Mr. Magoo with the proverbial wrecking ball whizzing by, inches from my head, and slamming into unwary bystanders or thick brick walls while I escaped unscathed. It was business as usual. I was an ignorant dope.

Around midnight, the safe atmosphere of my elephant grass nest began to evaporate as footsteps approached from my left. I heard an occasional muffled clanking of gear. The footsteps, though, soon became multiple pairs of feet and were so close that there wasn't time to wake up Gilbert and Smithers, the other two guys at my position. Quietly, I rotated 180 degrees, faced into the triangle, and switched my rifle to my left hand. The Viet Cong were now approaching me from my right side and walking through our formation without realizing that we were there. Ever so slowly leaning back and raising my rifle, I pointed the barrel in the face of the first guy, their point man, and held my breath, petrified. Moonlight was visible in his eyes and reflexively I squinted my eyes a little so he wouldn't see it in mine. When he passed in front of me, about three feet away, I was frozen. My rifle was then pointing toward the second guy. In the space of about half a minute, a full squad of VC waltzed past me. My after-guess was that there had been about ten of them.

There hadn't been enough room inside my skull at the time to count them. They were probably in the next province before I was able to exhale and relax the grip on my rifle. I didn't know whether to start crying, shit in my pants, or throw up. My urge was to do all three. The episode was awful, beyond terrifying. I thought they were going to kill me. My brain had been in overdrive, racing to outthink them. Shooting at them had been out of the question. It would have been suicidal for all of us to have them inside the triangle shooting out at us and our three positions of GIs shooting across the triangle at them and each other. I thought fast, came up with no plan, did nothing, and it worked. Like Magoo, I had emerged unscathed, but I was no longer thinking like Mr. Magoo.

When my hour of guard duty was up, I awakened Smithers but decided against trying to explain what had transpired. That would have entailed too much of a conversation and too much noise. It was a surprise for me in the morning to find out that none of the others had heard the VC squad passing through our position. When I filled them in on the story, they seemed only moderately interested, as if because it was over it didn't really matter anymore. What a dull group. They weren't in the least excited about what was definitely an unusual episode.

A lazy two-kilometer march the next day took us to a road where trucks came to pick us up. Thankfully, we had more than enough time allotted to make this move, so we hadn't fallen behind when I brought our column to a halt by banging into an ant metropolis. This was a basketball-sized nest, spherical, with outer walls of broad green leaves. Inside were tens of thousands of stinging fire ants. It was suspended in a bush about six feet off the ground.

Every once in a while, somebody walked into one and broke it apart. Today it was my turn. The nest cracked open like Humpty Dumpty and showered me with ants. They reacted poorly and began stinging the shit out of me as if I were a long-tongued anteater. My helmet and rifle fell to the ground as I went into spastic gyrations designed to get me out of my backpack, web gear, and shirt. The column ahead of me moved on. The column behind me held up with those near me offering assistance. They had been there before.

The delay wasn't inordinate, maybe a minute or two. Soon, Alvarez was back to see what the problem was. By this time, I was putting my gear back on and getting ready to go. Still he was disgusted, scowling, shaking his head in contempt over the delay, and saying out loud that someday I was going to get everybody all fucked up. He seemed a trifle histrionic to me.

For lunch back at Long Binh, we had hot chow and cold beer, Hamm's. It was always Hamm's or Pabst Blue Ribbon in this neck of the world. We were told that nobody was to drink more than two. Afterward, we walked to the southern edge of Long Binh where we were going to set up camp for the night. A few local majors and colonels showed up to pow-wow with our new company commander, Captain Burke. They were from G-2, the intelligence group, and said that the VC were trying hard to blow up the Long Binh ammo dump. As a result, units such as ours had been imported to run extra sweeps in the area and to send out increased numbers of night ambush patrols. There was a frank discussion about the ARVN being involved in what was essentially going to be an inside job. What a sorry state of affairs. Those guys were supposed to be on our side.

My unfortunate part of this little drama was another night on ambush duty. Ten of us went out half a click, about five hundred meters. Click was our slang for a kilometer, about three thousand feet. We set up our ambush in the usual fashion. About midnight, the sorry state of affairs became a fucking mess when the ammo dump went up. A mammoth roaring explosion shook the ground as a monstrous fireball lurched straight upward before burning itself out. Bob Reeves felt the explosion at Di An, several miles away.

The dump then erupted with blast after blast, which sent red, white, and orange fireballs in all directions. Red-hot chunks of scrap iron, shrapnel, and tracers flew everywhere. Glowing mortar and artillery shells sailed skyward, then drifted slowly back to earth, and exploded on impact. Some

of the time there were so many things going off simultaneously that you couldn't hear individual detonations, just a
continuous rolling roar. It was like every *Victory at Sea* film
I'd ever seen on one reel and it went on all night long.

I felt safe. My guess was that we were about a click away
and therefore wouldn't have anything bad land on us unless
God was feeling really irritable at the moment. Furthermore,
any VC with even half a brain would be hotfooting it out of
the area and would not want to fuck with us in any way. My
hours on guard that night were actually entertaining. The on-
going multicolored light show of explosions and secondary
explosions was the best fireworks display imaginable. Unfortunately, it wasn't the Fourth of July and there was no band
playing a John Philip Sousa march.

The next morning, we walked back to the beat of continuing explosions as the fire in the dump raged out of control.
Around late afternoon, it subsided and eventually burned out.
Stars and Stripes reported that several trucks and some small
sheds had been swallowed up in the conflagration. One GI
had been blown out of his bunk and suffered a broken arm.
Reportedly "hundreds of tons of explosives" had been lost.
According to *Stars and Stripes*, it had been "the largest ammunition dump in the world." Now it was a charcoal pit.

A squad-sized patrol in the morning produced nothing. We
had been searching the area just outside Long Binh for a tunnel entrance. Everyone knew that those bastards could dig
like moles and that they might have used a tunnel to pull off
the ammo dump caper. Personally, I doubted it, choosing to
believe that they had had assistance from inside the camp. It
seemed logical and easier.

In the afternoon, we swapped jobs with another squad.
They went out on another fruitless patrol and we guarded the
perimeter. When dusk arrived, we headed back out for a
night ambush pretty close to where we had been the previous
night. We hadn't quite picked our spot yet when Huish, who
was the caboose taking up the rear, spotted two VC off to his
right about fifty meters away. They also spotted him and
everyone dove for cover with no shots fired. A decision was

made to crawl into a nearby thicket and set up our ambush right there in case they traveled back that way later. We waited.

Huish's two gooks had made me nervous. Now, all of a sudden, the metal dog tags around my neck sounded like giant Chinese gongs. I took them off and hung them on a nearby tree branch so that they wouldn't chime every time I moved. All the rear-echelon guys had little rubber linings that covered the edges of their tags to dampen any metallic clinking. We didn't get them out in the field. Some guys taped their tags together to prevent any noise. After taking mine off, my next move was to pull the tear gas grenade from my web gear and attach it to the front of my shirt. I hadn't removed the dog tags before, but did reposition the grenade whenever I had the heebie-jeebies on ambush patrol, which was at least a quarter of the time. If we were badly shot up or nearly wiped out and had to run for our lives, my plan was to trail the gas behind me as I ran. With luck, that would choke them up and slow them down if they were chasing me. Anyway, my gyrations were unnecessary that night, and the sun came up without incident.

When we withdrew in the morning, I forgot about the dog tags and inadvertently left them behind. The loss didn't really concern me and I never asked how to replace them. Subconsciously, I may have wanted to lose them and had some delight at having done so. I was tired of hearing the story of how if you were killed, some moron at the grave registration office would put one of the little steel plates between your two upper front teeth then smack your jaw shut to wedge the dog tag in your upper jaw. This was to ensure proper identification of the body forever. As the story went, they did it that way in World War II, they did it that way in Korea, and they were continuing the fine tradition in Vietnam. I wasn't sure if it was true or just another jungle legend. It sounded so gruesome that I was quite sure that it would be exceedingly painful even if I were already dead. Honestly, I'd rather get seared with a red-hot branding iron for identification purposes than undergo the dog tag in the teeth routine.

Besides your name, serial number, religion, and branch of service, the dog tags listed your blood type. My original tags from basic training stated that I was A positive. After they were lost and then replaced during advanced training, I had mysteriously been transformed to A negative. If my tags were replaced overseas, there is no telling what I might have degenerated to, maybe monkey blood.

At the company club, back in Lai Khe, there was a radio that sometimes picked up Hanoi Hannah. She spoke English and proudly told us which infantry units had recently gotten their asses kicked, how many helicopters had been shot down, and which aircraft carriers were cruising the waters of Yankee Station or Dixie Station off the coast of Vietnam. She also announced how many U.S. servicemen had died during the previous week. At times, she even gave a few names. I thought it would have been immensely cool to have them find my dog tags and later have her announce my name over the radio as having been killed in action. I listened when I could but, of course, it never happened.

The brass were smarting from the ammo dump fiasco and wanted to nail a few local VC hides to the wall. It meant squad-sized patrols in the morning, squad-sized patrols in the afternoon, and squad-sized ambushes at night. It was getting repetitious. Today, the official army rumormongers, G-2 intelligence, arrived to inform us that the VC were planning to blow up a nearby seven-story electrical tower. It carried high-voltage power to Long Binh and would be a choice target. Around noon, we walked out to the tower and scouted the area for a good ambush site later that night.

For the remainder of the afternoon, we sat around with the rest of the company back at the bivouac area by Long Binh. While relaxing there, I was enveloped by a sense of doom. It wasn't just the heebie-jeebies or the willies, as I called the occasional attacks of nonspecific nervousness that we all experienced now and then. It was ominous. I truly believed that the VC were going to be out there that night. Something bad was going to happen. I might even get killed on that ambush patrol. The premonition was so strong that it was difficult to ignore. I was afraid. I didn't want to go out but had to. The feeling was uncomfortable and lasted for the remainder of the day and the first part of the patrol. This turned out to be the only premonition of my own death while I was in Vietnam. I was grateful for that.

At dusk, we returned to the tower and set up about a hundred meters away. We didn't want to be much closer because the area at the base of the tower had been laced with antipersonnel mines. An hour after we settled in, the tower was barely visible against the backdrop of lights from Long Binh in the distance. The minor mental breakdown that had afflicted me earlier had mysteriously disappeared. During my first hour of watch, it was a struggle to stay awake. I was locked in battle with my eyelids, trying to keep them open, when a rock landed in the brush a few feet away. That snapped me back to reality. Motionless, I awaited further developments. Another rock sailed in. Was it possible the guys at the next position were screwing around? No, that would be unfathomable; you don't throw things when you're in the dark surrounded by nervous teenagers with automatic weapons. Just then a little light went on in my head. The VC were out there with us and were trying to figure out our positions by drawing fire. Another rock landed.

A figure, crouching low, came at me through the brush on my right. Leveling my rifle toward him, I pulled the trigger halfway back before deciding to stop and cry out "Halt, who's there?" instead of just blasting away. My yell was way too loud. It should have been more of a whisper. The person coming toward me turned out to be Sharp. He told me to keep it down, asked if we were throwing stuff, and assured me that they were not.

"Keep cool, I think we got company," he said, then crawled away without any other suggestions or instructions. I was so upset at having come within milliseconds of killing Sergeant Sharp that the VC no longer concerned me. The feeling in my gut was awful. I would never completely forget it. The event dredged up memories of exploding the claymore in jungle school, which helped make the rest of the night even more unpalatable than it already was.

Over the next hour, several more rocks flew in. We played a patient waiting game and eventually the probing ceased for the night. I was a bundle of nerves by the time it was over. The next day, in retrospect, we all agreed that it had been wise not to give away our position with rifle shots but wondered if we shouldn't have lobbed a grenade or two. Who knows, we might have gotten lucky. We also decided that maybe it was a victory of sorts, if G-2 was right and they were out there to blow up a tower but couldn't do it because of us.

That night had been an example of OJT (on the job training). A lot of the Vietnam experience was OJT. We hadn't been trained how to deal with many specific situations, like how to react when the VC hide in the brush and throw rocks at your night ambush formation. We were smart enough to figure out to be quiet but not advanced enough in our thinking to heave grenades back. Like a lot of situations, we learned as we went. Next time it happened we would think of using grenades. That's the way OJT worked in a combat zone. You either got killed or figured out what to do.

My nerves were still agitated over having almost greased Sharp. We hadn't used passwords much so far. When we did it was often *soul* as the challenge word and *brother* as the response. We figured that the VC wouldn't know that one. Maybe we should have had a password every night to smooth things over and cut down on accidental shootings if someone had to go from one position to another after dark. It was a thought, but I wasn't in charge. Sharp was oblivious to how close he came to going home early.

When the sun came up, we left without incident and rejoined the company, where apparently there were no plans for the day. When the leadership realized this, they suggested digging more foxholes. We already had enough for everyone, so they then suggested that we dig them deeper. We agreed. We wanted to be ready if the Harlem Globetrotters happened by during a mortar attack and needed to use our holes. Satisfied that we were doing something, anything, they left us alone.

Later that day, there was a forty-minute lecture on field sanitation, malaria, hepatitis, and VD. Attendance was mandatory. It was so boring that I was damn near in a coma by the time it was over. The least they could have done to liven up things was show that sleazy VD film with the excruciating genital sores. Afterward, I showed my prick to the lecturer. His eyes lit up.

"That's jungle rot," he said. "Talk to your medic. He's got these little tins of powder."

I groaned as I thanked him for his sage advice.

We were turned loose to visit the base PX, which was closed because the REMF people who ran it didn't work past midafternoon. This turned out to be a blessing in disguise. Instead of shopping, we wandered around and found a watering point. This consisted of a cement slab with a little plywood put up around the edges for some, but not complete, privacy. Large rubber bladders were suspended overhead, full of water, like giant douche bags. We stripped down, turned on the spigots, and got our first shower since leaving Lai Khe. It made the whole day worthwhile. It didn't seem right to have to put on the same old grimy underwear afterward, but still it was a good deal.

We regrouped as a company and marched out fifteen hundred meters to a relatively safe area in the bush and dug in for the night. As usual, everyone put out claymores. I had procured a trip flare to put under my claymore, as some of the others did. The idea was that if a gook picked up your mine to swipe it or turn it around, the flare would go off and alert you. Vietnam was rife with stories about claymores being turned around so that when fired, the seven hundred steel .25-caliber ball bearings would fly back at the GIs.

I had heard that jungle legend a lot. A bigger problem seemed to be misguided GIs who set them up facing in the wrong direction to start with. In theory, these rectangular, freestanding, aboveground mines resembled miniature versions of a drive-in movie screen. Thoughtless GIs were setting them up the wrong way because they thought that was the way the "screen" was supposed to face. Accordingly, as a warning, they had large embossed letters on one side that said "front toward enemy."

The next morning, having completely forgotten about how clever I had been with the trip flare, I removed the blasting cap, then picked up the mine. POOF! The trip flare went off, giving me second-degree burns on my right palm and ring finger. The burns hurt so badly that I dropped the mine. Of course, the flash of the trip flare had momentarily blinded me. Now, staring down to see where the blasting cap and the mine were was like looking at a welding torch.

POW! The trip flare ignited the blasting cap, which went off in my face, tattooing me with pebbles. Fearing that the mine would go next and shred me with a cloudburst of ball bearings, I raced for my foxhole and dove in headfirst. The flare sputtered on for a few seconds, then died without igniting the mine. From the bottom of my hole, I was saying a silent prayer that all this had gone unnoticed, when I heard someone on the radio reporting flares going off, shots being fired, and troops jumping into foxholes. It sounded like we were being overrun by the enemy.

Soon, Fairman and Captain Burke showed up. It wouldn't be possible to fake or lie my way out of this one, so I admitted everything in matter-of-fact tones as if it was no big deal. Captain Burke had just recently taken over as our CO. He replaced Paone, who had done six months in the field and then rotated to the rear. Apparently the company-level officers only did half a year in the thick of it, then got put in a safer job for the rest of their year in the Nam. Burke was a career military man in his twenties who sometimes had the curious habit of wearing his wristwatch in a buttonhole on his shirt near its left collar. So far, he appeared to be an equable leader who took important issues seriously but didn't get too agitated over trivial matters. After being apprised of the situation he turned and walked away without comment. The captain was, however, shaking his head as if to signal that I was a dumb-ass. He was beginning to think of me as possibly the reincarnation of Sad Sack or Beetle Bailey.

The previous night, Tynes had tried to tell me not to forget the trip flare in the morning when I went out to collect my mine. He was probably fearful that I would end up doing what I had just done. Undoubtedly, he had never heard my father's frequent admonition about his children that, "You can always tell a Ronnau but you can't tell him much."

Fairman was a tad more outwardly agitated by the situation. He felt obliged to scowl contemptuously, as well as grouse out loud for everyone to hear. It was a part of his job description and, believe me, he did it quite well. Sensing a lack of sympathy, I decided not to mention my burned finger to Fairman. That would only prolong the agony of our encounter.

Mornings in Nam weren't easy and this one was typical. Breakfast for me was just coffee. Of course, the first few cigarettes of the day after not smoking all night, were smoked so hard it was almost like eating them. Then, just like clockwork, along came a bowel movement. Unfortunately, you had to go outside of the perimeter for this. We didn't want to deposit a bunch of smelly dumps inside our camp. That wouldn't be pleasant if we stayed at this location for any length of time. Besides, who on God's green earth wanted to be quietly eating breakfast and look up to see some guy's hairy ass taking a crap?

Often enough, I got a case of the willies when I was out there alone, squatting with my pants down. Most days, I just set my rifle on the ground while I did my business. However, whenever I had the willies I tried to hang on to it. It's hard to squat, poop, and wipe while holding a rifle in a serviceable fashion, but I learned. Fortunately, without fail the caffeine and nicotine acted like a high colonic enema, so that I never had to stay out there too long. The feeling of being exposed and vulnerable every morning during this ritual never left me, however.

We were required to shave regularly and this too was part of my morning routine. Small mustaches were acceptable but beards were not. We hadn't had a bearded president since Benjamin Harrison. Our commanders in chief shaved regularly and so would we. It was the army way. One or two days' worth of growth might be tolerated, but not much more. Some guys actually carried a can of shaving cream on operations out in the field. Not me. My way was to wash my face in the morning, then shave before washing off the soap.

I wasn't a fan of trying to shave without any lubricant. Back in basic training the drill instructors occasionally made us dry shave, without even water, and that wasn't fun. This was sometimes done as a group retaliation for a perceived offense, such as having left the latrine messy. At other times, the reasons were not readily apparent. It was sometimes ordered under the guise of character building even though it wasn't always very clear exactly which character trait they were working on. Fortunately for me, it wasn't so much shaving as an exercise in peach fuzz removal and as such was tolerable.

Another unpleasant aspect of mornings was dealing with our foxholes. In prior wars there had been fronts, so when you moved out the holes were simply left behind. There weren't fixed fronts in Vietnam. You might march east to west over a piece of turf one day then west to east over the same real estate a week later. The brass didn't want us to leave formations of bunkers or foxholes behind that might be used against us later. So, on most days during breakfast time, we were instructed to fill in our holes because we were leaving. It wasn't anywhere near as hard as digging the damn thing in the first place, but still, who wants to start the day shoveling a load of dirt?

Late afternoon brought an end to the operation. We weren't told if this was by design or just coincidence, but Tet, the Vietnamese New Year, started the next day. The United States had declared a truce during Tet, I guess hoping that it would turn into something longer and more permanent. We had declared a similar truce the previous couple of years but had still managed to end up with a fair number of soldiers killed or wounded during that time.

Our plans now were to head for a nearby clearing that would serve as our departure site. Just before we arrived there, Captain Burke came over to where 3rd Squad was, at the rear, and handed me as well as others several packs of matches. He told us to start lighting fires as we went. This would help the general process of defoliation and make it more difficult for the VC to follow us too closely. There was a letter from my brother Kelly inside my helmet. I reread it quickly, then used it as kindling to set a small field of elephant grass on fire. The grass was dry and easily ignited. In my return letter to Kelly, I told him how his letter had been used to help fight the Viet Cong.

Some of the greener vegetation we encountered refused to cooperate. This irritated Soja, who turned into a berserk pyromaniac and emptied his flamethrower onto the growing conflagration around us. He could make anything burn with that jellied gasoline. Of course, his motivation to assist was fueled by a strong desire to carry a substantially lighter load for the rest of the day. I forgot to ask him how he reloaded that thing and made the serious mistake of not asking him if I could shoot it at least once. That would have been an experience.

Helicopters transported us to the big airfield in Saigon, where we all crowded into the empty cargo holds of several mud-spattered Caribou aircraft for the trip home. There were no seats, just a floor. The engine noise was loud and precluded any attempts at conversation as the plane rattled and shook itself toward Lai Khe. It sounded like being inside a washing machine that was about to fly apart. The plane was narrow, with the walls close in on us and all the gear. I could see three bullet holes about head high on the right and one more on the left. I tried to work out how they'd gotten there. They could have been from four projectiles, or possibly from just three, these hitting the right side with only one crossing through and exiting on the left side. The two that didn't make it might have hit something like cargo, or slammed into the side of the head of an infantryman sitting there thinking that he was safe for a few minutes because he wasn't in the jungle.

Back on the company street, mail call preceded everything else. Afterward we were chauffeured, like conquering heroes, to the Lai Khe shower point to clean up. Our limousines were deuce-and-a-half pickup trucks. That night we were having a company barbecue, which were sometimes held to celebrate the last day of a big operation. Great quantities of hamburgers and hot dogs sizzled outside the mess hall on fifty-five-gallon drums split lengthwise and filled with glowing charcoal. Jones the cook was working hard. There was plenty of beer and the officers mingled with us common folk to wave the flag and tell everyone what a great job we had done.

Jamison was loudly holding court not far from the grill, sharing his opinions on many matters with anyone who would listen. His hair was drenched in Brylcreem, which he used in base camp but not in the field. A Bronze Star, without a V for Valor, hung on a thin chain around his neck. He got it earlier on Cedar Falls for searching some tunnels. No one was down there to shoot at him so he got the Bronze for effort without V for Valor. He called it his bragging star and was eager to tell us about it. I didn't learn anything useful from him but he was good entertainment while I ate a burger and barbecued beans.

When the food was gone, guys started scattering everywhere. My eventual destination was the company club. However, the beer wasn't free there so it was necessary to go get some Monopoly money out of my footlocker. Back in the hootch half a dozen guys were drinking beer and reading their new letters for the umpteenth time. At the far end of the room, Lopez was using a wet rag to clean up the radio. "Yeah, shine that thing like you shine Fairman's ass," Henley said out loud for Lopez and everyone else to hear. Henley was a large white kid from Texas who had been in Vietnam for several months. Often he was moody and quiet. Until a couple of weeks ago, he had been the radioman.

"Fuck you, Henley," Lopez responded.

"Yeah, you had to kiss Fairman's ass. Can I please be the radioman?" Henley said in a high-pitched mocking tone that was meant to imitate Lopez sounding like a little girl.

"I said fuck you," was Lopez's challenge as he stood up and stepped toward Henley.

The scene erupted into a fistfight. It was fast and furious with a lot of punches thrown and landed but no blood drawn. The other guys broke it up, restraining the pugilists, who were reduced to cursing at each other. The fight appeared to be a draw. Apparently, as best as I could figure, it had been over who would be the RTO and carry Fairman's radio. The radio was bulky and heavy but had certain advantages—like no walking point, no listening post duty, and no night ambush patrol.

After the excitement from the fight died down, I took off down the company street in search of a beer or six. The sign on the company club said that it was called Charlie's Place. It was supposed to be a clever play on words that referred to us or to the VC. A large rendition of the Playboy bunny symbol was painted over the door. I never, ever, not once, saw any type of female in the place.

Inside it looked like a small stateside, neighborhood tavern. The usual cloud of cigarette smoke often resembled an out-of-control prairie fire. There was a wet bar on the left with a refrigerator for beer, which came in cans rather than bottles. That made sense considering the circumstances. Sometimes there were whiskey drinks available. It was usually rotgut stuff that none of us had ever heard of. For a couple of dollars, you could buy the bottle, but then you had to leave and drink your firewater somewhere else. I don't remember ever seeing vodka, gin, or scotch for sale there but I didn't really pay that much attention to liquor in those days. Tables and chairs were scattered about the place beneath a couple of ceiling fans that sometimes worked. A television up high on a shelf behind the bar was almost never on. When it was turned on, it often only produced a blizzard of white snow and was quickly turned off. Once in a while, it managed to pick up AFTV (Armed Forces Television). I'm not sure where that broadcast originated. They showed the news, weather reports, and educational stuff. Nothing too negative was ever broadcast about our military efforts in Indochina.

Generally, the nighttime broadcast ended the same way they did at home when the networks shut down and went off the air at about midnight. The *Star Spangled Banner* was played to a backdrop montage of bellicose military scenes. It was the same every night. There was film of our air force pummeling German cities, marines raising the flag on Iwo Jima, fighter planes strafing a train, and finally the Enola Gay wiping out Hiroshima. On most nights, the mushroom-shaped cloud was my signal to stop drinking and get some sleep. I never felt comfortable staying up much later than that because I was fearful of what strange activity the sunrise might announce and how early it might occur. Besides, on most nights by the time AFTV went off the air I was crocked. For a lot of us, alcohol became an escape. Not too long after joining the Black Lions, I began getting drunk every night that I wasn't either out in the jungle or on guard duty at one of the base camps. If I was back at Lai Khe for the night with no specific duties to perform, I got tanked. It was that simple. That was my plan and I stuck with it. It helped make life more tolerable. More than a few guys in the unit were doing the same thing, so I wasn't the Lone Ranger in my approach to the use of alcohol.

The new company mascot lived in the club. This was a one-eared kitten named Brut, who spent much of his time prowling on top to the bar and sniffing at the open cans of beer. Originally he had been an enemy pet. A few weeks earlier, a 1st Platoon guy had lobbed a grenade into a trench, killing two Viet Cong and blowing one of the cat's ears off. The cat was taken into custody and not surprisingly found to be more than a tad deaf. Despite this handicap, Brut was a good listener. You could vent your soul to Brut, as I often did, and he wouldn't reveal your private thoughts to anyone.

There weren't any glasses in the company club, so most of us just drank straight out of the can. One guy had his family mail over a favorite glass beer mug. It probably helped him feel like he was back home whenever he got really shit-faced. He was at the bar, drinking heavily like everyone and pointing the cat toward flies on the bar. A tumultuous cheer erupted when Brut got his first kill of the night and the beer mug guy announced that it had been a VC fly.

My guess was that the average blood alcohol level in the room was somewhere in the low- to mid-200s. There was certainly no shortage of crocked guys with a compulsive drive to inform the FNG, me, what was really happening in Nam. Legends of the jungle were countless. After they killed you, the VC would cut off your dick and put it in your mouth. Our guys cut the left ear off dead VC for souvenirs. The VC were afraid of the ace of spades symbol, so having this card in your helmet band would help protect you. The VC would sometimes put an explosive device under a picture of Ho Chi Minh on the ground, knowing that our guys would stomp on it and get blown up. Sometimes they used reverse psychology and pulled the same trick with an LBJ picture. Our intelligence guys would interrogate two VC at a time up in a chopper. If the first guy didn't talk, he was thrown out and the second guy would suddenly develop oral diarrhea and sing like a canary. Lots of guys died from rectal bleeding in Saigon after VC prostitutes put ground glass in their drinks. One famous whore put razor blades in her cunt and sliced up somebody's dick. It was incredible. Our bar was the epicenter of jungle legend heaven. My mind was reeling. These guys were worse than sweet-and-sour tits from jungle school.

A few minutes' walk took me to the main enlisted men's club. This place was for everyone, not just our company. It was like our club in concept, but was larger, more crowded, and had loud jukebox music. As I approached, a group of four or five guys suddenly boiled out of the doorway into the street kicking and punching each other. The blows seemed so random and confused it was hard to tell who was fighting whom. It was quickly broken up and no one appeared to be really hurt.

I recognized one of the combatants as having been from

Charlie Company, a guy named Glenn somebody. I didn't know him well and never really would. There is no genuinely good time to be shipped overseas to a combat zone but for some people certain times are distinctly worse than others. As the story went, this guy's wife had been killed in an auto accident two or three weeks before he shipped out. They had two small children he had to leave with relatives. The working theory was that he was mad at the world because of his wife getting killed and his still being sent overseas. Accordingly, he tended to drink a lot, was not a pleasant drunk, and got into a lot of fights. His kids would become complete orphans instead of half orphans if he got killed in action. This made me think that there should have been some kind of rule that got a man's orders to Vietnam canceled when his wife died.

Not being a very good brawler myself, I decided against drinking at this club and retreated back to Charlie's Place. There I would at least know who was beating me up and could identify the assailant afterward, if necessary. On the way, a GI I didn't recognize passed in front of me running at full speed through the darkness. He was being chased by Ortiz, who was screaming and waving an axe. He sounded serious. The first guy ran right through a low-slung electrical wire and disappeared into the night with Ortiz in hot pursuit. One end of the wire hopped around with its sparks lighting a fire in the leaves. After regaining my composure, I moved away quickly before some authority figure arrived and made me do something.

A few beers later, it was time to bail out of Charlie's Place and get some sack time. My walk was momentarily halted by noises off to my left that sounded like a lost calf or some other small animal. The noises led me to a shallow drainage ditch next to the road. There was someone down there at the bottom, on all fours, drunk and groaning like a wounded animal on his last legs. I wasn't sure but it looked somewhat like Fairman. Deftly, I tiptoed away backward before he saw me and I was obliged to help.

My guess was that the events of the evening had been

everyone's way of letting off steam and dissipating the tension that had built up during a long operation out in the field. Half of the company was still out partying. For me the party was over, the beer had whipped me. I lay down on my bunk springs and slept like a dead man.

Naturally, in the morning hangovers abounded. Half of the company had four-alarm headaches. Mine was so bad that at first I thought it was some type of Asian meningitis. Then came the realization of why it hurt and the inevitable vow to never drink again under any circumstances. Unfortunately, we had to get up early. Not much chow was eaten. Breakfast consisted mainly of coffee and cigarettes for the survivors of the previous night's shenanigans.

Soon we were marching over, for the day, to guard a section of the southeastern perimeter that belonged to some other unit. With each step painful, shock waves traveled from the soles of my feet up the spine into the base of my skull. Halfway over, we noticed brilliant orange fireballs erupting over the airfield in the distance like California poppies blossoming suddenly after an early spring rain. It was a mortar attack. A second or two later, thunderous claps accompanying the orange bursts became audible. They were more intimidating. Great chunks of superheated tarmac flew skyward as the shells chewed away at the eastern end of the airfield. In the distance someone hollered, "Incoming round, in-fucking-coming round," as if the situation wasn't already painfully obvious.

I sank down to one knee. The explosions weren't close enough to suck the air out of my lungs or even strike much fear into my soul. They did, however, send off ground vibrations that I could feel entering my body through the knee I was resting on. The vibrations seemed to strike my skull in a synchronized way with the pulse from my heartbeat, making my headache worse. Maybe it was just my imagination. Everyone else had also stopped to watch the pyrotechnics.

With luck, the shells would stay over there and not come toward us. We gauged their changing proximity by measuring the time between the flash and the roar. The attack was a disappointing turn of events that I didn't want to get out of hand and involve me in any way. My goal for the day was to quietly pull guard duty while sitting in the shade like a lizard and drinking water until my dehydrated brain could replenish its internal fluids. The plan also called for the monkeys to cooperate and not set off any land mines on the section of perimeter that we were guarding, just to annoy us.

Suddenly, it was over. No more shells fell. A scattering of jeeps appeared and drove around in circles visiting the various craters. Only a few shells had managed to hit the actual runway part of the airstrip, which was made up mainly of dilapidated asphalt along with several areas of plain old gravel. There didn't seem to be much of that fancy Marsden matting or PSP (pierced steel planking), as the army called it at Lai Khe, like I had seen at other airstrips. A small shed on the far side of the airstrip burned unattended. No one raced to save it—maybe it was empty. Without doubt, after it had burned to the ground, the quartermaster's report would show that every broken, stolen, misappropriated, lost, or otherwise-unaccounted-for piece of equipment ever known to have been at Lai Khe was in that shed just before the fire. After ample gawking, we finished our trek to the perimeter. I walked with a semi-stiff neck so that my head didn't rock back and forth as I went. The rest of the day was richly uneventful.

That night TV programs were shown outdoors at the 701st Maintenance Battalion Motor Pool. The screen was a large plywood structure about ten feet high that had been sanded smooth and then painted chalk white. Recent weekly episodes of popular American programs were shown. *Batman* got a lot of laughs. *Combat* drew guffaws, snide comments, and boos. Westerns like *Gunsmoke* and *Bonanza* seemed to be the most popular. They were distinctly American, portrayed tough guys, didn't remind anyone of modern warfare or Vietnam, and generally lacked any young good-looking chicks to instantly fall in love with and get sad about. It was wholesome entertainment, the type of shows that even the Catholic League of Decency could endorse. The shows didn't seem completely normal, though, without commercials, which we would have enjoyed immensely because we were starving for all things American.

The few rusty folding chairs and wooden benches to sit on were quickly taken. Everyone else would try to find a comfortable spot atop the dead and injured vehicles that had been dragged into the transportation graveyard for repair or to be cannibalized for parts. These wrecks didn't look anything like what you would see in a stateside motor pool and were certainly grist for the worry mill. There were jeeps that had been blown completely in half and trucks with gargantuan holes in their cargo beds large enough for a refrigerator to fall through. Sometimes you could tell which tire had set off the mine because that quarter of the vehicle was missing. The tanks and armored personnel carriers were the most impressive. Some sported gaping holes through several inches of steel armor from rocket hits. All the metal that used to be where the hole was, had blown into the vehicle, then rattled and ricocheted around, bouncing off the inside metal walls at a high rate of speed until it found something soft to stick in, like a seat cushion or somebody's face. Many vehicles were so badly scorched from gasoline or diesel fires that some of their metal fixtures had melted. All things considered, this place made being a foot soldier and going most everywhere by ankle express a more palatable concept.

Even better than the entertainment that night was being able to sleep with my boots off. Most guys tried to prevent trench foot by letting their feet dry out this way at night. A lot of us, myself included, didn't want to get caught with both boots off if trouble started, so we alternated sides with one boot on and one boot off at night when we were out in the field. In some especially dangerous areas, like Phu Loi or the Iron Triangle, I wouldn't take off even one boot. That's also the way it was on LP or ambush or any place that gave me the jitters whether there was reason for it or not. In those situations, both boots stayed on all night, trench foot or no trench foot.

Part of the foot care program included having an extra pair

of socks. In the morning, you wore the driest pair and attached the other to the outside of your backpack so that it could be dried by the sun. After more ambush patrols than usual in the preceding week or two, the rot on my feet was beginning to win its war with the normal skin. A few bootless nights might turn the tide of battle and were certainly welcome.

In the morning we were told to pack up for an overnight trip. I couldn't recall any report of the enemy ever using tear gas and so decided not to bother with getting another gas mask. I figured the chances of the VC using gas as a strategic weapon were slim. In all probability, every bicycle on the Ho Chi Minh Trail was bringing down more urgently needed supplies—rifles, hand grenades, and mortar shells, to name three. The priority of tear gas on the Viet Cong's list of supply needs was probably somewhere between electric can openers and folding aluminum beach chairs. However, I still had to carry the canvas gas mask pouch so that they would think I was carrying a mask. That was fine with me. My little camera fit in there and I filled the rest of the space with candy. It had to be stuff like Abba-Zaba bars and boxes of Jujubes that wouldn't melt in the torrid Asian afternoons.

The day started with a truck convoy out onto Highway 13 going north toward Bau Bang. That's the same not-so-nice place where Chang the barber had been killed. Just outside the base, a well-muscled Viet Cong, shot full of holes and hanging by his ankles from an A-frame, was waiting to greet us. The frame had obviously been constructed in his honor. A cardboard sign hung from a piece of string around his neck: THIS TROPHY CAUGHT BY THE BLACK LIONS. Convoys didn't dillydally on Thunder Road so we were past him before I could get my Instamatic out and take a picture. What a disappointment. Still, it would be a good story to tell when I got home. It was doubtful that any of my friends or relatives had ever seen a man's body hanging by the side of the road unless, of course, they had lived in the South.

We spent what turned out to be a devilishly hot day patrolling up and down a section of the road on foot. It was hotter than usual because the shade we enjoyed when we patrolled in the jungle wasn't there. Most of the vegetation for about seventy-five meters on either side of the road had been either bulldozed or blown up by demolition crews. There was no place for roadside snipers to hide.

During the first few hours, some demo guys were out there with us. They cruised around at a leisurely pace in jeeps packed with all kinds of explosives. Occasionally they stopped to discuss this or that tree among themselves. Any foliage was suspect. The two of them stopped by me and chitchatted. They were about to apply their punitive powers to a denuded, thirty-foot tree stump and showed me a spool of detonation cord, the fabled exploding rope, which they then wrapped around the stump numerous times. When the cord detonated, it snapped the foot-thick tree trunk in half as easily as if it had been hit by Paul Bunyan's axe. It was interesting; I'd never seen that type of demolition work before.

While the demolition guys were ambling around blowing up things, a guy from our platoon named Webb walked in the middle of the road with a mine detector. He was just another 11-Bravo like me so I had no idea where he learned to work that thing. No one had taught me how in any of my infantry training. Webb stopped and dug in a few spots but never found anything.

The afternoon half of the day was distinctly different. The armored cavalry showed up. There were numerous tanks and APCs (armored personnel carriers) from the 1st Squadron of the 4th Cavalry. This group was also known by the nickname Quarterhorse. The plan was for us to run cloverleaf sweeps of the area east of Thunder Road. Cloverleaf described a search pattern in which we separated into four groups and all started at the imaginary base of a four-leaf clover. Each group then walked or rode along the outer edge of one of the four leaves until we all met back at the starting point. It was a way to divide up your troops and search a larger area in a shorter time without ever getting too far away from each other in case one group found the enemy and the proverbial shit hit the fan.

The unusual aspect of the afternoon was that instead of walking, we were all going to load up onto the APCs and spend the day being chauffeured around as passengers. This was a new experience for us. "Negative, negative, not that one," Sharp whispered to us as soon as we started climbing aboard a nearby APC. He then ordered us to get off and follow him as he walked over to another vehicle.

"Did any of you guys notice that there were about twice as many antennas on that track and they were about twice as long as on the other tracks?" He asked this as we walked.

A small, feeble chorus of no's answered him.

"That's a command vehicle of some type, maybe a battalion commander, maybe a second in command. It's a rocket magnet. The VC are taught to shoot at it first. If we make contact they are going to light it up like a Christmas tree. We don't want to be on it."

In this matter, a word to the wise would suffice. His logic seemed unassailable and I began to feel lucky that my squad leader had gotten me off of the doomed vehicle. It wasn't possible for me to see if all of the others avoided that APC or if it was taken by a squad whose leader had yet to decipher the meaning of the large antennas.

As it turned out, the armored experience was hot, noisy, and too metallic for my taste. Standing in an APC as it lurched along and rocked back and forth over uneven ground was hard work. It taxed all of your muscle groups, as if you were standing up in a roller coaster with no seat belt trying not to be thrown out. Because we didn't normally operate from inside tracked vehicles it made me think that perhaps the brass were looking for something specific in this area that we hadn't been told about. Whatever it was, we didn't find it.

That night, we circled the wagons on a flat space just off the road. A memorable breeze came along to cool us as we guzzled cold soda pop and water that had been trucked out to us. It turned out to be a very pleasant evening because each of us was a couple of quarts low, and a distinct euphoria and a certain sense of well-being accompanies serious rehydration.

About 1700 hours we heard heavy gunfire several hundred meters out. Two dozen VC had passed in front of one of our ambush patrols and been rapidly chewed up. Seven had been killed. They lay where they fell until the next morning, when they were found by the ambushers who had quietly held their ground until it was light enough to see what was out there.

Soon after the shooting, our listening posts were reporting movements at multiple locations just outside of our lager. The VC had advanced almost up to our perimeter. Word raced down the line not to shoot, all of the listening posts had been radioed to run for it, back to our position. Their job was done. As they approached many were whispering loudly, "Black Lion, Black Lion," over and over again as if they were chanting a mantra for self-protection. They were. Once again we didn't have a password that night when it might have helped. For the guys coming in, Black Lion was like a reverse password. It was what you said when you were approaching a friendly position and either didn't know the password or were afraid that they were going to start shooting without asking. It wasn't a planned thing, guys just did it when they were coming in scared. It worked. The LPs—running hard, short of breath, and panting like dogs—had just managed to reach us when our mortars plowed into the area they had just vacated. Numerous rounds crashed into the area the VC had been probing. Most shells hit the ground and exploded back upward, but some snagged treetops and exploded downward in showers of white-hot shrapnel. All the while, the mortar crews kept several mortar flares above us floating leisurely downward, suspended beneath small parachutes. This high explosive and illumination show went on for an hour. When it ended, everything was quiet.

We left superearly in the morning so that the platoon that sent out the ambush squad could reconnect with them. Everyone was agitated about getting that done, because there was safety in numbers and no one wanted that squad out by itself any longer than necessary. Plus, the brass wanted to inspect the VC, check for documents, confirm the body count, and look for blood trails. Each blood trail was added to the body count as half a point, on the theory that the VC's medical care was so primitive that half of the wounded would later die. And, of course, the lieutenants and captains in the field wanted as high a body count as possible for the colonels and generals back at the base camp. That's how you eventually became one of the colonels or generals back at the base camps.

We didn't get to see the ambush site, which was in the center of the direction we were moving toward. The 1st Platoon's task was to be on the left flank and provide security there for the formation as it moved out toward the ambush site. Once we got into position, we were stationary for most of the day. It was dull.

The Tet truce was over. Big deal! It was more of a quasi-truce. True, we had spent some of the time in our base camp doing nothing but we had also chased after the enemy on armored vehicles and sent out ambush patrols which had killed a few of them. In return, during this time, they had mortared us. Maybe the concept of a truce simply meant no bombing of North Vietnam and no massive multiunit operations in South Vietnam, but a continuation of all the small-unit actions during which we nickeled-and-dimed each other to death. That was what 95 percent of the war was anyway.

The New Year, the Year of the Sheep, was officially upon us. Valentine's Day was just around the corner. My former girlfriend, Jane Coogan, who had sent me a Dear John letter about thirty seconds after I joined the army, sent me a Valentine card. The message was that I was a swell guy even though she didn't want to date me ever again. Why did she bother? Fortunately, I'd gotten over her before leaving the States. Well, maybe I wasn't completely over her, but I had managed to accept the finality of the situation. A recurring theme in American war movies was the guy who gets a Dear John letter while in a combat zone and then psychologically unravels. We had ours, a guy named Willie Willis. He was a disheveled, unkempt, depressed, moody binge drinker. I wasn't close to him but was told that this all started after he got the letter. Before that, he reportedly was a neat, upbeat, sober, churchgoing Christian. I hadn't known him then.

My mom always got each of us children a box of good See's candy for Valentine's Day. She never failed. I'd miss that this year. I didn't want to miss sending her something even if there were no real Valentine cards available, so I wrote a Valentine's Day greeting on the ace of hearts from my deck of cards and mailed it off.

Our letters home didn't require postage. Stamps were an unworkable commodity for foot soldiers in Vietnam because our gear was often soaked by streams or rice paddies or pounding rains. Even without these drenchings, the humidity alone would curl a stamp right off an envelope. We just wrote the word *free* where the stamp went and the postal service delivered it. That went for all servicemen in Vietnam. Even though it only saved us eight cents for an airmail stamp, we thought it was neat: We were beating the system.

Bob stopped by to visit. The 1st Division headquarters had been relocated from Di An to Lai Khe. General DePuy, the commanding officer, wanted them closer to the action. Bob's 121st Signal Battalion, the communications center for the division, had been named Danger Forward and been the first part of HQ to be sent up to Lai Khe.

Unfortunately, when Bob arrived, there went the neighborhood. Lai Khe was in more of a wilderness area than Di An. It was like an army fort on the frontier of the Old West with wild Indians on all sides. This afforded the VC with the opportunity to take shots at division HQ that they hadn't been able to take before. Soon after division HQ arrived, so did the Viet Cong's massive 122-mm rockets. At that size it was really a monster. I think that they weighed over a hundred pounds apiece, with probably about half of that being the explosive part of the warhead. They were fired from a launcher by a two- or three-man crew and could hit Lai Khe from several miles away. Early in 1967, rockets were a rarity in our area. After Bob arrived, they became commonplace. Later in the year, everyone began referring to Lai Khe as Rocket City and some infantry units would extend their stay out in the boondocks at the end of an operation if the shelling of Lai Khe was heavy at the time.

Bob showed me photos as I got ready for a squad-sized patrol. His mom had put his name and address in the hometown paper, the *Press-Telegram*, for GIs who wanted more mail. All of the writers were young women, many of whom sent pictures. Bob was holding his own Miss America contest.

"You look like a fucking pack mule with all that crap on," he said to me.

Actually I was traveling light. On these afternoon patrols, we did carry a little extra ammunition because if we got in trouble we wouldn't have anyone else out there to help us. However, because we weren't going to be out for more than five or six hours, we left a lot of our normal gear behind— shovels, claymores, ponchos, C rations, personal items, and some canteens. I didn't even carry my camera. What a mistake that was. I should have taken half a dozen photos every day no matter what I was doing. Instead, I waited for obviously interesting shots to present themselves and ended up with way too few photos when I went home. In any event, on these short patrols we were each about fifteen pounds lighter than normal, which was a treat for us.

The squad walked down the company street toward the perimeter, then through the bunker line into no-man's-land. Bob was walking beside me, chitchatting and still flipping through photographs, seemingly oblivious to our movement and position. Before we reached the river, Sharp halted the squad and looked Bob in the eye.

"Son, you need to either gear up or go back," he announced out loud. Everyone chuckled, including Bob; we then shook hands and he retreated back inside the bunker line.

On the patrol itself, we didn't see any VC activity at all and not much imagination was required to figure out why. The air force was working over the area that we were trying to patrol. We marched as far as we could up to the point where we were afraid of being bombed ourselves. Streaking Phantom fighters rolled in just above the treetops and dumped their bombs out in front of us. A hot shock wave struck us in the face while the ground shook.

We couldn't communicate with the pilots because we didn't have the right type of radio and didn't know their frequency. Sharp contacted Lai Khe to find out why the air force was out there and what they were doing. Nobody seemed to know what was going on or how we could find out. The best we got was advice to pop some smoke, then move away from it to the southeast, and head back to Lai Khe. If anybody back at division could get through to the bomb jockeys, they would be advised of our presence, what color smoke grenade we had set off and what azimuth on the compass we were taking in our march away from the smoke. We managed to retreat without injury or the foggiest idea of what the air force was doing.

In the morning, the activity level at the heliport was out of control. Dozens of helicopters idled at full throttle as hundreds of troops were arriving, lining up, and boarding. The fluttering rotors blew out acrid exhaust fumes to greet us. Occasionally one of the choppers would rear up a foot or two off the ground before being settled back down by the pilot like a cowboy calming his steed. The entire scene exuded an aura of excitement.

The flight was short and peaceful, delivering us to an LZ that was undefended, as was the base camp that we were invading. Best of all was that the camp was right next to the LZ, literally only a two- or three-minute walk away. That was puzzling. Why would they build a camp so close to a giant flat space where we could land? It wasn't like they also had helicopters at their disposal. Within minutes, we walked unchallenged among the bamboo huts, gawking like curious tourists visiting an Oriental ghost town. Well-worn paths connected the various huts, some of which were storage and others living quarters. There were blackened pots by the now-cold fire, farm tools here and there, and clothes in the living quarters. As usual, the jungle canopy blocked any view of the camp from above.

The storage huts were bursting at the seams with rice. Unlike the huts we had seen in other areas, these had walls of sheet metal, not just roofs. In some places, the walls bulged outward because of the load. Most of the rice was in dirty brown bags still bearing the painted stencils from their place of origin. Many came from China or the Agency for International Development. About half came from Texas and California. Those bags sported a red, white, and blue flag on a shield logo with the words "A gift of the people of the United States." There was also a warning: Not to be sold. What they really needed was a warning: Not to be stolen.

I wasn't sure which was the more difficult task, diverting the grain from its point of entry at the harbors near Saigon, which presumably our side controlled, or actually lugging these fifty-pound bags over kilometers of mud, jungle, and unforgiving terrain while avoiding detection.

We spent the rest of the day demolishing the place. The huts were knocked down. The bags were gutted with knives so the rice could be spilled to rot in the mud or be eaten by rodents. Within an hour, the area between the huts was awash in a sea of rice several inches deep. We were forced to drag the bags farther and farther away from the epicenter of destruction in order to pour the rice onto wet earth. The sun belonged to the Viet Cong that day and beat down on us like an adversary. We had started our day of legal vandalism with youthful enthusiasm, even relish, but were worn out and dragging as it ended. Our last organized activity was to place all of the empty bags in a pile and burn them so that they couldn't be stitched up and reused. Of course, we all pissed on the rice before we left. One guy wanted to take a shit but we didn't have time.

While we were packing up to leave, it looked to me like Cruz was acting a little goofy and seemed to have a mild case of the giggles. Menendez was acting the same way. Cruz and Menendez were, as their names suggested, part of the Latin contingent within the company. My thoughts were that they were both Mexican but, not being very worldly, that's what I assumed about anyone who spoke Spanish. Cruz was more jocular and talkative than the average guy in Charlie

Company. Menendez was more reclusive and less talkative than average. They both spoke the King's English when talking with me or other non-Spanish speakers. But when speaking together or with other Latinos, they generally did so in Español. I wouldn't say that they were exclusionary but maybe they weren't as open to those that didn't speak Spanish as they might have been. Whether this was part of it or not I'm not sure, but I never did get to know them real well.

Later, Menendez told me that they had found some grass in one of the hootches that they had helped search and had impulsively smoked it. This was unusual, at least out in the field. Occasionally the sharp odor of marijuana was noticeable at night on the bunker line at Lai Khe. This was usually when no officers were around because anyone with two nostrils and a face that pointed forward could identify the smell. Even a guy like me, who wasn't a user yet and never did try the stuff in Vietnam, could detect it. Of course, I wasn't enough of a connoisseur to tell the difference between some primo Acapulco Gold or Panama Red and the local home-grown Vietnamese shit that had already been sprayed with noxious chemical defoliants by the air force.

Grunts smoking grass back at Lai Khe didn't thrill me, but it wasn't the end of the world. It couldn't really be much worse than pulling guard duty after drinking three or four beers.

If drugs besides marijuana were being used in Charlie Company, it was well hidden from me. Although hard drugs were not yet the major problem that they would later be for Americans in Vietnam, it is likely that at least some of the grunts in my unit were users. They wouldn't share that secret or want me to know because I was in all probability perceived as a naïve goody-two-shoes type of guy who would run and tell the scoutmaster as soon as I found out.

There were rumors about a white guy in our platoon named Henderson. The rumor was that he had been with the Green Berets and done an earlier tour in Vietnam. Now, for whatever reason, he was no longer a green beanie. Despite this, he had volunteered for a second tour of duty in the combat zone. As the story went, he had done this because he liked heroin and knew how to get it in the Nam.

Not long after leaving the camp we destroyed, we came across a stream. There were two types of streams in the jungle. There was clear and there was muddy. We tried to stay away from muddy streams for hydration purposes. Who wants to drink liquid dirt? If the stream was clear, the water was pure; it was that simple. Eyeballing the water was the only scientific test of potability we had. The two-foot-deep, ten-foot-wide stream we chanced upon after leaving the rice camp looked good. Its water sparkled like Irish crystal. We could see the bottom clearly; the water was cool and tasted great. We imbibed on the spot. I rubbed my hands together under the water to wash them before cupping a big drink for myself. It was quite refreshing. A lot of us topped off our canteens, as there was no way of knowing when we would encounter a stream of this quality again.

Resuming our patrol, we moved upstream for about fifteen meters, then followed the river's gentle curve to the right. Just around the bend was a big, fat, dead water buffalo lying half-submerged in the water. It was bloated like a pregnant cow carrying triplets and its flesh was rotting. The part of it that was out of the water wasn't dry, but instead wet with slime, a layer of saprophytic goo. Just looking at the dead beast put a bad taste in my mouth. A little farther upstream from the animal, we all rinsed out our mouths and canteens. It didn't work. The water didn't taste good anymore.

Several kilometers from the rice camp, we dug in for the night. There was a quiet born of exhaustion that evening. A full day of heat, sweat, and rice dust had left us covered with a tacky residue that felt somewhat like having been rubbed down with maple syrup. It was sticky and gritty and subjectively unpleasant. It made everyone move at a sluggish pace. Only an inner sense of necessity propelled us through the mundane tasks of digging foxholes and putting out mines. None of us wanted to do it, but we all wanted it done—sort of like brushing your teeth at bedtime.

Smithers and Gilbert were hacking away the weeds around

our hole as I wandered out in front, laying down a claymore wire as I went. On the return trip, I passed Mike Love, who was walking out his claymore. We exchanged glances but no words. Both of us just wanted to get this tedious shit over with and catch some sleep.

Seconds later, a lone mortar shell streaked silently downward, landing between Love and me with a bone-jarring explosion. The blast struck me from behind, smacking me between the shoulder blades and on the back of my neck. It hurt for a scant second, then faded. It made my eardrums quiver slightly, which was a little uncomfortable. At a distance of only about ten or fifteen meters, it was a miracle that I didn't get hit by any shrapnel.

The blast startled me out of my gourd and sent me scurrying for my hole as dirt clods bounced back to earth and the dust began to settle. To my astonishment, there stood Love, upright and unhurt. Slowly, rigidly, like an old man with an arthritic neck, he turned in my direction and stared, bug-eyed in disbelief. He was about the same distance away on the other side of the explosion. He hadn't been hit either, which made it a double miracle. Again we glanced at each other. When seconds passed and no more mortars fell, he turned and finished laying out his wire. I leaned against the foxhole and tried to calm down. I guess the VC had come home and found what we had done to their rice.

Maybe we had been saved by the soft earth in the area. It allowed projectiles to burrow into the ground for a few inches or a foot or so before detonating. Then the explosion and shrapnel were directed skyward rather than laterally at hapless dopes like me and Love. If we had been standing on a rock plateau or a concrete airfield, we might have been ripped apart by the ensuing metal shitstorm.

Rice, rice, the more you search the more you find. On the second day of the operation, tons of the stuff were everywhere again. Unfortunately, we were also beginning to find snipers along the way or they were finding us. Every once in a while a shot would ring out, forcing us to hit the dirt for a minute until we could determine where the shot came from and then fire back. What saved us was that the snipers were crappy shots. They didn't manage to hit any of us. Our marksmanship matched theirs. Every time we barraged an area, then searched it, they were gone and there was no blood. It wasn't much fun on the nerves.

The third day was more of the same. We returned to the original camp, then fanned out patrolling in circles farther and farther out from the camp. Every time we destroyed a rice hootch and started walking again, we would encounter another cache within minutes. This went on from sunup to sundown. There was enough rice in the area to feed an army. We were also finding more booby traps, usually in the form of grenades with the pin pulled under a bag of rice. Some were American grenades and some were the Chinese communist version, which we called Chi-Com grenades. It was awkward lifting or moving the bags while trying to look under them. This was about as good for the nerves as the snipers.

In the early afternoon, we spent about two hours dismantling a large hootch that contained about fifteen tons of rice. Our next stop was undoubtedly going to be another hootch, one we could see about fifty meters off to our right. However, as we took swigs of water and drags on our cigarettes, we noticed Alpha Company approaching on that side. If we didn't move with more alacrity in collecting our stuff and putting on our gear, they would walk right into the new hootch before we did. We decided as a group to move slowly and let A Company take the new hootch. Beck was the only guy I knew in A Company and I didn't see him among the approaching faces. I proceeded to put my gear on more slowly than usual.

Soon enough the new hootch was Alpha Company's property and problem. Unlike the others, it was surrounded by a bamboo fence. The poles of the fence were dried and faded with age and spaced so far apart that almost any animal could pass through it freely. There wasn't any logical reason for the fence to be there except to cause trouble. There was also a gate, which two guys opened to enter. As they did, a grenade exploded, ripping the two men with shrapnel and momentarily obscuring them in a hazy whirlwind of smoke and sparks and shards. A brown mixture of explosives and dust from the event drifted back toward the main body of A Company.

Both men were blown back a step and slumped to the ground motionless. There were frantic cries for a medic and a beehive of activity as all kinds of GIs, including their medic, rushed to their aid. Our Doc Baldwin also ran over to help. There were so many guys surrounding the two men that it was difficult to get a clear view of what was going on. A couple of guys from our platoon walked halfway over, but not any farther, to get a better look. It was like slowing down for an auto accident. They wanted to know what was going on but didn't really want to see anything too grotesque. It was way too sickening for me. I took only quick glimpses out of the corner of my eyes and didn't really see too much. What I did notice was that neither of the down men was moving, not even a muscle twitch. In my mind, I knew they were dead and it made me feel ill. I was happy to stay put. I didn't want a better view.

The tall guy near the center of the group stood there bent over at the waist looking down at the casualties. Maybe he was in charge. He seemed to be doing more talking than anyone else and gesticulating instructions with his hands. Soon he grew silent and began shaking his head like a ringside physician at Madison Square Garden signaling that the fight was all over. Activity on the men ceased and the guys in the group quietly stared at the men and at each other. It was sad. These guys had been dopus maximus. At absolutely every level of our training, we had been instructed to stay away from the obvious path when in unfriendly territory. Don't walk on trails, don't go through doorways, and never open a gate. Their parents would never know.

The rice-a-thon was definitely getting more competitive. We'd gone from unopposed to random sniper fire to a couple of dead guys. After saddling up, we continued our patrol to search for and destroy more enemy supplies. As we walked,

I was soon grappling with the notion of whether I should feel some guilt over the two fellows who had died. Nobody else was talking that way, but I was starting to think it. After all, we had seen the hootch first but let them find it and take casualties. Talking to myself under my breath, I quickly decided that the event was just part of the fortunes of war. I hadn't done anything wrong and didn't need to ride on this psychological roller coaster. In this instance, guilt would be wasted and possibly even harmful. It would be best for me to mentally ditch the entire episode, which I then tried to do.

About an hour later, Lopez spotted a gook setting up a claymore in our path. He fired a burst at the VC, who immediately abandoned the mine and took off running like a scalded dog. Lopez wasn't sure if any bullets had been hits.

It was disconcerting to think about how close this gook had come to scoring big-time. He would have obliterated half the squad if he had been allowed just a few more seconds before being spotted. He needed less time than it would have taken one of us to retie a bootlace.

The mine he abandoned was one of their horrific homemade jobs—a piece of sheet metal hand pounded into the shape of a pie plate, about fifteen inches in diameter. The plate contained a bottom layer of explosives, probably material from an air force bomb that didn't go off. The VC would open the dud bombs with hacksaws and scoop out the innards. On top of the explosives was a layer of wet cement into which pieces of metal had been embedded to serve as shrapnel. The cement was then allowed to dry. Inside the mine were sawed-off pieces of steel rod about two inches long and as thick as your thumb. It would have really been awful. In jungle school, we were told that sawed-up metal rods were the most frequently used type of shrapnel. However, if no rods were available, they would use any small metal item, such as screws, nails, bolts, and sometimes even coins.

Soon we found another shed. As it was being searched, I dug around in a curious eight-foot-square patch of dirt nearby that looked unusual. There weren't many plants growing on it, which seemed odd. About a foot down, I hit a layer of sheet metal. Next my shovel came up with a wire it had snared. Visions of the two dead GIs at the gate went through my head. I ever so gently untangled the wire and found a new place to dig a few feet away. Again I hit sheet metal, but without trip wires. Underneath was a cache of rice the CO estimated at thirteen tons for reporting purposes.

My reward for having found this underground storage site was being chosen to stay behind and blow it up while the others moved out of harm's way. It was a semi-frightening honor but I was stoked and certain that it would be fun. The resupply helicopters had started bringing us out lots of explosives to expedite the process of destroying the storage bins. We were finding so many that the manual labor approach was too slow.

Huish also stayed behind to take care of the aboveground shed. For my demolition project I used three blocks of C-4 plastic explosive wrapped in a bundle with detonation cord. On top of the C-4, I put three Chi-Com grenades that had been used in booby traps we had found and dismantled earlier in the day. This was to increase the explosion and get rid of the grenades, which we didn't want to lug around. Besides, just having one in my possession made me nervous. Their quality wasn't as good as the American products and it occurred to me that they might just go off for no reason. Last, my tear gas grenade was added for flavor. My thoughts were that, if they were able to recollect any of the rice, the tear gas powder might make it inedible. We lit our respective fuses in unison and then ran away quickly like burglars after the porch light goes on. The explosion that followed was tremendous.

Later in the day, after walking some distance away from the rice area, we stopped to rest. The squad members spread out a bit and sagged down among the plants. I sat down in some shade with my back against a tree. Wetness from the dank earth came right through the seat of my pants and underwear. Rather than spend the next four minutes of my five-minute break trying to find a dry spot, I just sat there. The steel pot on my head was heavy. Leaning forward, I rested my arms on my knees, put my forehead on my hands, and let my mind wander until my eyes slowly focused on a butterfly bomb half hidden in the muck and leaves between my legs.

How could it have eluded me? The canister was about the size and shape of a one-pound coffee can and had been painted a lustrous yellow, like a butterfly. At one end were steel tail fins, several inches long, which pointed up at me in an accusatory fashion. We didn't find these things very often because there weren't all that many unexploded ones. Most of these cluster bomblet units (or CBUs) went off when originally dropped. We were told that the initial duds were so erratic that they would go off later, secondary to simple ground vibrations or changes in temperature as the sun came and went. Now I had the feeling that this thing was so temperamental it might go off if I looked at it wrong. Some were full of ball bearings. Others were stuffed with hundreds or even thousands of little one-inch steel arrows. What was worse, having this thing one foot from my balls or two feet from my face? What would I grab if it started to smoke or go off? Gingerly, I moved away and alerted the others. I didn't have the nerve to drop even a sheet of toilet paper on it as a warning marker.

After hiking for about another kilometer, we made camp for the night. What a day it had been. I'd found an underground cache of rice, got to blow it up, sat on a butterfly bomb, almost had a claymore detonated at me, and saw two soldiers die from a booby-trap hand-grenade blast. That night's entry in my diary didn't start with the usual month and date. It got a title: A Day I Shall Remember Forever. Simple and bland, perhaps, but it certainly conveyed my feelings.

The next morning, we walked to a nearby landing zone at the crack of dawn and were airlifted out of the area and back to Lai Khe. Back in the company area, the first order of business was to line up for a head count. As formation was being held, about a dozen of us were called out by name to gather up front. Gilbert, Kirkpatrick, Sievering, and I were included.

Then a short, informal ceremony was held. This occurred every couple of months, whenever the company clerk had all his paperwork in order. We were all awarded the Combat Infantry Badge (CIB). This award was given to those in the army who served as infantry soldiers in a combat zone and survived more than a month. We all thought of it as the sign of a warrior and enjoyed wearing it whenever we were back at Lai Khe in mixed company with the REMF types. Actually, wearing the CIB all the time was military snobbery: We all believed that we were superior to those who never went out in the jungle. At the time, we didn't give much thought to the fact that we couldn't survive without the REMF troops. They trucked in our food, ran the PX, kept the helicopters flying, manned the base hospital, and a lot more. Without them, things would have been unimaginably rough for us.

Although getting the badge made me feel special, in my heart I knew that there were a lot of worse jobs than mine in the Nam. So far, I had figured out that these included any spot in an armored vehicle or a helicopter. I'm not sure that I could have filled those positions without having a slow nervous breakdown. I didn't want to get ripped apart by shrapnel inside of an armored vehicle or die by falling to my death in a helicopter. I was sure that both of those scenarios would certainly be more awful than getting killed by gunfire. With my imagination, the psychological burden of existing from moment to moment knowing that at any time, without warning, you could be suddenly blown up or shot down would have been hard to take.

After the ceremony, Sharp told me that I was now the squad's assistant gunner. Height, the current gunner, would be stationed permanently in the rear. His tour was almost over and the brass didn't want anyone to get killed at the last minute. Gilbert was the new gunner. Smithers, the guy with the least seniority, would take over for me as ammo bearer.

My guess was that this put me on track to someday become a gunner myself. All the other gunners and assistant gunners had been in country longer than I and would create openings at their positions when they rotated home, if they got that far. A popular theory or jungle legend was that gun crews had a shorter half-life in combat than others because they made such an easily identifiable noise and shot up such a storm of bullets that the enemy would shoot first at them if at all possible.

Back in the States, I had qualified at the shooting range with half a dozen or so weapons. Oddly, the M-60 had been the only one that I had ever been able to qualify on as an expert, the highest level. I remembered that during the training when asked what our weapon was, we were not supposed to refer to it as a machine gun or an M-60 or something else. We were to respond that it was a "7.62-mm, bipod-mounted, breech-loaded, belt-fed, gas-powered, air-cooled, fully automatic weapon." The string of words struck me as hopelessly pedantic and quite funny. That was probably why I remembered them.

Soon after the ceremony we were back on perimeter guard duty. The beat-up old sandbag bunkers overlooking the river and no-man's-land welcomed us home like an old friend. Sunbaked C ration cans from previous meals on the line littered the area. They had been licked clean by rodents in our absence and now drew fewer flies than before, which was a distinct advantage. The same old, tired magazines that we had read before lay atop the bunkers. We could relax there.

The army, in its own indescribable way, wanted everything to be tidy and would periodically send a gruff sergeant major walking down the line to bark at us about the unkempt appearance of the area. Stifling our sarcastic comments so as not to prolong the anguish of his visit, we would quietly shuffle around a bit and pick up a few cans and pieces of paper until he moved away to harass someone else. Today's visit was like all the rest. We ridiculed the sergeant major after he'd gone with sophomoric comments along the lines of "Gee, I'd really feel bad if the Viet Cong thought I wasn't neat." This was followed by childish cackles of laughter.

We spent the rest of the day lounging around the bunker in a state of pleasant boredom. Idle chatter continued well into the evening.

We were, however, still in Vietnam. Tynes, who had actually been watching out front, ducked down a bit and whispered to the rest of us that a light was visible out there in the jungle. Everyone quietly turned to look. Sharp, who was leaning against the bunker and facing away from no-man's-land, turned and looked hard. His brow wrinkled and he carefully squirted some spit out into the dirt as if it would help improve his night vision. In the distance, a solitary figure carrying a light of some sort walked out of the jungle and moved slowly toward us. At a hundred and fifty meters we couldn't tell if he had a weapon or if he was actually even a he.

Someone suggested that he was crazy or stoned. Another ventured that he might be playing the dumb-guy routine to locate our positions. Sharp instructed us to call the mortar platoon and drop a round out there to chase him off. I reached for the PRC-25 radio, hoping to get more involved.

The mortar platoon wasn't on the line. They set up their tubes back in the company area and waited to give us short-order mortar fire if needed. We worked it out among ourselves when the mortars would be fired and where. This arrangement was infinitely more expedient than trying to call for artillery fire. Artillery required that the CO or at least an officer be involved and give the order. Frequently, battalion HQ or even division HQ had to be notified and official approval obtained, depending on the target and target area. Sometimes before all the legal niceties of an artillery strike could be ironed out, choice targets managed to simply melt away, oblivious to the shitstorm that had almost engulfed them. With our own mortar platoon, there was less bureaucracy. The fire control system was a lot simpler—it didn't exist. Even a rookie like me with no rank and no radio skills could get the stuff fired off.

I'd never called for mortar fire before, or any type of fire, for that matter. Come to think of it, I couldn't even remember ever being allowed to talk on the radio up to that point. I'd done sitrep clicks on night ambush and listening posts before, but that was about it.

Doing the talking while everyone else watched gave me a sense of power and importance. It made me strain hard to observe all the formalities of correct radio talk.

"Four Six, Four Six this is One Six Kilo, fire mission, over."

"This is Four Six."

"Four Six, this is One Six Kilo. We need some high explosive one hundred meters to the west of our position, outside the line but south of the river, over."

"One Six Kilo, watcha got, over."

"Four Six, this is One Six Kilo, we have one Victor Charlie advancing on our position, over."

"Roger, One Six Kilo, we'll send out one shot as a mark, tell us where it lands, over."

The phrase, "Tell us where it lands" stayed with me and rattled around in my brain more than a little as we waited to hear the mortar tube report. All of us stared back into the dark recesses of Lai Khe as if we were going to see the noise. They were so far back behind so many rubber trees that we wouldn't see the flash.

THOUUMP! After hearing the dull and unmistakable sound of a mortar tube we turned our attention back to the figure with the light and waited for 81-mm of pain to land and scare this guy off so that we could all quit worrying and return to relaxing and doing nothing.

WHAMMO! It landed right on his head and he was gone, disappearing like some trick in a magic show. I was appalled. All of us had been staring right at him and were temporarily blinded by the flash. We couldn't see much of anything out there when our night vision returned. Either he had been blown to smithereens or was low crawling back toward Hanoi with his light off. There was silence.

Periodically during the night, I thought about the guy and wondered if he was dead and what we would find when the sun came up. For obvious reasons, I damn sure didn't want what we found to be an obvious noncombatant like a child or some Methuselah of a farmer.

There would never be answers to my questions. Sharp woke

us at 0500 and we left. The line was temporarily taken over by enlisted men from some helicopter unit. We would never find out what they saw when the sun burned off the usual morning mist that day. Having been the one that called in the mortar, I was more than curious. No one else seemed to really give a rat's ass. The army was treating me as impersonally as I had treated the guy with the light and there was nothing I could do about it, not even forget. It bothered me.

It rankled me for a while that I was not able to wait and see what had happened to the person with the light. Eventually, I got over it when I more fully absorbed the concept that for the military I was just another functionary. I didn't have any say in where we went, what we did, or how we did it when we got there, and it didn't matter to them in the slightest what I thought about any of it. I was just along for the ride, like a cork in a river.

Where we had to be that morning was in Tay Ninh Province on the Cambodian border. The platoon went as a group in the back of a loud, rickety, Caribou cargo plane. Again there were no seats, but there was about enough room for one platoon to sit on the floor with all their gear. It took us from the Lai Khe airfield and deposited us on a hard dirt runway next to a village named Soui Da (pronounced sooey dow).

The area around the runway was generally flat and fallow. The lack of cover lent itself to a feeling of nakedness and exposure. It wasn't a comfortable feeling at all. Sergeant Fairman didn't have to tell us twice to dig in. The area would soon become a permanent base camp for the 25th Infantry Division, which was also known as Tropic Lightning.

As we toiled, dozens of Hueys and Caribous came in unloading hundreds, then thousands, of grunts. Larger Chinook helicopters were bringing in artillery pieces and bulldozers. Tanks and armored personnel carriers were arriving by road. We were told that this was preparation for an effort that was going to be called Operation Junction City. It didn't take a rocket scientist to figure out that this was going to be the biggest operation we had ever been involved in. Besides the Big Red One there were troops from the 4th, 9th, and 25th

Infantry Divisions as well as the 196th Light Infantry Brigade, the 11th Armored Cavalry Regiment, and the 173rd Airborne Brigade. It added up to twenty-two battalions of Americans. There were also four battalions of Vietnamese marines and rangers joining us. The working theory going around was that their marines and rangers were much better fighters than the regular ARVN soldiers and as the story went, they could hold their own in battle. Not having worked with them before, I wasn't sure if this was reality or yet another jungle legend.

Tay Ninh Province could be described as a transition zone between the gooey muck of the Mekong Delta to the south and the thick jungle of Cambodia to the north. It was basically flat. Jutting abruptly upward out of this plain about two kilometers west of Soui Da was a mountain of dark black rock rising just over three thousand feet high. It was a geographical anomaly, this solitary peak on a flat plain. The Vietnamese called it Nui Ba Den. We called it Black Widow Mountain or Black Virgin Mountain.

There was a Green Beret camp on the very top of the mountain. With its commanding view of the province, it was an ideal location for radio transmitters and receivers. From the bottom, we could see the peak bristling with antennas. The VC owned the rest of the mountain and had honeycombed it with countless tunnels and caves. The Green Berets stayed off the sides of the mountain as much as possible and generally came and went from their fortified camp by helicopter only. Now we owned the bottom around the mountain. It was a unique arrangement.

As we sat around that first day, Soja was working hard to confirm our worst fears. He swore he heard somebody talking over at HQ about us attacking the mountain and going up its sides. Most of us were skeptical but it did set off a worried debate. We were all concerned. Although I had never attended even a single lecture at West Point, VMI, or The Citadel, I had seen enough war movies to know beyond the shadow of a doubt that the last thing I wanted to do was attack uphill against dug-in troops. I'd rather go over Niagara Falls in a barrel than try to fight my way up the sides of Black Widow Mountain.

A few feet away, Tynes was crouched over some C rations he was cooking. In his typically calm way he announced in a monotone, "I'm not going up that thing." Somehow I believed him. We all did, or at least we wanted to. Tynes always seemed to know a little bit more about what was really going on than the rest of us grunts. We weren't sure how he knew but he did. It was comforting. If he wasn't going up the Black Widow then the rest of us probably weren't going either. It was almost official.

Back at Lai Khe, Nancy Sinatra had arrived with a USO tour to entertain the troops. She had become a big star with her hit song "These Boots Are Made For Walking." Most of the infantry and armor were with us in Tay Ninh Province, so it turned into a show for the REMF. Later, when the singer learned of this, she returned to Lai Khe and gave a repeat performance. By this time some of the units were back at base camp and able to attend her show. In my book, she was a neat lady and had a heart of gold for doing that for us. It was too bad that C Company missed both shows.

The next two days were spent deepening our foxholes and filling sandbags in the morning, then practicing with our weapons in the afternoon. I fired my M-16 and had some fun. Gilbert fired way more ammo than the average guy, made a lot of noise, and appeared to be a much better than average shot. He might have been the best with a machine gun in the entire company. Later that day, Sergeant Alvarez, who had heard about it but had our names confused, complimented me on my superior skills with the machine gun saying, "I hear you shot the shit out of that gun today." It was like an arrow in the heart. I needed some validation. I needed someone to tell me that I was part of the team or that I was doing something right. Reluctantly, I told him that it had been Gilbert, that I was just another numbnuts out there with a rifle. It was demoralizing.

The next day, we continued the bunker-building craze. We also test-fired our weapons once again on the perimeter. It was unusual for us to do that two days in a row. A lot of armor and artillery guys joined us and it became a large, impromptu social event with everyone laughing, talking, and trying each other's weapons. Many non-issue weapons were being fired. There was an automatic shotgun, a few revolvers, and even a two-shot derringer. Several armored guys had the same type of modified weapon, a captured .30-caliber M-1 carbine with the stock and barrel sawed off. This created a kind of machine-gun pistol that wasn't very accurate but was a mountain of fun to play with.

We also saw the new black bolt CAR (carbine automatic rifle) test-fired. This was a shortened version of the M-16 with a telescoping stock. The weapon's firing mechanism was the same as before except that instead of a shiny chrome surface the bolts were covered with some type of duller black substance. The army was concerned about the jamming rate of the M-16. The problem wouldn't go away, despite attempts at increased cleaning and lubricating. The army then came up with the new black bolt. A few of the buck sergeants had been given these weapons to try out. It wasn't at all clear that there was any real scientific method to the experiment. Sadly, I didn't get a chance to fire one of them.

More than a few grunts in the company had already experienced problems with an M-16 jamming in combat situations and thought that we should be using AK-47s or something else more reliable. Because the brass couldn't contradict the party line publicly, most of them favored the M-16. They pointed out that at seven and a half pounds it was lighter than the Russian rifle by four pounds and therefore easier to carry. Also, because our ammo was half as heavy as AK-47s we could carry twice as much on patrol. In reality, a million rounds wouldn't help you much out in the field if your rifle jammed and wouldn't shoot. My loyalties stayed with the M-16 because I hadn't yet had a serious jamming problem in combat, but eventually I would. The high rate of dissatisfaction among the GIs with the M-16 was constant. It didn't matter. All the complaining in the world wouldn't change a thing. It would have been easier to teach a pig how to fly than it would have been to undo a multimillion-dollar contract between the Pentagon and the arms industry.

Around dusk, I meandered toward the north side of the dirt road that bisected our camp. I had to piss and didn't want to do it next to our foxholes, so instead was doing it off the road into the ditch beside it. Right away I noticed that the sound wasn't right. It had a ceramic quality to it, like a cow pissing on a flat rock. Looking carefully among the shrubs and weeds in the ditch, I saw that I was urinating on a large, unexploded, napalm bomb. Reflexively I stopped for a second, then finished peeing even though I was certain that if the bomb went off my stream probably wouldn't be enough to put out the flames.

After the initial deployment of troops into the Tay Ninh area, all pretense of surprise and secrecy melted away as battalion after battalion arrived. The operation was so large and obvious that everyone from Cambodia to Peru knew we had arrived. An airfield arose not far from the dusty base of the mountain as tarmac runways large enough to land cargo planes were laid down. A command post, as well as other small buildings, bunkers, and sheds popped up like weeds. This was no amateur act. All of us saw long sweeps and large search-and-destroy missions in our immediate future. The best rumors available at the time were that the VC and NVA in the area were well organized, good fighters. We were sure that they too could decipher the obvious that was unfolding around them and figure out that something big was headed their way.

A lot of artillery was arriving in the form of those huge 155-mm self-propelled howitzers mounted on tank tracks. They were a loud and gross display of firepower. Because the VC owned all sides of the mountain, the big guns were turned loose to pound them night and day whenever they were bored or needed the practice or just felt like it. Of course, it was a great show to watch, especially because we could see where the shells landed and the ensuing explosions. That was a sight we didn't get to see very often.

Watching one of the howitzers from the side about a hundred and fifty meters away, I noticed that you could actually see the artillery shell in flight for the first fifty or seventy-five meters. Not having noticed this before, I was fascinated and started drifting over closer to get a better look. On the way, I came upon a mortar pit whose tube was facing away from the mountain. A discussion ensued with the mortar crew about this visual phenomenon. They informed me that you could see a mortar shell in flight for more than fifty meters if you lay on the ground next to the tube and looked up as it was fired. They invited me to try it, which I did, getting a good view of a couple of mortars as they were launched. Afterward, while walking back to resume sitting around with the platoon and doing nothing, the question popped into my head, Where did those mortar shells go that they had just fired?

The next day things got going when the dozens of battalions in all the staging areas were dispersed to their starting points. The Black Lions were helicoptered out, en masse, to an area just south of Katum near the Cambodian border.

This was the actual start of Operation Junction City, a search-and-destroy mission in War Zone C. Like all of the division operations, it was named after a U.S. city, one with a fairly macho-sounding name. Early on in Vietnam, the operations were named after things—tough things like barracuda, buckskin, and marauder. Using cities started in 1966. Many Western cities like Phoenix and El Paso were used, maybe to please LBJ. My guess was that some major or colonel at headquarters suggested his own hometown. If the name had zip, it was used. If it was odd or inappropriate, it wasn't. Philadelphia was obviously out of place, for example, and no matter what your rank or position there probably wasn't ever going to be an Operation Truth or Consequences or an Operation Kissimmee.

The plan was to move the troops from the staging areas, like Soui Da, into positions surrounding two hundred fifty square miles of Tay Ninh Province that were held by the enemy. Hopefully, this would be a surprise and trap some of the estimated ten thousand men of the 9th Viet Cong Divi-

sion and 101st North Vietnamese Regiment that were believed to be in the area.

D-day for this operation could have stood for double day
because it took almost forty-eight hours to chopper all of the
battalions into their positions. We went out on day one. Our
landing west of Trai Bi, about a mortar shot's distance from
Cambodia, was uneventful. Five helicopters ferrying other
troops to other landing zones, however, were shot down the
first day. We also heard that five armored vehicles had been
blown up during their deployment.

Charlie Company spread out like a centipede down a long
stretch of Highway 4 running through a thickly wooded area.
It more properly should have been called Trail 4. I'd been in
supermarket aisles that were wider than it was in some places.
It was overgrown with weeds in some spots, washed out in
others, and paved nowhere. The Americans hadn't paid much
attention to this area previously, so it hadn't been salted from
stem to stern with mines and booby traps, which was nice for
a change.

Helicopters with public address systems hovered overhead
giving instructions in Cambodian. The basic message was
that we were not going to go past the highway and enter
Cambodia, but if any rockets or mortars came out of Cambodia at us, we would retaliate with artillery fire or air strikes.
Incredibly, one battalion of about eight hundred men of the
173rd Airborne had actually parachuted into their position a
couple of kilometers north of Katum, which wasn't very far
from us. The jump was largely unopposed and had gone well
with only about a dozen guys receiving minor injuries like
ankle sprains. We were all outwardly contemptuous, saying
that they were a bunch of show-offs, that the jump was unnecessary and had been done solely for publicity purposes.
Inside I was jealous, wishing that I had also gone in by parachute. Of course, I didn't dare mention this because I would
have been flayed alive.

During my advanced infantry training in Georgia, I had
actually signed up to join the airborne and had been accepted. My folks talked me out of following through with

the plan. Later, I rethought the issue and regretted being so weak-willed that I did what they wanted instead of what I wanted. It was an error in judgment on my part.

At a certain point, we moved off the highway and about five or ten meters into the jungle. There we formed a long picket line parallel to the road. Our job was to serve as a blocking force and nail any VC or NVA who tried to flee our way, out of the encircled area. Except for the obnoxious overhead babble in Cambodian, the day was pretty low-key.

When the sun disappeared, we walked back to an area designated as the battalion NDP and dug in. A battalion-sized NDP was large with sometimes as much as a couple of acres' worth of real estate inside the perimeter.

The next morning, we returned to the same section of road for more guard duty. This job was as simple as a paper clip. It was mindless, easy work. I had a sense of well-being. There were three of us at our position. The day was quiet and cool. My game plan called for me to lie down and doze off or daydream away the hours while I listened for enemy activity. Soon, I was flat on my back with my eyes closed and hands behind my head.

Every day, even before Vietnam, I took at least one small trip to Neverland. Often there was more than one trip per day. It was wonderful there because everything was perfect and I was completely happy. On this day's trip, I might have been catching the winning pass for the Rams in the Los Angeles Coliseum or been the wittiest guest imaginable on *The Tonight Show* with Johnny Carson. If it was *The Tonight Show*, the other guest would be some gorgeous creature that couldn't live without me, like Ursula Andress. Over the years I had shared some of these mental wanderings with my mom, who had nicknames for each of her children, and because of this she sometimes referred to me as Walter Mitty.

The current trip was going well until the footsteps came, the unmistakable sound of someone walking toward us, and Neverland had to be abandoned. The area we were spread out in was more like a thin forest than a jungle. However, tall, thick elephant grass in front of our positions limited the visibility to about fifteen or twenty meters in that direction. Every square inch of ground was covered with dry leaves that crunched loudly with each step.

I was flat on my back resting, with my eyes closed and my hands behind my head, when the steps first started. They were slow and deliberate with lots of time between steps so that he could listen for us. I managed to sit up without any discernible noise. Gilbert and Smithers had already been sitting and now tracked the footsteps with their eyes. Smithers, off to my left, welcomed me back to reality by pointing out front. As he did, his mouth grimaced and the skin on the front of his neck tightened like it does when you are trying to make something that you are doing a bit more quiet. The steps came toward us as slowly as it was possible to do and still be moving forward.

Gilbert was off to my right a few meters. The machine gun was between us and far enough away so that neither of us could get to it without making all kinds of dry leaf and twig racket. My rifle was in a death grip. The steps, which sounded as if they were just approaching the outer limits of our visibility, stopped for a moment, then began moving to our left rather than continuing toward us. We all glanced rapidly back and forth at each other and the noise. Soon, the steps reversed direction and moved back from left to right in front of us, eventually passing us by and heading toward Davis and Ilardi at the next position about thirty-five meters to our right.

Davis was now down on one knee aiming his M-16 at the noise. Ilardi was holding his grenade launcher with both hands but not aiming it. The M-79 grenade had a type of gyro device inside and had to travel some minimal distance like twenty or thirty meters before it would go off on impact. This was for obvious safety reasons. Once before, Ilardi had fired one that went up, whacked a palm tree, and then fell at everyone's feet. Luckily it didn't go off. If Ilardi fired at this close range, again it wouldn't go off but would fuck the guy up like being hit with a hundred-mile-an-hour fastball.

A few seconds later, the steps stopped moving past Davis

and went right at him. The grass parted and one VC emerged. Davis fired a quarter of a clip burst, which dropped him on the spot, where he lay groaning and slightly rocking back and forth. We all tensed up and waited to see if there was anyone behind him who would open up on us. After a few seconds, when it didn't occur, we breathed a collective sigh of relief. Cautiously, Davis walked over and confiscated the big fat AK-47 the gook had dropped. He then pointed his rifle at the wounded man while Ilardi dragged him back to the road. Doc Baldwin soon showed up to work on the guy, applying bandages before the VC was carted off and put on a medevac chopper. He was going to get better care than if he had escaped.

The scene didn't appear to be too shocking, so before he left, I wandered over to stare. His main injury seemed to be that one of the bullets had hit him in the low abdomen or pelvis. The exit wound on his backside had blown off about half of his left buttock. The crater where his left bun should have been was immense, at least as large as a medium-sized apple. I was sure that hurt. He had a few bandoliers of rifle ammo and a little knapsack but not much else. He was skinny. My guess was that he went hungry much of the time and had to eat what he found—such as bananas, coconuts, and bamboo shoots—just to survive. Nonessential resupply was probably nonexistent for this guy. If he smoked, he probably often had to go weeks or months between cigarettes. That was dedication we couldn't match. I'd give up and die after one day without a smoke.

That evening Sergeant Estes got shipped out on the supply helicopter. He was a squad leader I had always found to be pleasant and friendly. Unfortunately, he had developed a four-alarm fever, muscle pains, and sweating spells that Doc thought might be malaria. Doc later said that technically he should have called it black water fever. That's what they call it when you've had malaria before and now it has come back and also made your urine real dark, which was the case with Estes.

We had already sent a couple of guys back with these

symptoms since I'd been with the company. Still, lots of us, myself included, did not take the malaria pills regularly that they tried to give us. I'm not sure why. If Doc handed me a malaria pill, I took it. Otherwise, I forgot about it. We never got a final diagnosis on Estes. If we didn't have the label malaria, his illness would probably have been called bamboo fever or something like that. Anyway, Estes never returned from the hospital. It must have been malaria or something else equally serious.

After Estes left, the rest of the night was uneventful except for Smithers's noises. While sleeping he developed a seriously loud nose whistle. It sounded like an air raid siren, and made me anxious. It couldn't be ignored. In my nervous mind the whistle was broadcasting an announcement that all VC within earshot should proceed to Ronnau's foxhole immediately and cut off his head when he wasn't looking.

Experience had taught me not to awaken the culprit. They either got mad or woke up groggy and made even more noise. The correct procedure was to drop a leaf about the size of a playing card on the offender's face. Invariably he would brush the leaf off, rub his face, and roll over without waking up. Meanwhile, the whistle vanished. Occasionally a double-leaf treatment was required. This time one leaf did the trick. It was kind of childish but it was also practical and worked as well on snorers as it did on whistlers.

The next day, we heard footsteps in front of our position again but they didn't break through the grass and come into view. Nobody fired for fear of hitting the unknown, like lost GIs out taking a leak. My perhaps morbid fear of accidentally killing an American in Vietnam just wouldn't go away. It really made me edgy at times.

Back at the lager area for the night, I ended up at a two-man foxhole with Soja. Around midnight, while he stood guard and I slept, one or more VC walked up on our position. Ilardi, who was out on LP duty, heard them approach. Although he couldn't see who was walking toward us, he assumed that any honest-to-God noncombatants were at home asleep and not walking around the jungle in the middle of the night. Accordingly, he threw a grenade at the intruders, which nailed at least one of them. It went off about fifteen meters in front of our position and sent steel shards whistling in all directions. Some ripped into the sandbags on the front of our position and caused them to leak sand.

As improbable as it seems, the blast did not awaken me. This didn't jive with Soja who, seeing me still lying there, assumed that I had been struck and was down because of wounds. I awoke to him shaking me and asking in an agitated voice where I was hit. I pleaded noninjury as well as ignorance. He filled me in on what had transpired, then diagnosed me as being, in his words, fucking deaf. My excuse for not having awakened when needed was that with six siblings it could be loud at my house. It's quite possible some of my sisters' screams approached the decibel level of an exploding hand grenade. I had learned to sleep with loud noises at times.

In fact, I was simply exhausted, as were all of the enlisted men. There were limits to how long you could function when asked to stay awake every other hour all night every night. We went to sleep at about eight in the evening and got up at about six in the morning, giving us about five hours of sleep a night. That wasn't enough for us growing boys. Fatigue was becoming a problem. As this operation dragged on, more and more guys nodded off. Grunts all over the place were leaning up against a bunker with a rifle across their laps and zonking out. At times the numbers were such that it reminded me of the Gary Cooper movie *Beau Geste*, in which they propped up a bunch of dead soldiers at their fort to fool the enemy. The squad sergeants weren't unsympathetic. They weren't getting any more sleep than we were and therefore mentioned the problem to the higher-ups. This didn't yield any tangible results.

Our officers and platoon sergeants slept in the center of the NDP, didn't pull guard duty on the line, and generally got a better night's sleep than we did. They weren't unsympathetic to our plight but didn't have much of a say on how long these multiunit operations lasted. The decision makers, the field-grade officers, were back in base camp sleeping in a real bed with a real mattress. They probably didn't realize the magnitude of the problem. In any event, the situation wasn't corrected.

Sergeant Conklin struck me as exceedingly odd. There was something wrong with him, but I couldn't put my finger on what it was. He had managed to acquire an unusual device, a small electronic beeper with an earphone and a long thin wire that reeled out of the bottom. After putting the wire out in a circle around his position and plugging the end of it into a socket on the side of the beeper, he put on the earphone and slept until sunup. If anyone sneaking up on his position broke the wire encircling him, the device beeped in his ear. God only knows where he got the thing and I sure wasn't going to ask him. Hell, on most days, he was so schizoid that you couldn't get a straight answer if you asked him what time it was. I never saw another gizmo like that again, anywhere.

The center section of our camp wouldn't have slept so soundly had they realized that when the VC approached that night many of the sentries awaiting them were catching some Z's. Perhaps even Soja had been asleep. My ass was just glad that at least Ilardi had been awake.

While we had been guarding the road, other battalions had been on long sweeps through the cordoned-off zone. Now it was our turn again. The patrolling companies took up blocking positions and performed road security and the 2/28 Black Lions and 1/16 Rangers took off in different directions on search-and-destroy sweeps.

Right outside of our perimeter, we found a blood trail from Ilardi's grenade. The wounded man had really been ripped; he was bleeding like a stuck hog. There was so much blood that a blind man could follow the trail. Rusty-brown spots were spattered everywhere. Occasionally we found a used bandage. Maybe there had been more than one VC chopped up by the flying shrapnel. The average person only has four or five quarts of blood to lose, but this trail was two hundred meters long. It ended abruptly with no dead body and no visible grave.

The better part of an hour had been taken in tracking the blood nearly the length of two football fields. The point man and people up front were being slow and cautious. It wouldn't be much of a treat to walk up on a wounded enemy soldier who couldn't go any farther and had stopped to make a last stand and take a few round-eyes with him.

Amazingly, probing the ground searching for a grave turned up a landline, or Lima Lima as we called them. It was a communications wire as thick as your little finger buried four to six inches deep in the ground and running to the west, toward Cambodia. We started following it. Every few meters we would stop and dig down to make sure that we were still on top of it.

After a kilometer or so, a helicopter brought us out a German shepherd from the K-9 Corps with a handler, as well as an American who spoke Vietnamese and knew how to tap into the communications wire. The dog sniffed along and expedited the process of following the wire. We went a couple of kilometers more after the dog joined us. It was hard to fathom the man-hours involved—the time and effort required to install the line. It was mind-boggling.

By late afternoon, we still hadn't found what was at the end of the line. The CO thought there would be more than just a radio communication setup where the line ended. My feeling was that there could be anything, maybe even a company or battalion of Viet Cong or NVA, and I didn't want to have dinner with them. Much to our delight, the brass ordered us back to the lager area. Before we left, the interpreter got out his tools and tapped into the wire. He got into a short conversation with an NVA operator, who quickly figured out that he was talking to an imposter. The interpreter ended the conversation, he claimed, by saying, "Fuck Ho Chi Minh" and a few other unpleasant things in Vietnamese. He smiled broadly while regaling us with his version of the conversation. We could tell that he was quite happy with himself for having been able to insult an enemy soldier by cursing his leader. We then cut the wire in several places and headed back.

I was aghast. Although ecstatic over our orders to get the hell out of there, I was shocked that our intelligence people, the G-2 group, didn't want us to leave the line so that they could return later and try to tap into it just to listen. The situation didn't make sense, at least not to me. It appeared as if we were turning our backs on what could have been a veritable intelligence bonanza.

We were able to return safely to our night lager. There we were told that the Bravo Company, 1/16 Rangers who had gone in one direction that morning as we had gone in another, had suffered just over a hundred casualties that day, with twenty-seven killed and seventy-five wounded, when they bumped into a battalion of NVA. The story wasn't completely clear. Reportedly, more than 150 enemy had been killed.

Sometimes Fairman was hard to figure out. The day before, he had stopped by the gun position and asked why I still had a rifle if I was assistant gunner. Did I want to trade in the rifle for a pistol? That way I could carry more M-60 ammo. I told him no, that I already had a pistol and didn't want to be out there without a rifle. He told me to think about it. I did. Lots of guys had a rifle and a pistol. The other assistant gunners had M-16s. Hell, even the medics carried rifles in Charlie Company. Maybe he thought that I was traveling light and this was his way of telling me. Maybe he was just messing with me.

My plan became to increase my load of community property by two more belts of M-60 ammo. Now I was up to six hundred rounds of the stuff, which had to weigh as much as anyone else's community property. The second half of my plan was to not bring up the rifle subject again with Fairman. The plan worked. He didn't hassle me about it again.

The largest and most interesting discovery of the operation became our longest and most boring day. We were on a battalion-sized patrol. At midmorning, we came to a stop because some other platoon found a tunnel. While they searched it, our platoon spread out and provided security on the right flank.

After about two hours of security duty, we were beginning to wonder what was so time-consuming and so damn special about this tunnel. After about five hours, we started to get bits and pieces of the story. The tunnel led to an underground hospital. There were several floors of supply rooms, a triage area, operating rooms, and post-op areas. Bunks had been dug into the walls of larger rooms for about sixty patients. There was a good store of supplies, including stainless-steel surgical instruments, suturing materials, intravenous solutions, and quite a stash of medications, mostly antibiotics. All the patients had been evacuated. No VC or booby traps had been left behind to greet us.

The excitement generated by this find just about outweighed the tedium of sitting there all day as security. I watched Fairman and Sharp like a hawk. If there was any chance that they would ask for help to search down there or carry out medical equipment, I wanted it to be me. I was very anxious to get involved. In my mind, like a grammar school kid, I was muttering, "Please, please, pretty please with sugar on top." Had I said it out loud and he heard it, Fairman would have spit at me or thrown something in my direction. My help was never requested.

The hospital wasn't blown up before we left. B-52s probably wouldn't be effective. My guess was that rather than do a half-assed job now, they were going to send a real demolition team back later to do it right. That would be fun to watch. In the meantime, the hospital wasn't going anywhere.

The next day started off with a bang. Mail was brought out by a supply chopper in the morning before we went out on patrol. I received three letters, which I did not immediately open. Often, but not always, I'd refrain from reading my mail as soon as it arrived. I would put it off instead, so that I could prolong and relish the ecstasy of its arrival. My usual routine was to read one letter a day after sorting and rating them, saving the best one for the last day. Of course, each day's letter wasn't read until the very last moment, when it was almost too dark to read. In the meantime, each day's letter was pulled out of the safe confines of my lateral thigh pocket about once an hour so that I could visually inspect it and make myself glow with anticipation. Sometimes as we walked I would slip my hand into my pocket and feel the letter, squeezing it in an attempt to guess how many pages were in the envelope and if there were any enclosures, such as photos or newspaper clippings. These rituals were necessary for my survival in a shit world. They invariably lifted my spirits.

During the early part of that day's patrol, without fanfare, a light cloud of tear gas graced us with its presence. A stinging sensation in my eyes made salty tears run down my cheeks. Soon my nose began running in sympathy with my eyes. The noxious fumes weren't very concentrated and didn't burn our upper airways to the point that any of us were forced to actually don one of those hot, stifling gas masks. We all recognized what it was from having been forced to walk through the gas chamber during basic training. Without that experience, which had seemed cruel at the time, the gas might well have precipitated a panic among the troops, but it didn't. Everyone remained calm. Unfortunately, the jungle area we were in was quite dense and let in no breeze to help dissipate the gas. Despite our walking, we were stuck with remnants of the unfriendly atmosphere for about twenty minutes before we could no longer tell that it was with us. I guess we were lucky that no one started puking.

Even more surprising to me than the appearance of the gas cloud was the realization that no one seemed to know how it had come to be unleashed on us. Stories soon abounded that it had been dropped on us by the air force or fired in by howitzers from a nearby fire support base. None about the VC being responsible surfaced, however, probably because we didn't associate them with this type of ordnance.

All in all, it didn't seem to bother anyone too much except for a black kid from another squad. Maybe he'd had bad experiences with tear gas during race riots or antiwar demonstrations in his hometown back in the World. He was more agitated by the event than any of the rest of us and mused out loud that this was indeed an ominous development. He was fearful that the situation might get "worser." I sure hoped that he was wrong because if there was a bigger cloud of tear gas in our immediate future, I wouldn't have been helped much by my gas mask pouch full of Abba-Zaba bars.

The afternoon part of the patrol was just about as strange as the morning had been. A chopper landed and a colonel wearing immaculate fatigues got out to join us. Surprisingly, instead of walking with the CO or one of the other officers, he joined our squad and got in line just ahead of me and Gilbert. I could see a Big Red One patch on his shoulder but not his name tag. The patch was on his left shoulder, which meant that he was currently an active member of the division. His right shoulder didn't have a patch and didn't require one. Anyone, however, was allowed to wear a patch on their right shoulder of any division that they had previously served in and were proud of. It was an option.

He sure didn't have much gear, not even a rifle or a backpack. All he carried was a .45 pistol on his right hip and a canteen on the other. My guess, which proved to be correct, was that he would not be spending the night with us, not with that paucity of gear. He'd be gone by sundown.

We never discovered why he was out there with us. Most battalion-grade officers, such as majors and colonels and even higher-ranking officers, stayed in the rear most of the time, for obvious reasons. It was a lot less likely that they would get killed or maimed back at the base camp. There was also precedent for this approach. I'd read somewhere in one of my war books that so many high-ranking officers had been killed in one battle during the Civil War that President Lincoln had issued an executive order prohibiting the higher-ranking officers from being at the front lines if at all possible. They were supposed to run the battalions and divisions, not get killed playing hotshot out in the field which would then subject us unnecessarily to a series of inexperienced leaders.

The patrol ended without fanfare as we rejoined the rest of the battalion back at the main NDP. As expected, the mystery colonel didn't spend the night with us but was flown out by helicopter, unscathed, at sunset. About three hours after the sun went down, all was quiet and right with the world until a trip flare went off about fifty meters out in front of the fox-hole that was a few spaces to the left of mine. One of the guys on LP had been fumble-fucking around in the dark and had set off the flare by accident. Some grunt in the hole clos-est to the flare thought that it might be the enemy moving in and opened up with his M-16 until screams came back to "stop the fucking shooting." Nobody was hurt.

This lack of communication bothered me. On some nights not everyone was told that there were LPs out there and where they were. If you didn't happen to actually see the guys leave the perimeter, you didn't know that they were out there, sometimes right in front of your position. It was dis-concerting. Generally, I tried to tell those at the foxholes close to our planned location that we were going to be out there when I was part of an LP team. Still, you always had it stuck in the back of your mind that there might be some blockhead on the line who didn't get the message and might light you up if he heard noise from your location.

After the shooting, the rest of the night was uneventful ex-cept for a few small, mean-spirited, nocturnal insects. They were so tough that when you sat or laid on one of them, it would bite you, hard, right through your fatigues. It hurt like hell. Mercifully, they all went to bed about midnight.

MARCH

Hiking around Tay Ninh Province along the Cambodian border wasn't exactly walking in a public park with delicate flower gardens and neatly trimmed lawns. Thorns, thickets, and sharp branches were everywhere. As a result, the troops had lots of little holes and tears in their fatigues. This was deemed acceptable because it was both unavoidable and John Wayneish—it looked macho.

Unfortunately, my fatigue pants had tangled with the dreaded wait-a-minute vine, as we called it. These were long and hung down from the jungle canopy like those Tarzan swung on in the movies. It wasn't smooth like a rope, however, but instead had a series of hard, sharp, multipronged thorns along its length. They looked like grappling hooks, and would slice and dice your clothes or skin with ease. My right pant leg had been ripped open from the front pocket to the cuff. This apparently exceeded the militarily acceptable limits of sartorial disrepair, which is to say that it pissed off Fairman. He ordered a new pair of pants to be delivered on the next resupply day then groused about it to me whenever possible. He acted as if I had intentionally destroyed my pants through misuse and the U.S. government was going to have difficulty paying for the new pair without raising taxes. It was a chore to ignore him.

Resupply days were fun. They were sort of like Christmas, with something for everyone. A lot of real basic stuff was sent out, like soap, matches, toilet paper, and extra P-38s. Those were little one-inch metal can openers with a hole in them so they could be strung onto your dog tag chain. In general, there was also some toothpaste, shaving cream, writing paper, and envelopes. Most of us had run out of stationery by this point. I hadn't written home in a week or two because I was out of envelopes. It wasn't a very nice thing to do to my parents but there was no way around it.

After the semi-essentials came a few outright luxuries. There might be bags of candy, often M&M's, cartons of cigarettes, and sometimes a duffel bag full of cracked ice with beer and soda pop. There was no choice of brands, what came out was what you got. An attempt was made to keep the distribution fair and somewhat random so that the first guys in line didn't swipe all the beer. Each grunt stuck his hand into the duffel bag without looking and latched onto two cans. If you weren't thrilled with your selection once you saw what you had, you were free to trade. I always won because in general there was more soda pop than beer and anything that was iced and sweet was fine by me. I never drank beer out in the field, not once, because it diminished my alertness. Being less alert was unpleasant for me when I was in enemy territory, where there were always lots of well-hidden little people who wanted to kill me.

Not all the cigarettes were supplied by the army, which gave us a tiny little pack, containing four smokes, inside each box of C rations. These were mostly unfiltered Pall Malls or Chesterfields but sometimes Winstons with filters. According to the army, that was all we needed. I was up to two packs a day and would have to eat ten C ration meals a day to feed my nicotine habit. Not wanting us to lose the war because of a nicotine fit, the army went a step further and sent out a few extra cartons to help us out. I'm not really sure that it would have been enough.

Fortunately, the generous citizens of Birmingham, Alabama, had adopted the Big Red One as their official fighting force in Vietnam. A local kindergarten, the South Avondale Baptist Kindergarten, was sponsoring 1st Platoon and arranged for us to receive cartons of Old Gold cigarettes, the packages of which boasted good flavor because of their spin filter, whatever that was. We weren't sure who chose

Old Gold, maybe some of the church members had stock in the company, but that's what we got. They were a big hit with us. We enjoyed them immensely.

Interestingly, some of the GIs who smoked filtered cigarettes opened the packs from the bottom. This was an attempt to keep the filters clean and free from the incessant barrage of dust and dirt we were subjected to on a daily basis. Dirty smokes never bothered me, so I always opened my packs the regular way.

More five-gallon cans of water than we needed had been sent out. After all the canteens had been reloaded, I filled my helmet to the brim and attempted to take a sponge bath using a small towel. It was a semi-effective experience. I was a little cleaner but possibly not clean enough to justify the effort.

Around dinnertime, life got a little more complicated. Just as the sun was going down, along with our evening meal, Captain Burke arrived with an intelligence officer who wanted to brief us. He claimed that the VC were going to attack on foot around midnight at the point where Charlie Company's part of the line joined Alpha Company's line. He then announced a full alert—that is, everyone remaining awake and on guard for the night. All of the mortars would be zeroed in and waiting. Each company had one mortar platoon with three mortars. This meant that we had at least six mortars available. I wasn't sure if Bravo Company was with us at the NDP that night or somewhere else. There were hundreds of mortar shells already in our camp that had previously been brought out by helicopter.

An attack was certainly possible. We had been using the same battalion-sized NDP long enough for them to know exactly where we were camped out. Still, the idea that our intelligence people could figure out when and where a surprise attack would come ahead of time was hard to buy. We listened with healthy skepticism, believing that the VC were inscrutable and wondering how our G-2 guys could even hope to know what they were planning. Besides, we all thought of the G-2 people as a bunch of closet astrologers who spent their time at the Saigon Hilton drinking Mai Tais, sticking multicolored pins into maps, and making up this stuff to keep the generals happy. On top of it all, we damn sure didn't want to stay up all night. Sleepy theorized aloud that it would be just as safe to have the usual half of us alert and let everyone else wake up when the shooting started. Maybe that plan was an example of why the army didn't want seventeen-year-olds in a combat zone.

Sleepy had somehow lied about his age to join the army, without his parents' consent. He was still only seventeen. The rules stipulated that you could join before age eighteen only if your parents agreed and signed you up. You weren't allowed, however, to be assigned to a combat zone before eighteen. Sleepy had shared his secret with the enlisted men in the squad and, of course, none of us would fink on him.

The intelligence officer didn't stick around to evaluate the accuracy of his prognostications. He caught a flight out before it was completely dark, which, as if to add insult to injury, blew some more dirt on us and what remained of our dinners.

We spent the night sitting, waiting, staring into the darkness. No LP positions had been sent out. The hours crept by with each of us fighting off sleep, daydreaming, thinking our own thoughts. I moved my arm back and forth to catch some moonlight on my wristwatch. We'd repeatedly been told that if the VC tried a night assault they always started it before 0200 hours. That gave them enough time to succeed or fail and still get away before the dawn's early light brought the possibility of air spotters and either artillery fire or close air support with bombs or rockets. By the self-winding Omega that my friends Larry and Paul had given me as a going-away present, it was a few minutes past midnight.

Out front and off to the right we heard an increase in nonspecific noise coming out of the jungle. It moved closer to the NDP. POP! A tracer streaked out toward the noise. BOOM! A claymore erupted, followed a few seconds later by several more—much like the way that one dog in a front yard barking sets off all the other dogs on that street barking as well. Soon a lot of things were going off or exploding. The

strangely dark flashes of the claymores didn't seem to do a
very good job of lighting up the night like a giant Kodak
flashbulb might, but did send thousands of ball bearings flying out to greet our nocturnal visitors. POP, POP! More tracers were joined by the chatter of machine guns, then the
harsher, louder sounds of AK-47s being fired back. There
were also the sounds of M-16s being fired by both sides. All
of the VC units carried a lot of American weapons. Any
grunt worth his salt could listen to a shot and identify it as
being an M-1 carbine, M-16, M-60, AK-47, or some other
frequently encountered firearm. After you had heard them
a few times, it was easy. Soon there were so many weapons
being fired at once, with maybe over a hundred rifles and machine guns, that individual shots were no longer distinguish-
able.

We waited for the fighting to spread over directly in front
of our foxholes. All of us were wondering, with some trepidation, whether the VC were going to come out of the jungle
right in front of us and attack. Within a minute or two, our
mortars started and dumped about seventy rounds on the
area where the VC were. All of the rounds landed in the target area, none on our line or inside our perimeter. We were
grateful for that, because it was always a possibility. The
mortar barrage was apocalyptic. It was ending the attack
over there. My feelings were that I no longer needed to wait
for action in front of my position. It wasn't coming. The
number of exploding mortar shells was decreasing, as was
the rifle fire. Once again you could hear individual shots and
the occasional chatter of machine-gun fire. Not much was
being directed at our NDP anymore. Not wanting to be completely left out, I aimed into the center of where the fracas
was and slowly, methodically squeezed off half a clip of
shots. In my mind I was hoping and at the same time pretending that my effort was somehow necessary to repel the
attack. Gilbert watched but didn't join in. His face was expressionless. Smithers seemed enthusiastic but undecided
between my overkill and Gilbert's underkill. From the rest of
the 1st Platoon's section of the line, very few shots were fired

into the melee and only a couple other nearby GIs joined my effort.

A few more minutes went by. The big show then ended. The last shot came about thirty seconds after the penultimate shot. The time sequence made me wonder if the last shot had been somebody's rifle going off accidentally. Then there was silence. The air stunk of burned cordite and the moonlight penetrating the jungle was fuzzy from particulate matter in the air. Gilbert and Smithers began gagging and coughing. My tobacco-pummeled airways didn't seem to notice at all. With bleary eyes, we stared our way into the first light of morning.

First Sharp, then a few moments later Fairman, walked down the line exhorting us to get packed up and ready to move out. The sun was already up and the brass were chomping at the bit to see if we had knocked off any of the little suckers. The mortar barrage had been rapid as well as accurate. It was almost a foregone conclusion that we would find some sign of casualties out there. Because we hadn't suffered even minor injuries, this would be racked up as a one-sided victory. The score would be much like the Yankees going up against a minor-league team.

Our platoon was part of the force that would go out to do the search. This pissed off some of the guys because those that stayed behind in reserve would be allowed to catch a few winks. I wanted to go out and hoped we would see results. This wasn't just morbid curiosity. A lot of VC were in this area, and we would undoubtedly continue to make contact with them on a regular basis until we left. So far, there wasn't even a hint of a rumor that the operation was close to being over or that we were close to returning to Lai Khe. If we were going to stick around this place, our chances of survival would improve if some of our mortar shells had actually landed on the enemy and thinned out the herd a little. The best thing for us would be to find bodies stacked up like cordwood. There was also a widely held belief that if your unit gave the VC a bloody nose they would pick on another unit the next time. Who knows if they were really that organized or if this was just another jungle legend, but it sounded reasonable.

Not far outside of the perimeter, we found blood, a little here, a little there. It was like a scavenger hunt, with each guy trying to be the first to spot the next find. Toward the epicenter there were more recognizably tattered trees and uprooted plants. There were also larger blood splashes. Bloody gauze pads were scattered here and there as well as torn pieces of bloodstained khakis. One hedge, about the size of an automobile, was festooned with bloody khaki cloth hanging there along with globs of stringy vermilion pulp or clots and stuff that looked like chunks of human meat. That was bad, but the most dreadful sighting for me was a large pile of primordial ooze at the base of a tree with blood splattered all around it. It was sticky brown-and-maroon-colored crap with what looked like grape-sized bubbles embedded in the outer slime. It might have been guts from a disemboweled VC, but I wasn't sure, it could have been anything. It was terrible. After a couple of looks I backed off, fearful that if I kept staring I might spot something recognizable, like a finger or an eyeball. The sight of a slanted eyeball staring back at me might have caused me to faint on the spot. Furthermore, every fly in the province had arrived for breakfast.

There weren't any weapons or useful equipment lying around that I could see. Maybe the guys walking ahead of us had picked them up. Maybe the VC just hadn't left anything useful behind for us.

About a football field away from the blood and gore, someone found freshly dug earth in a small flat clearing. A little dirt was brushed away, revealing a hand, which was used to pull out a dead VC. This was done cautiously, because they would sometimes put booby-trap grenades underneath the body. The bottom of the grave was searched for weapons, which they would hide in there as frequently as booby traps. Undoubtedly they were hoping that some Americans would be too squeamish to search thoroughly for weapons under a buried putrefying body. They were probably right at least some of the time.

Jeep gunner returning fire at a well-known sniper whom we called Shooting Range Charlie.

An unidentified GI and Gilbert resting against a bunker after a long patrol across the river at Lai Khe.

The author, foreground, in an abandoned rubber tree plantation.

A large mine explodes on Thunder Road.

Easter Sunday mass at Lai Khe.

Moving into an NVA base camp with vehicles and tanks from Quarterhorse.

Search-and-destroy patrol through dense jungle inside the Iron Triangle.

Children from a nearby village selling soda pop. Unfortunately, if they could find our campsite, then so could the local Viet Cong.

Black Lions outside the village of Chaun Giao, which we had surrounded the night before.

The author, resting in the leaves next to Highway 4 near the Cambodian border.

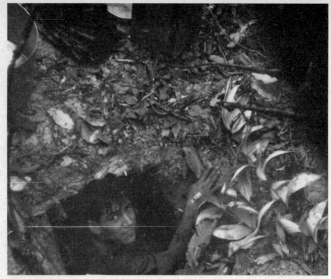

This volunteer tunnel rat found an air force pilot's parachute and dog tags in this hole.

Platoon members digging up an enemy grave to check for buried weapons.

Sergeant Sharp on the roof, tearing apart a hootch full of bags of rice.

Headstone of a sixteen-year-old girl, Tran Cung, in a graveyard where we stopped to rest and collect wild peppers.

Third squad in high elephant grass. We were lost and trying to find a place to hide before sundown.

Bob Reeves, a friend from high school, driving a deuce-and-a-half on Thunder Road to Lai Khe. (Courtesy of Robert Reeves)

Sergeant Fairman cleaning his M-16 before an operation. (Courtesy of Mancil Fairman)

Kirkpatrick wearing a flak jacket for a convoy on Highway 13. (Courtesy of Fred Kirkpatrick)

Cordova sent this photograph of himself on the outskirts of Long Binh to his parents. (Courtesy of Arthur Cordova)

The flip side of this scenario wasn't very pleasant either. It would take a VC with a cast-iron stomach to retrieve a weapon from underneath the body of a friend or someone he knew that had been decomposing for a week or two underground. It would be even worse if the VC didn't have access to a shovel and had to do part of the work by hand.

No weapons or booby traps were found. My only involvement with this unfortunate fellow was as an onlooker, about twenty meters away. The scene wasn't ghoulish at all. There was so much moist soil stuck to him that to me he didn't look like a dead guy, he just looked like a dirty guy. His eyes were closed and his face was expressionless. If his wounds were in front they were covered by the dirt. I certainly couldn't see what type of injury had caused his demise.

Eventually, almost every officer and sergeant in the company took advantage of his rank and walked over to take a closer look. Captain Burke held court by the grave. There was a lot of radio talk as he compared maps with the other officers. Someone boot-flipped the dead gook back into the grave, facedown.

As they milled around, looking at maps and discussing what to do next, a number of the lieutenants and sergeants unconsciously smoothed the loose soil around their feet and kicked small amounts of it back into the grave. By the time we left they had unintentionally damn near reburied the guy. Normally, we didn't put out an intense effort to rebury VC. On occasion, someone with a Christian heart would throw a few shovelsful of dirt back on them, other times they were just left to rot or be eaten by animals.

After the blood, guts, and bodies of the first half of the day, the second half was a lot less interesting. We didn't find anything else until we neared our encampment on the return leg of the patrol at dusk. As usual, we had used a different route coming back than we had used going out. That was standard operating procedure, so that they wouldn't figure out what path we were going to take and jump us by surprise.

As we got closer to our NDP and the troops that had stayed behind for the day, we found another dead guy. He had made it about a hundred meters from where the mortars had fallen. My guess was that after receiving life-threatening gunshot or shrapnel wounds, he fled the scene, probably at a dead run. After going two or three hundred feet he ran out of gas or blood or oxygen, came to a stop, then lay facedown on the soft earth, and passed away. His feet were pointing back toward the battle site.

There were no important documents on him, or weapons for that matter. Besides a shirt, the dead VC was wearing those light beige-colored shorts that a lot of Vietnamese men wore. They always reminded me of swimming trunks and seemed oddly out of place in a country with probably only one public swimming pool for every three million people.

Unfortunately, 3rd Squad drew ambush patrol again that night, precipitating a considerable amount of grumbling, certainly more than usual. This wasn't because we had been up all the previous night and were tired. From that point of view, ambush was a blessing, with two hours of sleep instead of only one between on-guard hours, because we regularly used three-man positions on ambush. The grousing was because the brass wanted the location on Highway 4 again. There had been an ambush patrol somewhere nearby on that road every night since the beginning of Junction City. It didn't seem prudent. The enemy might figure out our routine and turn the tables on us.

My two cents' worth got thrown in on the side of the grumblers. They were right, this was troublesome, and we should probably try someplace else. Sharp didn't tell us that we were being a bunch of worrywarts so I think he agreed with us even though he couldn't say it openly. He did say that we could pull it off by acting like soldiers and being careful. He stressed the importance of being quiet, but not doing that by falling asleep.

The first hour on ambush that night found me sprawled out on my back with my ankles crossed and hands behind my head as I relaxed and stared up into the dark sky. Like most nights, I was saving my journal writing for later on when the boredom factor reached near-catastrophic proportions. As usual, my helmet was serving as a pillow. There were no stars to watch that night, but every so often a passenger plane, complete with running lights, cruised by at high altitude. It seemed odd to have a war going on with commercial airliners flying overhead. Every time I saw one a fleeting sense of sadness filled me that I wasn't on it and headed home. The others felt the same way.

Rifle fire unrelated to the plane could be heard in the distance. There seemed to always be rifle fire within earshot in some direction. If it sounded more than a city block or two away you ignored it, which I did.

Overhead, about a thousand feet up, a parachute flare popped open. We didn't know who called for the flare, but it wasn't us. Maybe the main force back at the NDP had the heebie-jeebies left over from the previous night. Despite the flare's brilliance, it didn't improve our vision all that much, because of all the odd forms and bizarre shadows created by the light as it descended through the trees and vines. A kaleidoscope of lights and shadows moved around me as the flare lost altitude. Not wanting to be spotted, I remained motionless, trying my best to look like a fallen tree or pile of dirt.

A second and third flare popped open, then drifted lazily downward, trailing gray smoke and gently rocking back and forth in the breeze. Watching their descent was pleasant and semi-hypnotic. What I didn't realize was that one of the heavy metal canisters used to launch the flares was now silently streaking down at us without warning.

A heart-stopping metallic clang rang out as the canister transected a three-inch-diameter tree, then bounced off the ground next to my head, and sailed off into the jungle. "Bejesus!" I screeched, managing to jump from a lying to a standing position in one movement. Sharp filled me in on what it was. How myopic. Of course the canister had to land somewhere. I hadn't thought that it might fall on me. This was idiocy of unparalleled dimensions: Chunks of metal the size of Chrysler engine blocks were falling out of the sky and I wasn't even wearing my helmet. It was another lesson in survival. From then on, I wore my helmet whenever flares were launched. At the same time, I was cognizant of the fact that if one of the canisters landed right on my crown, helmet or no helmet, I'd end up with a very short neck and my head wedged between my lungs.

By now, we were two weeks into the operation. The VC and U.S. forces were nibbling away at each other in numbers that were starting to add up. We were picking each other off in ones and twos all over the operational area. If you added in the hundred or so killed or wounded in the 1/16 Battalion during their big battle, our operation had contributed substantially to the American casualty figures for the week.

At home, America got the casualty figures for the previous week every Thursday evening on the network news. Some people specifically watched that particular broadcast to get the figures as they followed the war from week to week. Estimated VC casualties were also given and were always several times greater than ours. Ours had been getting higher lately. According to *Stars and Stripes*, the last week's American casualties—from February 26 through March 4—had been 232 killed, 1,381 wounded, and 4 missing, for a total of 1,617. That was over four hundred more than the highest previous week which had been in January during Cedar Falls. It didn't seem like a lot of casualties when you considered that we had about four hundred fifteen thousand servicemen in Vietnam. It did seem like a lot when you considered that most of the casualties were coming from that minority of servicemen that made up the primary combat units such as armor, artillery, infantry, and aircrews.

The casualty figures were big news everywhere, even in *Stars and Stripes*. One of their photographers was sent out to join the 1st Platoon on morning patrol to get some pictures of the men in action. Not being at all shy about appearing on the cover of the newspaper as Sergeant Rock, personally leading the conquest of Tay Ninh Province, I struck macho poses at every opportunity. My helmet was worn farther back so that you could see more of my face. My rifle was held higher than I normally carried it so that it would be more visible and for once I actually wished that I had brought a bayonet with me. It would have looked rugged on the end of my M-16. Each pose was carefully held, without moving for a few seconds, so that the photographer would have enough time to snap my picture if he wanted to do so.

He didn't even come close to taking my picture. If it wasn't bleeding or on fire he wasn't going to waste any film on it. On top of everything else, the dope didn't have a weapon, not even a pistol. He wouldn't have been worth a pitcher of warm spit to us if we got into trouble. He probably imagined that the VC would treat him with civility because he was unarmed and more of a correspondent than a combatant. How idiotic! In any event, the patrol didn't make contact and the photographer didn't take a single picture of me or anything else.

We rejoined the company for the afternoon and it was awful as well as absurd. Some genuine Saigon commandos were coming out to see us set up an ambush. We had to do this at 1500 hours because they had to get back before dark. We were told to put on a good show. The brass even gave us some multicolored camouflage face-paint sticks, which I hadn't seen since basic training. We put weeds in our helmet bands and helped cover each other with leaves after we got in our prone positions. We did a lot of stuff that we didn't normally do to show these guys what a "real" ambush was like. Talk about stupid, this was it.

Fairman wandered over to kibitz. He laughed, made sarcastic comments, and offered gratuitous advice. He began kicking a small cloud of dirt in my direction. "Let me help you there, Ronnau," he said, with more than a trace of gaiety in his voice. "You look like you need some more camouflage." Some of the dirt settled on the little beads of sweat covering my arms, neck, and face, creating a layer that was sticky and unpleasant.

"Why thank you, Sergeant," I said in mocking tones.

"You need to be well covered up," Fairman announced, kicking a few more toe loads of dirt on me.

The sun broiled us like pork chops on a grill. We were miserable. Unfortunately, our audience was about half an hour late and, on top of it all, when they arrived we couldn't make rude or obnoxious comments because they were all captains and majors. What a waste. It was ludicrous to the max.

The next day was payday. We got to have all this fun and get a salary too; what a treat. The army was going by the book even if there was a war in progress and sent a paymaster out to the field with a box of money and a bunch of blank money orders. As usual, I sent a $125 money order home. Like half of the GIs in Vietnam, I was saving up to buy my super-duper dream car when I got back to the World, complete with red and yellow flames on the hood and wheel wells. The rest of my pay, thirty or forty dollars, I took in military currency. It was more than enough to last for a month, considering that most of the time we were out in the boondocks where no purchases were possible.

My base pay was $100 a month. They were still paying me as a Private E-2 even though everyone was supposed to be promoted to E-3 or PFC just for getting off the plane in a combat zone. They gave us each an extra $8 as overseas pay and $65 hazardous duty pay for being in a combat zone. Working the math, it appeared that my combat pay for the previous night's dusk-to-dawn ambush patrol had been about $1.07.

No taxes were taken out because we didn't have to pay on money earned in the Nam. They did gouge me for $4.42 for Social Security. That seemed to be in really bad taste—forced collection of retirement pay from the troops, many of whom weren't going to live to see retirement. Oh well, at least we got paid. I'm not sure that was true for our counterparts.

The day after we got paid, we were sent out on a platoon-sized patrol, which was without significant consequences, though it did include a short period of high-grade fear and near panic. Art Cordova, a savvy Mexican from Albuquerque with seven months of Vietnam under his belt, was walking point. Suddenly, he was spooked by a couple of deer that darted out in front of him. They were a species about the size of a Great Dane that we don't have in the United States. It was unusual because we didn't see large animals very often in Vietnam. Most were smarter than we were and had already left the area. During my entire time in the army, I never met a single person who actually told me that they had seen an elephant or a tiger, Vietnam's two most majestic inhabitants. Such encounters must have been rare.

The same was true for the exotic, large-beaked birds you might expect to encounter deep in the jungle. Occasionally we did see some small, nondescript birds that looked like common sparrows or grackles but that was about it. We never saw anything close to the brightly colored, parrotlike creatures that let out loud shrill yells in every war movie set in Asia when the outnumbered GIs were trying to be quiet and hide from the enemy. My assumption was that the larger birds, like the larger animals, had fled the area.

The deer had succeeded in making Cordova jumpy and more alert. Later in the day, he was still on point. Sergeant Sharp and Lopez with the radio were behind him. As we moved along, Cordova spotted a typical electrical detonation wire that was often used to set off mines. He immediately began yelling, "Claymore, claymore, claymore!" I hadn't seen such a look of terror on a person's face before then. Nor had I seen people stoop so low while moving away so quickly, like crabs at the seashore suddenly scampering for their lives trying to escape from the tourists. Likewise, I also crouched over and moved away rapidly.

When no mine went off, we cautiously moved around the wire and followed it to each end. There were no VC and no explosives at either end. Still the wire had struck terror into the squad.

Six weeks before my arrival, the platoon was digging up a grave when seven guys were blown away by a claymore. Four had died. All these guys, then, had already seen the wrath of a claymore up close. After this day's scare, everyone was jittery for a while and seemed to have a little bit of a nervous giggle when we discussed the possibilities.

There must have been a village nearby. When we stopped for the day and dug in, a couple of local kids, about ten years old, showed up to sell soda pop and snacks. They had metal buckets with a little ice in them for refrigeration. The sight of ice-cream bars for sale almost made me pee in my pants with excitement. I hadn't tasted an authentic dairy product in months. Visions of tasting the sweet, vanilla goodness like that only found in the center of an orange Dreamsicle flowed through my head. After one bite, I heaved the ice-cream bar at a nearby bush, hard. I was bent. The taste was flat-out awful. My guess was that they were made with either pig milk or buffalo milk. For a minute, I thought I was going to start retching. The children were also peddling small bread pies, which I declined to try. I did buy a lukewarm Coke for thirty piasters to wash away the taste of the alleged ice cream. Unfortunately, it occurred to me that if the local grammar school kids knew where we were digging in for the night, the local Viet Cong probably did as well.

Whether they knew of our whereabouts or not, the VC didn't mess with us that night, or during the next day's patrol. The patrol was fruitless. Because we didn't find anything, we kept looking. Thus it was way too long. It exhausted me. War is a young man's game. Half of the war movie stars that I'd ever seen were too old to complete a trek like this.

When we choppered out to return to our NDP for the night, my spot was next to the open door. Usually when in this position, I leaned back a little so that if I got shot or for some other reason lost consciousness I would fall back in, not out of the door. On this trip, I leaned back inside the helicopter, out of fear that I would fall asleep from fatigue and tumble out.

By 0800 hours, the following day the sky was bright and the air already warm. We milled around, fully equipped and ready to go, for about an hour while the company officers and platoon leaders conferred with the battalion brass. After much radio chatter and comparison of maps, the order of march—a determination of which companies and platoons would lead the way and which would walk on the flanks or take up the rear—was finalized. Radio frequencies were assigned and coordination of activities with supporting artillery and helicopter units was completed.

Someone asked Fairman what was up for the day. He gave a flippant answer but didn't spill the beans. He then told Captain Burke that he was going to move the platoon across the NDP to wait for our marching orders. He didn't seem to have a solid reason for doing this when the captain asked, but was given permission nonetheless.

We ended up standing next to an ammo point, three feet deep and thirty feet in diameter, full of every type of ordnance a grunt would ever dream of carrying. We didn't give it more than a passing glance until Fairman began speaking. He said that we were going to march eight kilometers to a large NVA camp on the Cambodian border. If no one was defending it, we would move in and take over, then destroy it. Someone asked what would happen if the NVA were defending it. Fairman calmly repeated that even if Ho Chi Minh and the entire North Vietnamese Army were there, we were still going to move in, take over the camp, and destroy it. We would attack. He then said in a disinterested monotone that if any of us weren't carrying enough munitions or just decided that we wanted to carry a little more, the ammo pit was open for business. We could load up with whatever we wanted. It wasn't until later that I realized that psychologically, Fairman had played us like a fine violin.

Soon the pit looked like a department store sale on the day after Thanksgiving. Troops dug through containers in earnest, searching for the particular type of grenade or bullets they wanted. A number of guys put on extra belts of machine-gun ammo. With an NVA base camp in our immediate future, I also decided to increase my load. This was accomplished by putting on two more hundred-round belts of ammo. My torso was now crisscrossed by eight belts hanging from my shoulders. They were heavy, cumbersome, and made it easy to understand why chain-mail armor disappeared in the sixteenth century. Nonetheless, I carried eight belts every day for the rest of my tour. The thought crossed my mind that if I took a slug or possibly even a piece of shrapnel in the torso, it might actually set off one or more rounds. Fortunately, the most comfortable way to loop on the belts was with the business end of the cartridges pointed away from my head.

After rooting through the ammo pit, we still had a few minutes to kill before heading out for the day. As we stood there, Fairman told us that we were lucky to be out in the boondocks because last night while we were sleeping, the VC had slammed our base camps at Long Binh, Bien Hoa, Di An, Lai Khe, and other sites with over a thousand rounds of mortar fire. Some of the shots might actually have been rockets. There was damage and there were casualties but Fairman didn't have the specifics. Lai Khe's share of the pain had been more than a hundred rounds.

Our march was uneventful and the camp was fortunately undefended. The site was very impressive compared to what we had seen. In addition to the usual storage bins and barracks, there was a mess hall with enough benches and tables to feed dozens at a time. There was also a separate kitchen, complete with metal stools, ovens, and all manner of cooking utensils. Clearly, this setup was meant for more than a couple of guys with a few weapons. A staging area of this magnitude was designed for a company or battalion-sized force and meant that there were a lot of troops around the area even if we couldn't see them at the moment. It was food for thought, even worry. Maybe they were watching us and counting our numbers to shape their plans. We smashed or fragged everything that we could, then set the place on fire before leaving.

That evening as we sat around the lager area a brief flurry of shots rang out on the perimeter off to our right, about a hundred meters away. We weren't asleep yet, but it was already dark enough so that we couldn't see what was happening. We just listened. The whole thing was over in half a minute and forgotten by us in about five.

In the morning, we were told that a couple of VC, not seeing where they were going, had inadvertently walked into the perimeter. The GIs and VC had simultaneously spotted each other and traded shots. Two GIs from Alpha Company had been killed. Nobody knew if any VC bodies or blood trails had been found. When we went out on patrol, our route of march did not take us to the area near where the VC had been shot at the previous evening so we weren't able to look for blood ourselves. Within a distance of one or two clicks, we hit another camp. This one had rifles, mortar shells, and a boatload of small-arms ammunition. Weapons were like gold. This haul would make the brass at Lai Khe and Saigon very happy.

Interestingly, lots of munitions from the communist-bloc countries were made to be one increment larger than ours. We had a .50-caliber machine gun, they had a .51. We had an 81-mm mortar, they had an 82-mm. With their size differential, our ammo fit in their weapons and could be fired, but their ammo couldn't be used by us in our weapons. It was a machination born of the Cold War, which they envisioned as including multiple armed conflicts all over the globe until either capitalism or communism won out and reigned supreme.

The most interesting find of the day came out of a small slit trench covered with a crudely camouflaged roof. A 4th Squad guy went down to look for treasure. He stuck his head out and handed me a piece of cloth to pull up. It was a complete air force parachute. The pilot's dog tags were also in the trench, which made me think that he had been captured. Unfortunately, I didn't get to check his name for future reference before the tags were passed up the chain of command so that the higher-ups in Saigon could be notified.

A day later, we choppered out for a company-sized patrol and found nothing but the air force. F-4 Phantom jets were bombing and strafing right in front of us. I'm not sure why. Maybe something was out there that needed to be driven away before we arrived.

The strafing was very different for us. Usually close air support was just bombs. The F-4s didn't have built-in guns. They were only able to strafe if a special pod containing a Vulcan rapid-fire cannon was temporarily attached underneath the jet. We didn't experience this very often. These Phantoms flew right overhead with their 20-mm cannons frothing at the mouth. The slugs were being fired out so fast that it wasn't possible to hear individual shots. We just heard one long, odd, mechanical shriek that is hard to describe. Empty brass casings were falling among us. Some struck the ground with a loud metallic clang and then bounced away. We found a couple of dud cannon shells on the ground. When they didn't fire, the cannon mechanism apparently just spit them out along with the empties. At about a pound or more each, they could have easily impaled us like giant ice picks or even exploded on impact. Wouldn't that be a world of hurt? There certainly are a lot of ways to get killed in a war and most of them are unpleasant.

Back at the lager area, mail call was a gas. There were several letters from my mom with a bunch of newspaper clippings from the *Los Angeles Times* and the *Long Beach Press-Telegram*, which we all read enthusiastically. According to the paper, during the week of February 14 to 21, while we were busting up all those hootches, we had in fact been on a separate operation called Tucson. We hadn't heard this.

Could the communication between the top brass and us spear-carriers at the bottom get any worse? We truly were, as the saying went, "the first to go and the last to know." It took old news clippings from the other side of the planet with a little map to show us where we had been, what the name of the operation had been, and how much VC stuff we had captured or destroyed. It was pitiful. I felt like Buckwheat in the *Our Gang* shows. Everybody told me what to do but nobody told me why or what was happening.

A front page story about Junction City said this was the biggest operation of the war. The previous record holder had been Cedar Falls. The headline was HORSESHOE TRAP and the subheadline, PARATROOPS LEAD WAY. This irked everyone and provoked guffaws and much cursing. There was also mention of antiwar protests at home. The hawks on television and in the news had been saying for years that there was a direct correlation between increased antiwar activity at home and increased VC activity in Nam. They spoke as if one caused the other. You couldn't prove it by me. I didn't detect any connection.

Ortiz came to see me. He wanted a five-cent bag of Choo-Choo Cherry, which I gave him. It was like Kool-Aid powder, only better. My mom put a five-cent envelope of the stuff in some of the letters that she sent. There were other flavors, like Rootin-Tootin Root Beer and Indian Orange. It surprised the hell out of me that other mothers didn't send their kids this type of stuff. It was wonderful.

Ortiz was grateful and handed me a glob of C-4 plastic explosive about the size of a tennis ball as a thank-you gift. For boiling water to make coffee or cocoa, C-4 was the fuel of choice. There was about a pound and a half of the stuff in each claymore. Just crack open the plastic case with a bayonet and scoop it out. Take a piece the size of a walnut and knead it like bread dough to get all the lumps out. Then light it with a match or a cigarette. It would burn white-hot for about half a minute, giving off enough heat to run a steam engine, bring a metal cup of water to a full boil, or make a can of pork slices with gravy so hot that you couldn't eat it. However, serious caution was required. If you weren't a deft baker's apprentice and failed to get all the lumps out, the stuff would sometimes explode.

Soja had been the first one to show me how to cook with C-4. He had also claimed that it could be used as chewing gum. After popping a small glob of it into his mouth he chomped away. Watching cautiously, I waited to see if his face would explode. Using that stuff for gum didn't seem necessary: A small pack of Chiclets already came with each C ration meal. My desire to not appear like a complete pansy compelled me to chew a small piece. It was rubbery and tasted very much like Ronson lighter fluid, which I had once accidentally gotten in my mouth. The stuff must have contained nitrates, like those in TNT, because it gave me a sudden headache, a sharp pain in the forehead like you get from eating ice cream or a Popsicle too fast. I spat it out almost immediately.

One of the most important aspects of using C-4 for cooking was that you had to be very cautious with the remains of the claymore. They had to be carefully hidden. The army disapproved of destroying a forty-dollar antipersonnel mine to heat up a few cups of java.

There were rumors that some guys reassembled scooped-out mines and carried them instead of full ones to lighten their load. To my mind, this story was so improbable that it didn't even qualify as a jungle legend, which might be true. No 11-Bravo worth his salt would put a nonfunctional mine in front of his foxhole at night. He wouldn't be fooling anyone but himself. It was inconceivable.

Another less effective way to heat chow consisted of mixing insect repellent in one of the little tins of C ration peanut butter. This concoction would burn slowly like a poor man's Sterno. It would heat food but wouldn't make it real hot or boil water. Being calorie-starved and often fighting off weight loss, I didn't use that technique but instead ate all of my peanut butter. We almost never tried to cook on fires made of kindling. Much of the time, everything was too green or too damp to burn. When it did burn, you looked like an Indian sending smoke signals to the enemy.

Our next patrol was with tanks and armored personnel carriers from the 1st Squadron 4th Cavalry, Quarterhorse. One of the vehicles, an APC, had GOOK SCOREBOARD painted on it in block letters with numerous little stick figures below the words. The figures were VC wearing the typical cone-shaped hats. By my count, it looked as if they were claiming eight or nine kills which would have been a hell of a lot for any one vehicle or person. It reminded me of planes from World War II with rows of little bombs or Nazi flags painted under the pilot's window. It was kind of clever.

There were distinct advantages to this type of patrol. For one thing, we got to walk at a more leisurely pace with the armored vehicles. They couldn't just step around things like we could on foot and had to proceed with more caution and planning. If the vegetation was too thick or gullies too steep or streams too deep, they had to back up and go another way. Often we would end up on their flanks, cooling our heels while they went through the gyrations of turning the fifty-two-ton monsters around and picking a new approach to get from point A to point B.

Also, the tank commanders really enjoyed firing that big 90-mm cannon. They loved to blitz things with the touch of a button, which really cut our workload. We would find a hootch or bunker, then instead of busting our butts dismantling the damn thing, we'd let the tanks annihilate it with a couple of cannon shots. While they lowered the barrel, we ran for cover, sticking our heads back up after the blast to gawk at the remaining shambles.

Perhaps best of all was the amount of supplies those guys carried. They had too much of everything. They had C rations by the case and washed them down with gallons of soda pop. Most armored vehicles in the Nam carried more Coke and Pepsi than a small late-night convenience store. Alcoholic beverages in the field were frowned upon so the vehicles carried only about half as much beer as a convenience store. They couldn't afford to supply us all with canned drinks, but were generous with their five-gallon cans of fresh water. This was wonderful for us. It meant that we didn't have to ration our water or follow the usual practice of never drinking the final few gulps of water in your last canteen. With them around, we could drink like a sailor on shore leave. If we ran out of water, the armor guys would let us refill our canteens.

Despite the obvious amenities of armored life, the tracked vehicles were viewed with simple disapproval by the grunts. They were too loud, too hot, and above all way too dangerous. They drew rockets and mines like a garbage can draws flies. They were always bursting into flames. We thought of them as being rolling barbecue pits and wanted to avoid riding in them if possible. The tankers, those GIs with an MOS of 11-Echo had the highest death rate in Vietnam, even higher than helicopter crewmen and infantrymen.

Whoever was responsible for sending Quarterhorse out with us had inside information and knew beforehand what we were going to find. It was the biggest, most elaborate camp yet. Dozens of frame structures were connected by wooden sidewalks. They even had electricity, provided by several gas-powered generators. Each generator was so large that it took about eight of us to lift it onto an armored vehicle, without which it would have been impossible to remove them. It was backbreaking labor for us to drag the damn things only a few feet, let alone carry them for miles through the jungle from the nearest road. The amount of human effort that the little people must have expended to get the generators to this camp in the first place was hard to even imagine.

Some huts had electric lights. Fifty or sixty bicycles had been used to bring supplies down to this terminus of the Ho Chi Minh Trail. In a sewing room were five large electric sewing machines, a lot of gray clothing material, and a big pile of white bras with an overly generous cup size by Asian standards. I never figured that out. Maybe it was the start of some sort of new secret weapon. The assembly line in a claymore mine factory was quite impressive and serious food for thought. A lot of small- and medium-sized pigs milled about in corrals. The armored people swiped those to eat later or give to villagers. That was logical because we couldn't carry them. Officers pilfered the few silk VC flags available. That was the natural order of things. Actually, the VC didn't have a flag of their own, they just used the flag of North Vietnam. I guess that said something about who was really running the show for the VC.

When we left the area, all the armored vehicles had stuff piled so high that they looked like Jed Clampett's truck on *The Beverly Hillbillies*, moving west. There was no way that we could have removed all those weapons and contraband without Quarterhorse. My souvenir for the day was a machete with engraved writing on the blade. The words appeared to be Chinese rather than Vietnamese.

We weren't very good at sneaking up on the enemy. We certainly weren't as good as Jeff Chandler's troops in *Merrill's Marauders*. My suspicions were that the real marauders weren't as quiet as the movie version. It wasn't reality. Even without tanks clanking along, it's hard to move two hundred men on foot quietly. The VC always heard us and escaped.

They wanted to win guerrilla-style, knocking us off with booby traps and snipers. In general, they avoided large unit battles where losses could be high. That's why the camps were empty. It was their battle plan.

At dusk we dug in. Tynes sat down next to a tree for a breather. ZAP! A snake in the tree took umbrage at the encroachment and bit Tynes on the leg, just above the knee. The bite went through his fatigues and left a couple of punctate fang marks. Not having been subjected to this type of assault in inner-city Los Angeles, Tynes was unprepared for it and became quite agitated. Sievering hacked the critter to death with an entrenching tool.

We weren't used to dealing with snakebites. They didn't occur very often. A decision was made to medevac Tynes out, no matter what the amateur herpetologists in the crowd said. That way, he could be observed in an aid station in case he developed serious medical symptoms. It was pretty dark when he got lifted out. Of course, being infantry, we weren't smart enough to send the dead snake back for identification so the doctors could figure out an optimal treatment plan for Tynes.

At the last minute, Sievering and I were sent out about fifty meters as a two-man LP. Everything went well for the first few hours. Then one or more VC who were probing our lines were spotted by the foxhole position from our platoon that had the Starlight scope that night. This was a device that allowed you to see at night. The lead VC was within twenty-five meters of the perimeter, which meant that he was behind us, between our LP and the rest of the company.

We were oblivious to the intruders until I took over the radio at 2300 hours to start my next hour of watch. At 2305, I put on the headphones so that I could give the sitrep clicks when called. In the headphones I heard the grunt with the Starlight scope telling the CO that he had spotted a VC just outside the perimeter. The VC was off to the side a little so that the position's claymore wouldn't hit him if fired. Captain Burke radioed back to not shoot and give away their position. He suggested that they keep observing the enemy and not pop their claymore unless the VC changed position, so that he might get hit by it. The conversation ended.

The episode was unnerving, to say the least. Not knowing which position had the Starlight scope meant that I didn't know if the enemy was behind me to the left or behind me to the right. The situation made me listen hard for noises around me. A couple of times I held my breath for a few seconds so that I could hear everything possible. My head moved slowly from side to side as I stared intently into the darkness surrounding me. There wasn't much moonlight available that night to help me see. I was tense. During the remainder of the hour, there was no more radio traffic and no mines exploded.

At midnight, I whispered a short explanation of the events to Sievering before going to sleep. My remaining hours of guard duty that night were definitely more jittery than usual. I still didn't know where that VC was. The next day, when we rejoined the company, we were told that the VC had been spotted moving away from the area sometime after midnight and had simply disappeared.

We were also informed that all of us were going to spend the day digging trenches from foxhole to foxhole all the way around the perimeter of the NDP, just as they had done in World War I. It was as if General Pershing had resurfaced at the Pentagon and was giving orders. For the last couple of weeks, we had used this same spot as an NDP. When we were out on patrol, other units occupied it. When the other units went out, we used it. There was no doubt that the VC knew where it was. It appeared that our leaders agreed with Julius Caesar who believed that if you held a position in enemy territory for two weeks, or a fortnight, then you should build a fort for your protection. That was the plan. We were going to upgrade our defenses with trenches.

Sharp seemed to enjoy being a ditchdigger. He mused that being inside the perimeter for a day of excavation work meant that we weren't outside taking chances. As he put it, we could dig a few meters of trenches and be one day closer to going home alive. Still, it was fun to get back to road security the next day. We were close enough to the NDP that we were covered by the safety umbrella of our mortars, not close enough to help with the trench digging, and not far enough away to be finding any base camps.

It was a banner day for me. I played mail call roulette and won. Letters were sent out to the field every few days. Packages from home were not. If a parcel came, you were informed of its arrival and asked if you wanted it sent out to the field or held for you at Lai Khe. The catch was that whatever you got you kept. There was no way to send your package back to your footlocker in Lai Khe. If the package was a complete set of *Encyclopedia Britannica*, you could lug it around for the duration of the operation, however long that was, or throw it away. Earlier, one of the guys had accepted a package that turned out to be a large stuffed teddy bear. After two days of valiant effort, he tossed it into a stream and watched it float away. We wanted to shoot at it but Sharp vetoed that because of the noise.

My package was like Christmas. It was small, wrapped in light brown paper from cut-up Safeway grocery bags. There was extra white string and Scotch tape, more than normal, to fend off the physical insults of the army postal system. The weight and feel told me instantly that it held two paperback books. Seeing my mother's writing on the address label told me that they would be good ones. They were: Truman Capote's *In Cold Blood* and Noah Gordon's *The Rabbi*.

As soon as we had settled in at our road security position for the day, I began the Capote book. For a short while, I was transported back to Kansas. It was a pleasant diversion. Then Fairman steamed by at a furious pace. His face was flushed as he issued commands without breaking stride or even looking at us.

The 3rd Platoon had choppered out to go on patrol. Now they were pinned down by enemy fire and our platoon was being sent out as reinforcements to help bail them out. We were to gear up on the double, move out onto the road, and then jog down it a short distance to a clearing where helicopters could land and pick us up. Soon the sounds of chopper engines in the distance turned into a squadron of the Yellow Jackets, from the 1st Aviation Battalion, fluttering in just over the treetops and settling in a clearing. The flight was too short to be relaxing, only five or six minutes. The start of our descent signaled its end, the angle of our descent signaled its urgency. As usual, the clicking and re-clicking of rifle bolts, a true measure of the infantryman's anxiety, was audible over the whirr of the engines. Some guys pulled the clips out of their rifles several times during the short flight to make sure that they were really still full of bullets.

At about three hundred feet, Smithers and I stepped out onto the port-side skid. The east side of the landing zone appeared to be on fire. Occasional tracer bullets flew around at odd angles. One sailed up our way and disappeared over the door gunner's head. It made me flinch. The door gunner immediately went nuts and fired a hundred rounds or so back at the tracer's origin. At about two hundred feet, a gunship just off to our left fired off both its rocket pods, which unleashed two dozen of the missiles and sent them crashing into the trees below. This unexpected volcanic eruption startled me so badly that I had to grab the door gunner's seat to keep from falling overboard and doing a swan dive into the landing zone. The exploding rockets seemed to set off the rest of the door gunners, so that now they were all firing simultaneously into the jungle around the LZ during the last precious seconds before we landed.

Thankfully, when we touched down, the water in the rice paddy landing zone was only a foot deep and didn't slow us down much. We quickly made it to the edge of the paddy, where we bunched up against the rear and left flank of the 3rd Platoon, which was pinned down near the top of the embankment that led up and off the LZ. Green smoke swirled around us. That was the color de jour, which signaled to the helicopters where we were and where they shouldn't fire any rockets or machine guns. Small-arms fire crackled at the top of the embankment and beyond. No one that I could actually see was doing any firing. We were all hugging the earth and wondering what was happening in front of us and why couldn't we get off the LZ.

All I knew for sure was that this place was beaucoup bad shit. It also occurred to me that it was probably preferable to go in with the first wave whenever possible. That way, if the LZ was hot, like this one, and all fucked up, like this one, you would at least be more likely to know what was going on, given that you had been there from the beginning. Maybe it would help you survive. Those in the second or later waves were stuck in the same mess but were less likely to understand it. That could be a recipe for trouble.

My torso was dry, on the embankment, and my legs in the water of the rice paddy. Above us, the shooting waxed and waned with bullets flying out over our heads on a regular basis. Up the embankment about ten meters was a thick tree trunk that kept getting hit by bullets. Some spun off the hardened wood and landed in the mud or water around us. The really hot ones hissed. None were close enough for me to snatch as a souvenir.

A large, somewhat overweight guy from 3rd Platoon named Ciccarelli was to my right and slightly up the slope from me. Of course, being the bulkiest guy in that platoon, he had been given the flamethrower. They used the same logic everywhere. Whether you were big with fat or big with muscle, you still got the heaviest and most difficult weapon there was to carry. Maybe this was because it appeared less painful to others than watching some shrimp or middleweight lug around a seventy-pound piece of equipment.

As the minutes passed, gravity slowly pulled Ciccarelli down the hill a few inches at a time until he ended up next to me. After giving me a smoke, he breaks into this long, comical, woe-is-me monologue about how he ended up in Nam. It was all a mistake. He joined the army to play the French horn, which is what he did for a living in civilian life. He thought that if he was in a band he wouldn't see combat. He had it all figured out. Then, as soon as he signs on the dotted line, they take away his French horn, put him in the infantry, send him to Vietnam, and give him a flamethrower. Every sentence had the word *fucking* in it in about three places. The whole thing was well polished and hysterical. You could tell he had told it before. It made me laugh out loud and my eyes water, which didn't seem right given that just up ahead everyone was shooting and trying to kill each other. Still, it was definitely funny.

Our problem at the moment was a machine gun and a couple of riflemen in a bunker next to the LZ. Our return fire had not penetrated the structure or silenced its occupants. About this time, we heard the calls "Flamethrower up" and "Where's Ciccarelli?" They were going to incinerate the bunker. Ciccarelli's eyes grew so large that he looked like a cartoon character as he struggled to raise his bulk up to a crouching position.

Up above, the bunker let out a muffled roar as an M-79 grenade caught the edge of the firing port and exploded. The Viet Cong then rapidly piled out the back way with their wounded and the skirmish was over. After the dust cleared, it was messy inside. There was blood everywhere. The parched sandbags drank it up, leaving the stains dry to the touch, not gooey. I'm not sure why I touched the blood to check whether it was sticky, but I did. Actually the scene inside the bunker was quite tame, with blood only, no globs of anything or pieces of anyone to be seen. I was glad that it ended this way. I'm not sure that my mind could have handled seeing the results of involuntary cremation. Plus, I certainly didn't want to hear their guys scream like in the movies when people get burned to death. That would have been way too horrifying.

The sandbag bunker seemed odd. We used a lot of sandbags, but they didn't. In fact, before this I hadn't seen them use even one anywhere. Maybe I shouldn't have been so surprised: After all, they managed to steal everything else from us.

We had four or five wounded, all minor injuries, good for a story to tell back in the World but none requiring evacuation. None of the wounded were even in my platoon. Despite the sometimes harrowing experience of having been pinned down for forty-five minutes by enemy fire, we were all fine.

My sweat glands had outperformed my trigger finger. None of us in the 3rd Squad had even fired so much as a spitball during the entire episode.

As we regrouped and moved away from the area, Ciccarelli's eyes were back to their normal size. He bemoaned aloud matter of factly that a grenade launcher had ended the stalemate because, as he said to anyone who would listen, he had wanted to "barbecue me a piece of ass." Somehow I doubted it.

This was one day that I wouldn't have to write home about. Despite my juvenile mentality, I was with it enough to know that the last thing a mother wanted to hear was that her baby boy was anywhere near actual shooting or danger of any sort. Early on, I had fibbed and wrote her that I was working as a carpenter. Most of my time was spent in the rear constructing hootches from wooden ammo boxes. My letters spoke of army life and army chow but not of hostilities.

That afternoon, we were told to put a roof on our foxholes before nightfall. A load of empty sandbags had been flown out to us for that purpose. We were to fill them with dirt and then build short support walls on the sides of our holes to hold everything up. The roof would be a layer of logs that we had to chop, covered by two layers of sandbags.

We groaned and proceeded with the speed of a three-toed sloth. Later, we were informed that this was for our own protection. There was going to be a massive B-52 strike at dawn a scant four hundred meters from our lines. If they miscalculated the crosswinds or the bombardier even sneezed during the delivery, we might end up being a direct hit. Now we couldn't move fast enough. Every bunker had a protective top before the sun went down.

The much-anticipated air strike started just before sunrise and was designed to catch the enemy still asleep and exposed. During the pyrotechnic ruckus, the ground shook back and forth like a healthy California earthquake, except that it lasted one to two minutes instead of one to two seconds. It felt like an eight on the Richter scale. The loud rumble of multiple, sequential explosions filled our ears. Th wasn't just a few dozen bombs. This was hundreds and hundreds of quarter-ton and seven-hundred-fifty-pounders going off. It sounded like a herd of locomotives headed our way. The gray predawn sky turned into bursts of burnt-orange flashes shooting upward. It was as if the sun were trying to suddenly jerk itself up into the sky but for some reason could not complete the task. We watched the show, grateful that it was on them and not us. Thank God the VC didn't have an air force. The air strike was much more frightful than the Long Binh ammo dump explosion.

Search and destroy that day was a little strange. We were spread out, mixed in with armored vehicles heading east. The terrain was flat and open with numerous little groves of trees and clumps of shrubbery here and there. We could easily walk around this vegetation but it did partially obscure our vision at times.

The sky was overcast. A heavy rain beat down on us all morning, which wasn't unusual. We all got soaked to the bone, which also wasn't unusual and didn't bother us very much. We had all adapted long ago to sometimes being forced to exist like Aquaman. I was so used to being wet that I made no attempt to stay dry. The only thing that being rained on during the day meant to me was that I had to cup my cigarette to keep it from being extinguished. Otherwise, it was business as usual.

The strange part came in midafternoon. The rain abated and seemingly all was peaceful. Then three Phantom fighters showed up and made passes way off to our left where the jungle's edge met up with the semi-open, plateau-like area we were walking through. After their initial pass overhead to see what the area looked like, they started dropping napalm bombs on subsequent passes.

The glistening orange light from the flames ricocheted off the wet ground and struck us broadside with its warmth. though the clouds of fire were two or three football ay, I could feel the heat on my face as if I were sitt to a blistering campfire. It was the largest conever seen. Soon the area looked like hell on a bad day. The VC must have really hated that stuff. It would have been dreadful to have it land anywhere near you.

We marched on. Being out in the open with tanks, we knew that the bomb jockeys could see our position and wouldn't dump any of that stuff on us. The situation was kind of odd because we hadn't heard any shots and didn't have any reason to suspect Viet Cong activity in the area being bombed. We were far enough away from the napalm so that it was possible that another unit with which we hadn't made visual contact was over there. Maybe they had called for the instant inferno. As was often the case, we never figured out the situation.

Tynes was back. During his short stint in the rear, he had failed to die or even become seriously ill from the snakebite. Now, having been the beneficiary of a short respite from the everyday drudgery of army life in Vietnam, he became a prime contender for the first rotten assignment that came along. That turned out to be a night on LP with me and Ilardi.

The three of us sneaked about fifty meters into no-man's-land at dusk and were settled down in what we felt was a good spot as the light started to fade.

"He's coming around. He's coming around," someone yelled from inside the NDP. As a rule, things that came at night in the Nam weren't very good. My mind immediately wandered back to the most recent cause for nerves, the gooks inside the perimeter the other night. Was it possible that another one had stumbled inside our lager and was trying to get out, coming our way? Standing up and facing back toward the battalion, I pointed my rifle and took a couple steps in that direction. If I was going to trade shots with this guy, I wanted to be closer to the main force.

Tynes was hunching down and eyeballing me curiously. Whispering, I asked him who he thought was coming. By now he was in a prone position and looking at me like I was from another planet. In a stern monotone he answered, "He said 'incoming round.'"

About then, the first of a half-dozen mortar shells came crashing down. With no foxholes, all we could do was hug the ground. Half the rounds were between us and the line. The rest were just inside our section of the line. Nothing was hit, no one was hurt, and it ended quickly.

Sometimes, when there was no wind and it was quiet, you could hear the unmistakable sound of a mortar tube being fired. When this happened, it was possible to holler out a warning before the first shell arrived. If that didn't happen, then there generally was no warning until the first explosion erupted because mortar shells streaking down on you don't make a lot of noise like incoming artillery fire. Six rounds was a lot if even a hint of daylight was left. Usually they would fire just one or two shots and then drag off the mortar and hide before spotter planes or Huey gunships could locate them and retaliate. We were called on the radio as soon as it was over.

"Lima Papa one, this is One Six, sitrep, over."

We gave them two clicks and then tried to wish away the rest of the night.

All was calm as we reentered the perimeter the next day. We expected that. We hadn't detected any flurry of activity after the mortars or heard any helicopters, therefore guessed that no one was hurt.

Next, the whole battalion headed back to Soui Da. After a month in the field, we were a tired and tattered group, ready for a change of scenery and underwear. A lot of the guys wanted to get back to Lai Khe to visit Disneyland and get laid. Some just wanted to spend the night in a safer place where you didn't have to sleep with one eye open. My vision of utopia was centered on a hot shower. Never in my life had I gone a month without bathing, worn the same fetid shirt, and rotated two pairs of grimy socks. After four weeks of continuous wearing, my shorts could have been used as an illegal biological weapon. The entire situation was nasty. It might take awhile under the faucet just to wash off the topsoil.

Interestingly, despite the length of our unwashed state, it didn't seem like me or the other guys were giving off an overly putrid stench. Perhaps that was just my perception, attributable to olfactory nerve burnout. Maybe the smell had snuck up on us so gradually that our noses hadn't noticed and slowly became immune to the odor. I do remember one time being back at Lai Khe in a cleaner state and walking past a company returning from a long stay in the field. Now those guys were really grody. They smelled worse than a dead skunk split open by a car by the side of the road.

Before being transported to Lai Khe, we had to spend one day at Soui Da in ready reserve until the units taking over for us in the operation could get safely into place. To his ever-lasting credit, Captain Burke accurately assessed just how worn-out we were and allowed us to simply lollygag around rather than trying to conjure inane tasks for us to perform, which some officers would have done. The brass were just as wiped out as we were and also ready to relax a bit. Fairman was so excited at the prospect of returning to the company club, the land of unlimited suds, that he was almost friendly. It was as close as he would come to a good mood that I ever saw.

We spent the time sitting in groups making conversation, smoking, and relaxing. Because we weren't on the move, we had the luxury of time to boil water for coffee and to heat up our Cs before devouring them.

A few feet away, Soja had perched a can of beans and meatballs atop a little ring of pebbles. Carefully he prepared then lit a small chunk of C-4 underneath the can. His skills at kneading were suspect at best. Halfway through the burn, his C-4 erupted with the force of perhaps a couple of fire-crackers and showered him with boiling gruel. He groaned out loud, then cursed a bit under his breath. There was ac-tually a patch of first-degree burn on his right lower jaw and neck. Even though it was riotously funny, I didn't dare laugh out loud because he was really mad and would have pounded me.

The early morning flight out of Tay Ninh Province was a dream, except for the landing. Bright sun and cerulean skies carried us back to Lai Khe and one or more days out of the jungle. Even the temperature was pleasant, about 70 degrees.

Everyone was in a good mood, including Soja, who had forgotten about his soup burns.

At the heliport, as we came down for the landing, a gust of wind from several helicopters landing in unison on our right suddenly tipped our helicopter drastically to the left. Fighting to keep from being blown completely over, our pilot gunned the engine and swung it back to the right. All of this caught me completely by surprise and rolled me right out the door. The ten-foot fall was cushioned by all the gear on my back, which I landed on with a thud.

Although I escaped serious injury, my trigger finger had hooked a sheet metal screw in the doorway and ripped a bunch of skin off of the inner surface. My pride was more injured than anything else. I cursed loudly at the stupid jackass pilot, then walked away, bitching that he was supposed to land us, not dump us. The outburst was simply to camouflage my embarrassment at having fallen. I was well aware that the pilot couldn't hear a word I was saying.

To my chagrin, I later discovered that the fall had cracked the plastic cap off my can of Pepsodent tooth powder. ("You'll wonder where the yellow went when you brush your teeth with Pepsodent.") The white stuff was now spilled all over the inside of my backpack. I thought that I had outsmarted the whole world by not bringing a tube of toothpaste that might get squashed in my gear.

That day's mail call included several packages for me. My mom sent socks, as requested. Everybody's mother had to send socks. Socks rotted and wore out fast. The army at Lai Khe didn't seem to issue them, I'd never seen them for sale in the PX, and—as incredible as it might seem—they weren't readily available on the black market in the village at Lai Khe. It was strange. Socks were a necessity. Your feet wouldn't survive without them.

My brother John sent me malt syrup because I had complained in a letter about missing a good chocolate malt more than anything. Now all I had to do was find vanilla ice cream and chocolate syrup.

My friend Larry sent me a jar of Bravisol, also by request.

The stuff was a creamy soap with a fine abrasive pumice mixed in. My face was developing blackheads the size of manhole covers. I hoped the new soap would help. Part of the problem was the cheap ink used in *Stars and Stripes*. Copies were sent out to the field with every resupply helicopter or mail call. The ink blackened my fingers and there was no way to easily wash my hands. Eventually the ink transferred to my facial pores.

Was this a case of a buzzard's luck or what? Our first night back had been spent in drunken debauchery, with the entire company exhibiting significant symptomatology of the fuck-'em syndrome. Now, on the second night, they were going to send out just one ambush patrol: It was us again, 3rd Squad 1st Platoon. Why me? God must have been getting back at me for sins committed in a previous life.

As usual, we walked through no-man's-land, then crossed the river at the shallow spot. On this night we turned left, or west, and walked a little before entering the jungle and disappearing from the sight of GIs on the Lai Khe perimeter just as the last light of the day was dying. Moments after we settled into our site, the guys guarding the bunker line came on the radio. They thought we had turned west but wanted us to verify it, which was unusual. They then warned us that there were three dinks with weapons on our side of the river, just at the jungle's edge, east of the shallow spot and moving west toward us. Now that the line was sure of our location, they were going to proceed with plans to light up these guys.

A chorus of maybe a dozen rifles and machine guns went off in the distance, lasting less than a minute. It sounded more than a city block away but we paid attention anyway. Who knows what they hit? The line called to reconfirm that we were still all right and mentioned that they couldn't actually see if any of the targets had been wasted.

The next morning, we took a new and rather circuitous route back to the river, where we crossed at a different and deeper spot. In fact, it was neck-deep with a modest amount of current, which jostled us around a bit as we crossed. During the crossing, Tynes lost his pistol. We couldn't go back without it. According to the higher-ups, losing a weapon, leaving it for the VC to find and kill somebody with, just wasn't done. They would rather see the entire squad and all its weapons vaporized by the blast from a Chinese nuclear warhead than have to explain to division HQ how we lost a weapon without dying or being injured.

Fortunately, the water was clear and maybe a swimmer with his eyes open could find the weapon. Tynes was an illogical candidate and we all knew it. Sure, it was his pistol, but none of us thought of a ghetto black kid as likely to be a good swimmer. I think Tynes agreed because he didn't jump in. Being downright skinny, with little fat for insulation, I'd had my ass chilled to the bones when we crossed the river. That was enough for me, so I didn't volunteer.

Huish jumped at the opportunity. He liked doing odd tasks and being the center of attention. Wearing only his pants and boots, he jumped headfirst into the stream. Except for a few celery-green plants, the river bottom was mostly tan sand, a distinct contrast to the gunmetal-blue .45 pistol. After only three short submersions, Huish came up with the prize.

Tynes was most grateful. He probably would have been fined as a punishment or had the price of the pistol taken out of his pay as restitution. I was also grateful. It didn't seem likely that the VC would ever find a small weapon lost on the bottom of a river. That didn't bother me. My concern was that if we didn't get our caravan moving soon the mess hall would close, and we would miss breakfast. In the vernacular, we needed to Hotel Alpha (haul ass).

There wasn't as much of a rush as we thought. We got breakfast and had time to spare. As it turned out, 3rd Squad was going right back out on a nineteen-hundred-meter day patrol. Because we were going to cross the river again shortly, there was no need to hurry and change into dry clothes and boots for the day. After eating, I sat on the edge of my bunk like a pile of wet laundry until it was time to go.

It was a nothing patrol, just damp. There might have been a little of the silent rebellion involved because we had been out on ambush the night before. Anyway, I don't think we went out but about half of the planned nineteen hundred meters.

Afterward, we changed into dry clothes and were sent to pull guard duty at the gate that led out of Lai Khe onto Thunder Road going north. A duster was stationed there with us in case anything formidable and unfriendly came our way during the night. A duster is an armored personnel carrier with the roof cut off and a twin-barreled 40-mm antiaircraft gun mounted on top. It was known as an ack-ack gun and was what the navy used in World War II newsreels to shoot down kamikazes.

We felt safer than usual with the duster nearby and enjoyed shooting the bull with the crew. They also had a Starlight nightscope, which they let us play with all evening long. We took turns and looked hard for any sign of something suspicious for them to shoot at. We wanted to see that ack-ack gun chew up the terrain in front of our positions. It didn't work out that way, but we enjoyed the possibilities.

We were lucky to be where we were that night because there was a small attack back at Charlie Company. It could have been a fate worse than death but turned out to be more like a Marx Brothers movie. A few mortar rounds sprinkled around the company area, falling in quick succession. The only casualty was the shithouse behind our hootch, which took a direct hit through the roof and was obliterated. Most of us would rather have been hit by chunks of red-hot shrapnel than the stuff that came flying out of the 55-gallon half drums under the craphouse seat. The stench alone was enough to drive vultures off a meat wagon. It was a relief being sent on perimeter guard duty the next day, away from the stinky mess until the sun dried it up. The flies and gnats must have thought that it was Christmas come early.

After lunch, we took turns visiting the PX and the barbershop. There was only one barber on duty, the ancient one, facing a mob of waiting grunts. Everyone had gotten pretty shaggy during the last operation. The long-haired look didn't sit well with the brass. It never does. Accordingly, the word was put out that four weeks in the boonies is no excuse for long hair. We were all to get to the barbershop and shape up ASAP.

Huish sat outside the barbershop nursing a Coke. Not being a spit-and-polish type of guy, he was using this as an opportunity to get off guard duty, goof off, and not to restore his military appearance. He would horse around until it was his turn for a haircut, then leave, saying he couldn't lollygag there all day, that it was somebody else's turn to be temporarily relieved from guard duty.

At the PX, much to my surprise, there was something to buy besides paperback war novels and cans of condensed milk. They must have just recently received a shipment of goods. The rear echelon types hadn't had time to buy up everything.

A small transistor radio and wristwatch made my shopping list. Fortunately, I had brought my ration card: They actually checked it and marked off what I had bought. The ration cards had something to do with curtailing the black market and protecting the local economy. According to the card, I was limited to buying three radios and two wristwatches during my year. My limit on televisions and electric fans was one each. I didn't foresee a big run on those items from guys in my unit, given that there was no electricity in our hootch. As strange as it seems, the ration card also warned that I wasn't allowed to buy any liquor until I was twenty-one. I could die for my country but couldn't buy its booze.

The real miracle was that I was able to buy batteries for the radio. They were often sold out. In fact, all of my future battery purchases would be made on the black market inside the village at Lai Khe. These deals were always brokered by Kim, a twelve-year-old youngster who billed himself as our houseboy. His name wasn't really Kim. We called him that because his given name sounded like a drawerful of silverware being dumped on the kitchen floor and was impossible for the enlisted men to pronounce. Kim had paltry English-language skills but knew some words, such as *radio* and *battery*. He told me the price, I gave him the money, he returned with the batteries, and kept his commission. Kim also got our laundry done. He hauled our bags of dirty clothes into the village and returned with them in neatly folded batches for a dollar or two worth of piasters. He could even get them starched if we wanted, but not many of us did.

Back at the bunker line, I proudly displayed my new radio. Interest ran high at the prospect of some finger-snapping, toe-tapping musical entertainment. Of course, everyone was anticipating their own brand of sounds, be it rock 'n' roll, country and western shitkicker, blues, or something else. Unfortunately, the only English-language station available was Armed Forces Radio and they weren't playing music at the moment but instead a live speech that President Johnson was giving to the Tennessee legislature.

At first we thought it might be the important announcement we all wanted to hear—that a peace treaty was about to be signed. Any enthusiasm for LBJ and the radio evaporated when it became apparent that this was just more of the same old rhetoric. He said that we were the good guys, that we were doing the right thing in Vietnam, and that we were in fact winning the war. But for now, no, you're not going home because, no, the war isn't over, so let's get out there and win one for the Gipper. I still thought of our military efforts in Indochina, to help the South Vietnamese, as being a noble cause but was quietly disappointed that no real progress toward peace was included in President Johnson's remarks.

The speech didn't prompt much discussion of the politics behind the war. Nothing ever did. There was some grumbling over the failure of the two sides to get together and settle the matter, but that was about all. Politically, we were a mottled group. Some favored our military efforts, others didn't. We talked about it so little that I really didn't know which side of the fence most members of the group were on. Quite a number of grunts didn't seem to have strong feelings either way: They had just been sucked up in the mess. America has a war, there's a draft, and you go. They didn't know college or other fancy deferments from Shinola.

The officers and sergeants also seemed to be outwardly

neutral on the politics of the war. They told us what to do and how to do it without mentioning the global picture. They were going to lead us through our little slice of the war without talking about the whole pie. They never gave us a rah-rah song and dance that they expected us to come back carrying our shield or being carried on it because we had to win this war for God and for country to save our nation. That was fine with me. It was probably better that way.

For us, reality was trying to finish our tour and go home in one piece. We had to do this as a unit, not as a collection of individuals. In part, it meant ignoring our differences on the subject to the point of barely discussing them. This was accomplished with great ease, in much the same manner as racial differences were handled: They were largely ignored.

Just as the political extremes of "Hell no, we won't go" or "My country right or wrong" were infrequent in Charlie Company, so were black power slogans or nigger jokes. Even though most of the GIs in Charlie were white, I only remember a couple of racial comments during my entire tour in Vietnam. A guy from Arkansas who didn't want to do something told some whites that he "would rather suck snot out of a dead nigger's nose until his head caved in." Another time, Cordova did the "Eeny meeny miny moe, catch a nigger by the toe" thing when talking to a small group of guys that included two blacks. He apologized, said it was just a rhyme, and remarked that he wasn't particularly prejudiced. They didn't seem too upset, at least not on the surface.

I'm sure that many units did have serious racial problems but it seemed to me that Charlie Company in 1967 wasn't one of them. Maybe it was more common in noncombat units where people didn't depend so much on each other. They could survive it. We couldn't afford it and needed to stick together.

At times, life didn't seem all that bad. Not only had some other group been made to clean up the exploded shithouse mess, but another squad had been given that night's ambush patrol. Third Squad was going to relax a bit while pulling guard duty on the bunker line.

The ambush squad exited the perimeter, then walked east and parallel to our line of positions for a while before heading off into no-man's-land toward the river. Menendez was one of the guys stationed at a bunker a couple of spaces to my right on the line. As the squad passed in front of his position he stepped forward, pointed his finger in the lead man's face, and announced, "I'm going to get you a dust-off tonight." He stepped back, then repeated the sequence with a couple of others in the squad. By the time the last guy in the squad went by, he was pointing his hand like a gun and rhythmically chanting, "dust-off, dust-off, dust-off."

The whole scene was out of character for him because he was normally not a very outgoing or talkative person. Everyone was looking at him like there was a big joke that they didn't understand, either that or Menendez was nuts. He was! I'm not sure if it was a case of just being crazy or a combination of crazy being helped along by his continuing to use drugs, but he was definitely certifiable that night. After the ambush patrol went by, everything seemed to quiet down. Menendez explained that he hadn't been serious about what he had been saying.

Minutes later, it was nearly dark. Menendez picked up an M-60 with two belts of ammunition and walked out into no-man's-land. When he kept walking, Sharp began yelling for him to return. He shouted something back over his shoulder that we couldn't understand. When he got closer to the river crossing, he raised the gun up and pointed it toward where the ambush squad had gone into the jungle. He then cut loose, shooting wildly into the jungle with three-round bursts. Then, for whatever reason, he decided to turn in our direction and shoot at us for awhile. The bursts at us seemed longer, like five-rounders. Maybe it was just my imagination, because the bullets were coming at me and I was scared as hell as well as unsure of what was going on. Menendez was only about seventy-five meters away. At that distance, the tracers covered the ground between him and us with frightening speed. Each one seemed like it passed right next to us. Between bursts we could hear him screaming. Of course, we were all hiding behind the bunkers and trying to get down as low as possible.

It was quite a spectacle with bullets streaking in all directions. He blazed away, dividing his efforts between the ambush squad across the river and us back on the bunker line until he had fired off all two hundred shots. Eventually, when we thought that he had run out of ammo, two Spanish-speaking guys he considered friends crawled out and talked him into giving up. Seriously, they should have received medals for their efforts. Menendez was out of his mind and might have killed them both.

We never saw Menendez again. He was taken over to the aid station, where a couple of orderlies put him in a straight-jacket, then sent him to see a psychiatrist and have his frontal lobes rotated or whatever those guys do. Afterward, he was shipped home and probably given a Section Eight. Section Eight is army talk for a discharge because of mental problems.

The next morning we put on heatstroke blazers and motored south in trucks on Thunder Road to the army base at Phu Loi where we were deposited in an area called Reno site. Nobody seemed to know or care how the place got its name. Likely it was named after some guy that got killed. It was a staging area, a place where you put troops that were being held in reserve in case of trouble somewhere else. Reno site was simply a flat dirt yard inside the Phu Loi base camp. It was about the size of half a football field. There were rows of three-foot-high sandbag walls crisscrossing the area. We used them to sit on or lean against but they were mainly intended to corral the blasts and block shrapnel if there were any mortar attacks. There were also a few fifty-five-gallon drums for trash and a couple of wooden outhouses, but not much else.

Soon after we arrived at Reno site, some of the others noticed that Sergeant Conklin was no longer with us. He hadn't been on any of the trucks in our morning convoy to Reno site. In the last few days at Lai Khe, Conklin had been mouthing off that he had been on his last operation. He wasn't going out in the field on patrol again no matter what. Despite being halfway to a twenty-year pension, he would risk it all and suffer the consequences if we went back out on assignment before his tour of duty was over. He had only nine days left in the country and was consumed with worry about getting killed before he made it home. Because of this, he had tied himself into such psychological knots that he could no longer function as a soldier.

He was suffering from what we all called short-timer's fever, a condition that should have been considered a bona fide psychiatric affliction. Lots of guys got it. Near the end of their tour of duty in Vietnam, they were overwhelmed by an inner drive telling them to protect at any cost the hard-won survival that they had battled for all year long.

It was my impression, after listening to several months' worth of conversation about survival odds and chances of death and probabilities, that the earlier in a tour that a GI was exposed to death, the more nervous he was about getting killed toward the end of it. Maybe it was easier on the psyche to be introduced to combat in a gradual sort of way. In any event, it appeared to me that if two guys had been in country about the same amount of time and had both seen about the same amount of blood and guts, the guy who had seen it the earliest was the more nervous of the two toward the end. It was like he was afflicted with some type of early-carnage syndrome that made him fret openly about the situation, worry about it constantly, and talk out loud about the possibility of dying on his last patrol.

Early in his tour, Conklin's platoon had been nearly wiped out at Loc Ninh. Now, as the saying went, he was "so short he could jump off a dime" and was convinced that he would get zapped if he went out in the field again.

We had ignored Conklin. However, Fairman, a lifer, bristled with hostility whenever the subject of not going out came up. Talk was free. Until Conklin actually refused to go somewhere with the company, there wasn't much Fairman or anyone else could do about it. Well, that time had come. Conklin was convinced that the platoon was headed for hot shit within the next nine days and had refused to join the convoy.

While we were at Phu Loi, Sergeant Conklin explained his actions to some type of military review board. As clear-cut as it was, his case was adjudicated with amazing speed. Fairman smiled when the subject came up. There seemed to be mirth in his voice, which he made no attempt to conceal, as he explained to us that Specialist Four Conklin, no longer Sergeant Conklin, would stay at Lai Khe until his tour was over and forfeit several months' pay. Fortunately, Fairman had not been part of the official proceedings. He would have tried to give Conklin the Private Eddie Slovak treatment.

It seemed a trivial punishment, but it wasn't. He might not be allowed to reenlist and would see a lot of years of effort toward a pension go down the drain. However, there was a definite quality of mercy in the sentence, which reflected the temper of the times. Cowardice in previous wars would have bought him a trip to Leavenworth. In any event, no one that I knew was really close to Conklin, so the matter was quickly forgotten without much conversation.

Of course, there had been some politics and favoritism at work in this situation. Height, who had been as short as Conklin a few weeks ago, had been pulled off the gun crew and kept in the rear for the tail end of his tour. The brass didn't want the enlisted man closest to going home to get killed at the last minute. That would be too hard on company morale. We needed stories of survival to serve as sources of hope. If he could make it, so could we.

It was the same for Medal of Honor nominees. They were heroes and had to be protected. Once nominated, assuming that it wasn't posthumously, they were either shipped to the rear or sent home to be safe, same as in World War II and Korea.

Conklin's chances of being allowed to stay behind for the last few days of his tour would have been better, perhaps even likely, had he handled the situation quietly, not made such a public stink about it. He was also hurt by the fact that he was not well liked and was perceived, by me and I assume others, as somewhat of an oddball or weirdo.

After a while at Reno site, Sharp asked for three volunteers for shit-burning duty. I raised my hand. Before I went overseas, my English professor at Long Beach City College, Mr. Booth, had pointed a crooked finger at me and offered some advice. He had served with the marines in China not long after the Boxer Rebellion and suggested, from his military experience, that it would be wise to "keep your mouth shut, your bowels open, and volunteer for nothing." He had been right.

The army solved the piss problem with piss pipes. These were pipes or metal canisters that artillery shells had been packaged in, pounded halfway into the ground. They were everywhere. Each had a piece of wire screen over the opening to prevent flies from congregating. We peed into these things, which helped direct the absorption of our nitrogen waste products back into Mother Earth and kept the GIs from just whizzing willy-nilly everywhere, sometimes creating stinky little miniswamps of urine that people might walk through.

The shit problem was more complex. What do you do with almost half a million dumps a day in a land with virtually no plumbing? The army answer was simple. Have the troops crap into fifty-five-gallon barrels that would periodically be dragged out of the outhouse, mixed with diesel fuel, and set ablaze. It was disgusting, but it worked. Two other guys and I had to drag out three of those things. They were actually half barrels, which held only about twenty-five gallons each. We poured on diesel fuel, stirred it around with a stick, then tossed in a match. Talk about air pollution, this stuff was indescribable. Sending a cloud of it downwind toward a nearby village was as close as I would ever come to being charged with war crimes.

The rest of the day was relaxed and upbeat. Rumor had it that there was some type of night operation being planned but that until dark our time was our own. Most of us just sat around Reno site rereading our old mail, writing letters, napping, smoking, and shooting the bull. A couple of guys went looking for the Phu Loi PX to see if they had anything not for sale at Lai Khe. They missed the PX but found the base brothel and dove in. They returned with tales of a local whore named Phu Loi Fanny. She was a minor celebrity, the pride of the base.

According to a white corporal that I didn't know, she had literally hummed the "Star Spangled Banner" while giving some guy a blow job. The corporal, whose eyes were two slightly different shades of blue, seemed to be in a manic mood and appeared animated as he described the action. He claimed that Fanny had hummed on key, didn't miss a note, and could do more things with your dick than a monkey with a flagpole.

Another guy, MacChesnay, verified the story. MacChesnay and I didn't have much in common so we didn't talk much or really know each other. MacChesnay was currently thrilled with himself as he announced proudly that he had previously fucked an American, a Puerto Rican back in the World, and now a Vietnamese lady. He talked about their relative qualities like some sort of self-appointed sex connoisseur.

His plans for further research on the subject included taking his R & R (rest and recreation) in Taiwan so he could screw a Chinese woman. He had heard that some of them actually had slanted cunts. It was becoming clear again to me why I didn't talk with him much. Besides this nonsense, I also didn't converse with him because he sometimes had the really irritating habit of telling anyone who would listen about his dreams. They were stupid, not worth hearing about. He acted as if they were riveting tales and we should be hanging on his every word. Dream tellers seem to think their stories are of interest to others while most of the people who listen, in fact, do so to be polite, wishing they were somewhere else.

All American bases, including Lai Khe and Phu Loi, hired lots of locals for manual labor purposes. Some of these people were given make-work jobs, not because the help was needed, but because it was believed that this would help stabilize the nation's economy. All bases had platoons of two to three dozen ladies that walked around all day picking up cigarette butts or other litter. Usually there was one GI, bored out of his mind, who led the ladies in an endless parade around the base. At the end of the day, they left the base and returned to their villages before curfew. Of course, some were VC or VC sympathizers.

After work on this day, as they were headed home they suddenly veered into our area to dig through the trash cans for discarded Cs. Apparently they always did this when they saw troops stationed in the Reno site staging area. Fairman went nuts, bellowing in Vietnamese, *"di-di-mou, di-di-mou,"* for the gooks to go away. That's what *di-di-mou* meant, go away. He had been warned that they had tried to put explosive devices in trash cans in the past and had all been warned not to come back to this area. All the women, of course, pretended not to understand him. This made him boil over even more, so he ordered us to set all the trash cans on fire to prevent the women from rummaging in them. When all the cans were ablaze, the women drifted away amidst a high-pitched, rapid-fire dialogue in Vietnamese. We couldn't understand what they were saying but it didn't sound friendly. Afterward we stood by one of the barrels for a while and watched the flames until Fairman cooled off.

A little while later, Sharp told us to pack up and be ready to leave on foot. He wouldn't elaborate on the plan. We thought this was odd. We never started to go somewhere en masse at dinnertime just as the sun was getting ready to set. Behind us, the metal fifty-five-gallon drum that we had idled by to watch the flames erupted in a violent explosion of about grenade strength. It was ripped completely in half. Maybe Fairman had been right in his approach to dealing with the ladies.

Soon the company walked out the gate. Next came a five-click march over a flat pebble-strewn wasteland growing only small bushes and clumps of the toughest types of weeds. The topsoil was dry and the walk dusty. Seemingly in the middle of nowhere, we were told to stop walking and start digging foxholes for the night. Not wanting to be caught after dark without an adequate hole, I attacked the earth with a vengeance. Soon the sweat was rolling off of me. Sharp saw this and came over to tell me not to dig so hard. Our evening maneuver had been a decoy attempt to trick the VC. We weren't spending the night there. We hoped that any locals who saw us moving this way believed we were, but we weren't. As soon as the sun was down, we were going to do a double-time speed march to the village of Chaun Giao, one kilometer away, and surround it.

That's exactly what we did, arriving abruptly and sealing off half of the village while a company of ARVN sealed off the other side. The ploy had worked and a number of VC were stuck inside. Fortuitously, the 3rd Squad ended up with great protection. We were behind a four-foot dry mud berm surrounding our sector of the village perimeter. It was as hard as adobe. The bad news was that we were spread real thin and I was alone at my position. Mortar flares were going off behind us periodically. My instructions were to not let anyone out, turn back anyone who tried to leave, shoot them if they persisted, and try not to kill any friendlies.

Some of the VC would sit tight for the night and then try to bluff their way past the interrogation teams in the morning. Others would fish around, probing the perimeter for a spot to pass through during the night. Not long after we arrived, curious children came out to stare at the soldiers. Some of the women also came. Our somber attitude and pointed rifles sent them back inside, and everything was quiet for a few hours.

Near midnight, three men dressed in brown khakis walked out to the banana trees about thirty meters away from me on the edge of the village opposite my section of the berm. The lead guy went down on one knee and stared in my direction. The other two stood behind him in the shadow of the banana tree leaves. There was a little extra light from a parachute flare way off behind me. I didn't see any weapons, but I would have expected any VC to hide their weapons before trying to sneak out.

My weapon was pointed at the guy in front. Maybe he didn't see me, because only my head and rifle were above the berm. Also, his night vision might have been hindered by the flare in the sky behind me. After a few seconds, the lead guy stood up and started walking toward me, his two companions following. Even though there was already a bullet in the chamber, I recocked my bolt as loudly as possible. The front man stopped, looked right at me for the longest time, a few seconds, then turned and walked back into the village, the other two still following.

No one else tested my section of the line again, though they did test others. Over to my right about fifty meters, a small group of VC waltzed out. The lead guy was shot dead in a brief flurry of American gunfire. The other VC then threw hand grenades in all directions and scattered. In the confusion, a few made it out and escaped. The rest retreated inside the village.

When the sun came up, we found blood trails. Inside Chaun Giao, a piece of bloody cloth was spotted next to a shallow water well. A grunt jumped in, splashed around a bit and came out with an AK-50. This was an upgraded version of the standard AK-47 with a lightweight plastic stock in place of the old-style heavy wooden one. There were also some minor changes to the magazine receiving mechanism. A Viet Cong medic was captured in a small tunnel under one of the huts. Several others were taken into custody as VC suspects.

Although there was much activity inside the village, most of the next day was quite dull for those of us standing guard on the outside. Out of sheer boredom, I planted a four-by-six-inch American flag on a stick in the top of the earthen berm at my position so that I could watch it flutter in the breeze for something to do. It had been in my backpack for uncertain reasons.

Around midday, I made up a story that most of the guys in 3rd Squad, including myself, were out of water and volunteered to enter the village with a bunch of canteens that needed to be filled. My gambit was approved.

For the next hour, I wandered around the village. Americans and ARVN were searching the huts. Groups of villagers sat as they were being given a talk of some type. Lots of food, rice, and canned goods were handed out. A team of U.S. medics had set up shop in the center of the village around a card table covered with medical supplies. It looked as if every mother in the village was dragging every child she had to be checked. Every so often, I could see a helicopter overhead and hear its loudspeakers going in Vietnamese.

After sufficient wandering around, I returned to my guard position and resumed the monotony of the day. Thankfully, the activity in the village was ending and things were winding down. A company of ARVN soldiers left the village, passing by us. One was carrying a World War II M-1 with a launchable grenade in the barrel tip. That weapon was one step above a flintlock. It was so antiquated that you didn't even see them in war movies anymore. I offered him my M-16 in trade, which he gladly accepted. A large grin creased his face as he started to walk away. He thought that I was serious. The transaction reduced me to belly laughs. Who would want his old blunderbuss? The ARVN didn't seem at all surprised, but maybe a little disappointed, when I retraded weapons. If Fairman had seen this event, he would have been stricken with apoplexy.

The company spent most of the next day marching or preparing to march. We moved slowly, stopped often, and changed directions a couple of times. The ground vegetation at the knee-high level and below was unusually thick. We didn't seem to cover much ground.

Our platoon stopped once to destroy as hideous a booby trap as I had ever seen. It was composed of a trip wire about a foot off the ground that ran to two 60-mm mortar shells attached to a tree at about the height of my Adam's apple. They were rigged to go off together. What a squad buster that would have been. There could easily have been half a dozen of us killed with the one blast. A couple of short, leafy tree branches had been placed over the mortar shells to conceal them. The leaves were by this time dead and brown, which made them stand out from the more verdant surrounding vegetation. Perhaps it was this that first drew the eyes of the point man, Kirkpatrick, to the threat and saved us all. We destroyed the booby trap in place with plastic explosives.

Later, we had to clear away vegetation to get down to the ground where we would dig our foxholes. This went smoothly until Tynes bumped into a large snake, which then slithered off toward Huish. Tynes was agitated and even stuttering as he called a warning to Huish, then delivered a monologue on why he didn't want to spend the night out here with a bamboo viper. Breaking out matches, he started several small fires near where the snake had been. The fire burned away from us, out toward the snake, but it also spread back toward us, our gear, and our incipient foxholes. Sievering was the first to object, protesting loudly as he was forced to rescue his backpack and rifle from the flames. We all followed suit, then passed the time brushing embers from our clothes and changing our positions a bit whenever a cloud of smoke encroached on our breathing space for too long. Eventually the fire burned itself out.

The second objection came from local VC, who apparently deemed the smoke from our brush fire a signal beacon for targeting purposes and dumped a mortar round on us. It struck a tree in front of our foxholes and went off like an airburst at a height of about thirty feet. Irving, who was standing next to me, was the only casualty. He groaned as a piece of hot shrapnel sliced a two-inch laceration into his right forearm but didn't stick in him. It was ugly but not life-threatening. Doc bandaged him up. He would get a Purple Heart but that was about all.

He certainly wouldn't get a trip back to base camp to see a real doctor. As far as the infantry was concerned, if it stops bleeding and no parts are missing then it ain't serious. Doc didn't suture wounds out in the field, so Irving would end up with a much larger scar.

To top it off, we didn't even get to spend the night. After

everything, the thick foliage, the snake, the fire, and the mortar explosion, we were sent out on ambush.

Ap Bau Bang, which we called simply Bau Bang, was a badass area. Maybe that's why our platoon patrol the next day was only two clicks long, two thousand meters, out from the NDP. We were pretty close to being done by early afternoon and had returned to within a hundred meters of the rest of the company when a radio call came from Sergeant Alvarez. His squad had found a fresh pile of human feces, which he reported to Fairman. There was no mention of toilet paper, which would have been unusual, because the Viet Cong generally didn't have it to use in the jungle. I'm not sure what they used, probably soft leaves or small tufts of grass unless they were near a stream, which they could use like a bidet. Fairman told Alvarez to hold up, then he contacted Captain Burke back at the company to plot out a strategy.

Halfway through the patrol, Gilbert had given me the gun to carry. He was more worn-out than usual and wanted to carry my light M-16 for awhile, so we swapped weapons. He didn't make this request very often. At twenty-three pounds it was easy to understand how the gun could grind you down on occasion. Fortunately for Gilbert, he was thicker and more muscular than I.

We stood there for a couple of minutes, dead in the water, waiting for all the radio conversation to iron out our immediate course of action. Momentarily the gun rested across the back of my shoulders to spare my arms the effort of holding it up. In front of me a milk-white butterfly circled around and around a long Tarzan vine hanging down from a tall tree. It was somewhat larger than the average monarch butterfly in California and had a single tulip-red stripe on each wing.

As the butterfly floated and circled only a few inches from my face but oblivious to my presence, a squad of Viet Cong soldiers with M-1s, M-14s, and a BAR (Browning automatic rifle), hidden in the jungle directly in front of us, opened fire. All the weapons going off simultaneously created quite a racket. The loudness was astonishing. It started at the maximum level. There was no crescendo. We were hit with a wall of noise that was thick enough to lean on.

Two slugs caught Love in the right shin and almost tore his leg off. Another grazed his head, ripping his right ear half off, and leaving him barely conscious. Alvarez took hits through the pelvic area, which left him writhing on the ground. Webb, the next guy in line, stepped forward and began returning fire as did the rest of the squad. Then Webb's rifle jammed and so Alvarez heaved his back for Webb to use.

Out front someone screamed, "Medic, medic." It was a sickening sound, like the noise when someone fell and struck the back of their head hard on concrete as you watched. It induced a mild nausea in me. Indefinable qualities in the voice let everyone within earshot know that somebody was hurt very badly. Gilbert asked for the gun, and we swapped weapons again.

Fairman was now out in front between Alvarez's squad and us. Almost immediately, he bumped into two guys moving back, away from the wounded and the shooting. Holding his rifle horizontally, he smacked them both at once, hard. He intended to either turn them around or break them in half. He cursed at them loudly to go back and start shooting, which they did.

Fairman then turned away from his radioman and began shouting and gesticulating wildly for us and another squad to move left. He was screaming at the top of his lungs and pointing which way to go. Our platoon still didn't have a lieutenant so Fairman continued to be in charge. Doc Baldwin flew by from the rear running right toward the shooting. I was hollering at various people to get out of his way as he approached. Simultaneously, about twenty of us, two squads, started moving obliquely to the left about thirty meters, the way that Fairman was directing us to go. He went with us. Alvarez's squad and the other of our four squads remained where they had been when the shootout had begun and returned fire at the VC. Our repositioning was a chaotic maneuver. We were tripping over bushes and bumping into each other as we went and not really understanding what we were doing.

We were a jumbled mess by the time we got to where Fairman told us to stop and start returning fire at the trench that had ambushed Alvarez. Smithers was on the absolute left end. Gilbert and I were next to him, which was all fucked up, because the machine gun was always supposed to be in the center of the squad, never isolated on the end. The first guy to our right was Sergeant Condor. He was supposed to be leading his squad, not mixed in with ours. This was the best example yet that I had seen of the fog of war. In part, this phrase referred to the fact that actual combat was often quite chaotic and plans sometimes went completely awry. At times, squads and platoons and even whole divisions got disorganized, mixed up, turned around, and out of position. Frequently, not even those involved understand what is going on or how it had happened.

We cut loose on the enemy even though we couldn't see them. We were firing into an area of exceedingly dense jungle, we could hear sounds of gunfire, and see periodic muzzle flashes, and an occasional tracer. That's where they were. Gilbert worked the gun while I connected belts of bullets together for him and fired my rifle. Whenever a tracer came out, I immediately launched a half dozen slugs right back at it. Next to me, Smithers fired until his rifle jammed, then he pulled out a grenade. This really made me nervous because he was an FNG with only a few weeks in country. I told him to put the grenade away, then we swapped rifles so that I could try my skills as a gunsmith on his weapon. It didn't work, so I reclaimed my rifle, took his spot on the end of the line, and he moved over to help Gilbert with the gun.

It was easy to become frustrated with the lack of visibility from the prone position. We couldn't see much over the plants in front of us that were only a foot and a half high. Standing upright to fire helped a little. I could see where their camp was and my tracers zooming into it without seeing any distinct VC. The jungle was too thick for that. Twice

I stood up to shoot and reeled off a full magazine. It was exciting to get up quickly and fire then try to get back down before they shot my ass off. I got a charge out of seeing if I could get away with it. Both times when I stood up, the more experienced guys like Cordova and Tynes started yelling at me to get down, that I was a fucking idiot, that I was going to get hit and so on, so I stopped doing it.

As jumbled as we were, our position was good. We had been at six o'clock with the VC at twelve o'clock and Alvarez in the middle. Now we were at ten o'clock. We had flanked them and were blasting away from their side. Most important, we could be as wild and reckless with our gunfire as we dared because our wounded were no longer between us and the VC.

Behind us, Fairman was at it again. We had all been huffing and puffing when we arrived, now after a few seconds prone and shooting we had regained our breath. Again Fairman stood up, danced around, waved his arms like a crazy man, and pointed toward the enemy position. He wanted everyone to stand up right now and walk forward shooting and reloading as fast as we could. "Just keep moving," he screamed at us, "and don't stop." This was scary shit. We were going to reenact Pickett's charge at Gettysburg with everyone using live ammunition.

Without some type of final signal that I can actually remember, we all got up, pretty much in unison, and charged forward. Every gun out there was on rock and roll. Tracers from both sides flew in all directions. The air around us was supersaturated with burned gunpowder and appeared slightly gray. It was unreal. Each of us was playing Russian roulette and we knew it. The guy to my immediate right let out a groan, crumpled up, and fell after being shot in the stomach. A few steps later, Sergeant Condor, the next man down our impromptu line on the right, yelped like a swatted puppy as a bullet went in the front of his shirt and out the back. It left a puffy, red welt on his side but didn't draw blood. He stumbled forward for a step or two before crashing into the ground on his face. Soon he was back up on his feet again, moving forward and shooting right along with the rest of us.

This was beyond a doubt the wildest and most crazy thing that I had ever done in my life. It was hard to believe that I was really there, marching forward toward a trench full of people shooting at me. We were quickly closing on their position. I didn't know if we would end up blasting each other at point-blank range when we got there or start hand-to-hand fighting or what. There wasn't enough time to figure it out and I wasn't mentally composed enough to do so before we got there. The charge had covered about thirty or forty meters and had taken less than a minute. I was hyperventilating when we arrived and my heart was beating like an out-of-control Morse code machine.

Gilbert had burned up almost an entire hundred-round belt as we walked. I had squeezed off about fifty shots from three different magazines. Oddly, and as incredible as it might seem, during this mess, I was aware of the fact that I was throwing away government property when I pitched empty magazines aside rather than save them. I could reload faster that way. It was a perplexing reaction. However, being in a position where I was allowed to do this helped me feel more like a real soldier.

The camp was empty when we got there, except for one dead Viet Cong soldier lying in a trench. Other wounded enemy soldiers had left two blood trails leading out of the camp, one to the north and the other to the east. Well, at least we hadn't been skunked. We continued our march, shooting and reloading, through the camp and out the back into the jungle behind it until we had overrun enough terrain to make up a reasonable defensive perimeter. Then we stopped and reorganized, putting the various squad members in their correct positions with adequate spacing.

As we stood there as a blocking force in case the VC came back, the other platoons headed our way to help us move our wounded to an LZ site to the south. Artillery had been called for and was now flying overhead toward the VC escape routes.

The enemy's bivouac wasn't extensive. There was the

shooting trench, which was now full of empty brass casings from what we figured to have been about ten shooters. There was a fairly deep water well, metal pots, clothes, and rice. I found an empty pack of Ruby cigarettes from England, which struck me as odd. Sharp found an exquisite little ceramic bowl the size of a grapefruit. The top was covered with a piece of brown paper that had a couple of loops of clean white string holding it in place. It appeared pristine and delicate and strikingly out of place. Inside was a little bit of clear water and one plump crab, someone's gourmet treat.

Some poor Viet Cong had carried it around as a treasured goody to be savored. As long as he had it, there was at least one small, definite bright spot in his immediate future that he could look forward to, no matter how shitty the rest of his existence was. It reminded me of the infrequent cans of really enjoyable C rations, such as peaches or pound cake. I would carry those around for days before eating them, which couldn't be done when we were on the move and I was just trying to cram down calories. The really good stuff had to be eaten when we were settled in somewhere so that it could be consumed slowly and savored.

The camp appeared tattered. There were bullet marks on every tree limb more than an inch in diameter. So many leaves had bullet holes, sometimes more than one, that the place resembled a broadleaf tobacco farm after a bad Carolina hailstorm. Counting my own cartridges, talking to a few others, and doing some simple math led me to believe that during this brief encounter we had fired about four thousand bullets at them.

Cautiously, I lowered a trip flare inside a bucket on a rope down into the well. That really didn't improve our vision very much. Sharp threw a VC grenade in but it was a dud and failed to explode. We talked about a jungle legend that a smoke grenade would poison the water. For this reason, putting them in water wells or reservoirs was outlawed by the Geneva Convention. I popped a yellow smoke and dropped it in. It fizzled, farted, sank, and went out. If this jungle legend were true, it would have to be the unburned chemicals that fouled the well.

Periodic shots began to ring out in the jungle around the camp. All of the radios were starting to go off again. Fairman and Sharp were becoming agitated and signaling that we were to leave quickly and move south. Two guys asked if they could throw the dead gook down the well. Fairman didn't see why not, so down he went with a splash. That would really foul the well and make my poison smoke grenade seem rather tame.

Moving south through the foliage, we soon came to the western edge of a clearing, where we stopped. Simultaneously, another platoon was entering the same clearing, which encompassed about two acres, from the northern edge. This open space was not where the medevacs were landing, just an area that we had to go through to get where our wounded had been taken.

As we stood there, a VC rifleman hidden at the southern edge of the clearing started shooting at us. We dove for the ground. Before I could fire even one shot back at him, a viper, as fearsome in appearance as God could have made him, came through the weeds, flicking its tongue and moving straight toward my face. It was only about three feet long, but when your chin is down at ground level a snake looks enormous. It moved at me quickly, unafraid, as if it planned to crawl up my nose or down my throat.

Springing like a cat, I jumped a few feet to the left, away from the reptile, and landed with my torso on solid ground but my legs dangling over the edge of a Burmese tiger trap. The rectangular three-by-four-foot hole was built for humans by the VC. It was several feet deep and studded with dozens of sharpened punji stakes. It was concealed by a lattice of thin bamboo poles covered with leaves. Luck was with me. Had I fallen all the way in I'd have been a human shish kebab.

There was now another VC at the south end of the clearing. He had an M-79 and was lobbing grenades out into the area where the other platoon seemed to be bogged down. The sight and sounds of the grenades exploding out in front of us made me shudder. After some of the blasts, we could hear pieces of shrapnel whizzing around. Hastily, we opened up on both shooters with everything we had in an attempt to help out the platoon in trouble. It seemed like it took them forever to leave the clearing and retreat back to the north.

The launched grenades were so slow that you could visually pick them up in flight and follow their trajectory to impact. Their speed was probably only one or two hundred feet per second, like a good tennis serve. I had fantasies about shooting one down if it was fired more toward us. That would have to be done with the M-60, not my M-16.

Fortunately, the dink with the M-79 had visual blinders on and fired only straight ahead, at the exposed platoon, which made a bigger and better target. None of the shots were off to his left at Gilbert and me. For this, I was grateful. We were already close enough that it was possible we would eat some shrapnel before this mess was over. After some of the grenade explosions we could hear pieces of metal whizzing in our direction. Thankfully, the VC never changed his tactics and fired any rounds directly at us. That was fine with me.

Just as the last members of the exposed platoon were retreating to the north and getting out of the open clearing, a launched grenade, one last, long, lucky shot, sailed in and exploded. Two Black Lions were seriously fucked up but not killed.

As if the VC, snakes, and tiger traps weren't enough, some tanks showed up to join the festivities. They drew fire and responded with canister rounds, which we called beehives. These 90-mm shells were like Napoleon's grapeshot rounds, except that instead of firing clouds of miniballs they sent out swarms of little one-inch arrows called fléchettes. We had all heard the story of these being used in battle and then afterward dead VC had been found nailed to trees or with their arms stapled to their chests. Perhaps it was just another jungle legend. On top of the beehives, the armor guys were going crazy with .30- and .50-caliber machine guns. They rolled right through whoever was shooting at them and ran into us. A lot of their fire came in our direction before things got straightened out. During this mess, two more of our guys got shot. One was hit in the right eye with no exit wound. The other was hit in the abdomen. Later Doc Baldwin told me that the guy who was gut-shot couldn't move from the waist down, but that he didn't know if the paralysis was permanent.

It wasn't all that clear that these last two casualties, of our nine for the day, had been hit by enemy fire. There was a lot of scuttlebutt that they had been hit by the tanks, but no one knew for sure. There was also a lot of talk that the lieutenant of the other platoon had not acted quickly enough to resolve the situation when they had been caught in the clearing with grenades being launched at them. As the story went the platoon sergeant, Sergeant Smith, had taken charge, given orders, and got everybody moving.

We didn't have to stretch our imaginations very far to believe the part about Mark Smith. He was a tough, no-nonsense platoon sergeant. Sometimes he carried a pump shotgun instead of an M-16. His nickname was Zippo Smith. I think that was because even though he didn't smoke he still carried around a shiny Zippo lighter he used to burn down hootches. He would eventually get a battlefield promotion and become an officer. That didn't happen very often. In Vietnam, battlefield commissions were as rare as hens' teeth.

When the first casualties, Alvarez and Love, were carried to the LZ, the dust-off helicopters from Phu Loi wouldn't come in to land because of the artillery fire sailing overhead. Colonel Marks, the brigade commander, had flown out to evaluate the situation in his own helicopter. He landed and jumped out carrying a grenade launcher as the wounded were thrown into his vehicle and evacuated. Marks remained on the ground. All of us grunts thought that this was a spectacular show of support on the colonel's part. I had previously heard stories of high-ranking officers who flew through heavy shit to pick up wounded troopers from places into which the medevacs wouldn't fly. Up until now I had thought that it was maybe just another jungle legend. Shortly after

Colonel Marks landed, the artillery fire was suspended briefly to accommodate the medevac choppers.

Soon all of the wounded had been evacuated by helicopter. Those of us who remained on the ground then circled the wagons in a defensive formation around the landing zone and secured the area. A head count was hastily organized to ensure that no one was unaccounted for. This was not necessarily easy, considering the fog of war. With multiple wounded being dragged in different directions by people from other squads and then thrown onto different helicopters and nobody keeping a master list of who went where, it was easy to see how someone could be lost, overlooked, or simply left behind. Apparently, the consensus was that everyone was accounted for because no attempt was made to go back toward the VC camp to search for stragglers.

When all of the wounded had been removed, the artillery fire was restarted. A decision was made that we did not need an ammunition resupply then and there, it could wait until the next day. After about thirty or forty minutes spent in a defensive posture at the landing zone, the company marched south about a kilometer to a place in the jungle where we dug in and spent a quiet, uneventful night.

Morning was on us like a pistol shot. The usually slow hours of nighttime guard duty had sailed by briskly, almost enjoyably. There was a lot to write in my diary. When not writing I was lost by myself, deep in thought. The nighttime hours spent on guard, alone and contemplating what had transpired, were needed to sort everything out in my mind. In the darkness I had replayed the day's events over and over, ruminating on the possibilities. What should I think about all this? Would Love's leg have to be amputated? What if I had been shot up? Could I have done anything differently? Would the guy who couldn't move ever be able to walk again? Had I performed well enough? It was gratifying to me that it had never even crossed my mind to chickenshit-out like those two guys Fairman had blocked from running away.

I felt bad for Alvarez. The rumor going around was that, despite being told to hold up, he had moved forward with the

RTO, Love. This had gotten the two of them clobbered and
the platoon into a shoot-out without the immediate help of
the rest of the company. With luck it wasn't true. If it was,
then I hoped he wouldn't realize the extent of the carnage
that followed after he went down. Jack might find his own
wounds and whatever disability they brought easier to live
with than the wounds of the others. Maybe he hadn't heard
Fairman's order to hold up. Maybe I had the entire story
wrong.

Another way to look at it was that we found the human
feces, knew the VC were close by, and knew we were going
to find them within a short time, with some of us getting hurt
in the process. You could make a case that by going first into
the path of almost certain harm, Alvarez had sacrificed himself and was a hero.

I also thought about Fairman. We get bushwhacked and he
turns into Audie Murphy. First he moves forward to rally and
reorganize the troops. Then he directs us in a crafty flanking
maneuver that looks like it came out of a textbook at West
Point. Then he leads the charge on the enemy position. He
did everything except yell, "Fix bayonets!" like in the movies.
I had to appreciate his military skills even if the guy didn't
think of me as much of a soldier. We had our military tit in
the proverbial wringer, and he had gotten us out of it.

Everyone seemed to have dealt with the situation in his
own way and accepted it with equanimity by the time we
started out on a three-thousand-meter sweep the next morning. Even though there were a lot of wounded, nine, and some
of the injuries were horrendous, we were all fully aware that,
once again it was the other guy who got hurt. Just before
moving out, Sergeant Fairman announced that he had been
informed by radio that all of our wounded had survived the
night. The grim reaper had not joined us.

Unfortunately, Lieutenant Judson had rejoined the company. He seemed to spend most of his time back at Lai Khe
serving as the company executive officer. Maybe that was
the captain's way of keeping him from causing problems in
the field, where lives might hang in the balance. That was

fine with me. My guess was that he had been sent out because of the losses the day before. Fairman didn't need his leadership abilities, which were minimal, but the platoon could use one more guy packing an M-16, provided he could shoot straight.

That morning, a supply chopper was sent out to restock us. The quartermaster delivered enough munitions to replace all that we had used up the day before. In a nice gesture to us for having been in such a bad shoot-out, he sent out some 32-ounce cans of fruit cocktail. What a treat! Each platoon got two cans. Right in front of us, Lieutenant Judson put one can in his backpack for himself and told a sergeant to let the platoon divide up the other can. I could hardly believe what I was seeing. What an asshole. He hadn't even been with us during the firefight. It was difficult to figure out what was worse, his being so self-centered or his acting that way in full view of everyone and not caring what any of us thought.

Still, the fruit cocktail was insignificant compared to bullets. Thankfully, there were plenty of those sent out, both plain ball ammo and tracer rounds. Which to use was the shooter's choice. You simply picked what you wanted. My routine, until then, had been to use a tracer for every fifth bullet that I put in a clip. My logic was that every fifth round in the belts of M-60 ammo was a tracer. That's the way it came, like it or not. Besides, shooting tracers was fun and gave me a sense of power.

Now my thoughts had changed. Tracer bullets were for World War II fighter pilots. They would be helpful for far-off targets, with good visibility, when you were unsure of how close your shots actually were to the target. But in the jungle they weren't helping me much. They were, however, possibly showing my intended target where I was shooting from and giving away my position. Maybe the VC didn't use tracers as much as we did, not because they couldn't afford the luxury, but because Victor Charlie had already figured out all of this. In any event, I decided to stock up on only plain ball ammo then and in the future.

However, under no circumstances would I get rid of the

special clip carried inside my backpack. It was full to the brim with nothing but tracer rounds. I called it the death ray and used it only when we were having target practice on the perimeter. Firing it looked like the spaceship ray guns in *War of the Worlds*. It was really cool, even though it dirtied up the inside of my barrel something fierce.

All of the tracers that I had seen flying out of the enemy camp the day before had been red. I was beginning to think that the story about the enemy using green tracers was just another jungle legend. Over time, I would see a gazillion tracers fired in both directions and never would see green.

After finishing with resupply, we were subjected to another dose of Lieutenant Judson's antics. He positioned himself in the middle of a nearby road, picking his teeth with a matchbook, and casually staring up at the sky, like some farmer wondering if the far-off clouds would bring rain. His mind wasn't with us as he checked his watch frequently, not wanting to miss the start of the heavyweight championship fight that Armed Forces Radio was going to broadcast live from New York.

Apparently, his royal highness intended to waltz on down the road while listening to his transistor radio as half of the platoon on either side of him provided security. We were to do this while fighting our way through the most ornery thickets imaginable just a few meters off to the side of the road.

How preposterous! Everybody and their mother knew that it wasn't considered wise to travel along roads or trails unless you wanted to get into trouble. It was hard to believe that Judson would put people in jeopardy simply to hear a sporting event. We were flabbergasted. All we could do was shake our heads in disgust and pray for an early knockout.

In the seventh round, Cassius Clay pummeled Zora Folley into unconsciousness with a series of jabs that changed the course of an infantry patrol on the other side of the world. (Most white fans still called him Clay, not Muhammad Ali.) After the post-fight commentary, the lieutenant pocketed his radio, and we moved off the road and went in another direction. Judson irked me so badly that I wouldn't have pissed on him if his eyeballs were on fire.

We moved toward a once fertile but now fallow agricultural area that the brass wanted checked out. Acres of parched farmland passed beneath our feet as we traversed an abandoned valley, claimed by the war. The area was so dusty and desolate that tumbleweeds should have blown by us. A stream in the middle of the valley still boasted a few inches of water, which supported greenery along its winding course. With yesterday still fresh in our minds, we moved cautiously, scanning the tree line on the other side of the valley as well as every shrub or bush in sight large enough to conceal a midget.

For reasons unknown to me, we had an artillery escort that day. Every few minutes, we would hear the dull freight-train rumble of an artillery shell that flew over our heads and exploded one to two hundred meters in front of us. They marched ahead of us like that all day long. Around midafternoon, a short round landed beside our column, sending a blizzard of shrapnel in all directions. No one was hit. We all looked back and forth at each other, then watched the wind dissipate the brown cloud of dirt.

Later, we changed course again and moved toward one side of the valley where there was a road. The brass were sending us back to Reno site for the night and a small fleet of trucks was waiting for us. Just as we approached the vehicles, another errant artillery shell landed. Shrapnel punctured the metal door and splintered the wooden side rails of the nearest truck. The explosion evoked nervous laughter and snide comments.

We had heard one jungle legend to the effect that sometimes bored artillerymen would put multiple can opener holes in a C ration can, then attach it to the tip of a 105 shell. Supposedly, this made the projectiles shriek like a wailing Irish banshee, announcing that someone on the ground was about to die. In theory, the cannoneers thought that this was good fun. The game also made the shells less accurate. However, neither of the two shells that had fallen near us that day sounded different, as if they might have been tampered with before firing. We viewed the misdirected shells as just another close call, one of a zillion in the Nam.

Good Friday was spent on Thunder Road motoring back toward Lai Khe. There was a lot of pissing and moaning going on in the back of my truck. The advent of a major holiday, one usually associated with a big family meal, had as usual produced increased talk of home, the war somehow ending, and everyone being back in the World with loved ones. Unfortunately for our morale, someone had procured a copy of Thursday's *Stars and Stripes*.

Photographs of Ho Chi Minh and President Johnson were on the front page under the headline U.S. PEACE BID REJECTED. The story said that Uncle Ho and LBJ had exchanged personal letters on how to initiate peace talks and they couldn't agree on anything. LBJ had offered to stop bombing the North and stop increasing the number of troops in the South if Ho would also stop sending more soldiers into the South and agree to secret peace talks. Ho responded that he wouldn't agree to talks until we not only stopped the bombing but also pulled out of South Vietnam. Of course, there was also a lot of babble about how they each wanted peace the most and it was all the other one's fault that they couldn't even agree on what day of the week it was. In the meantime, both sides should just keep killing each other.

Inside was a backup article, no doubt orchestrated by LBJ, which quoted former president Truman as saying that the American people should all get behind LBJ and give him "their full support" and that "Our hopes and prayers are with him."

None of us had known that there had even been any peace overtures between the two leaders. It had all been quite hush-hush. *Stars and Stripes* should have left it that way for Easter weekend. We were amused that Ho's letter addressed LBJ as "Your Excellency." Other than that, the guys were not only disappointed but also pissed off. The antigovernment comments in the back of that truck were exceedingly caustic and hostile.

Back on the company street at Lai Khe, we had a head count and listened to a few announcements, one of which was that our squad had ambush patrol across the river that night. Mail call followed immediately. Besides letters, my haul included a package about a foot high, wide, and deep. It was from my folks, but had no doubt been assembled by my mom. My plan was to not open it, but to set it inside my foot-locker so that I could think about it, guess at what was inside, and mentally savor whatever it contained during every hour I was awake on guard until the ambush was over in the morning. That approach would distract me with pleasant fantasies and make the ambush pass more quickly and enjoyably. The plan worked well.

When opened the next day, it revealed that the folks had tried to mail me Easter Sunday in a box. Inside were brightly wrapped candy bars, packs of chewing gum, homemade cookies covered with either little blue and yellow candy stars or Redhots. There was also a bright gold, plastic, king egg full of half-dollars and quarters. My folks hid a king egg somewhere in the house every Easter. All in all, it was like receiving a small carnival in the mail, not as good as being at home but still nice.

Our ambush had been a snooze. The rest of Easter week-end was spent within the mentally comfortable confines of guard duty on the perimeter.

Orders were cut issuing Purple Hearts to the nine who had been wounded in the firefight. They were receiving a little piece of history. The government was still giving out Purple Hearts from the stockpile ordered for the invasion of Japan. The medals were older than the men receiving them.

Fairman had applied for a bronze star for Doc Baldwin. Doc had stood up and sprinted into the kill zone to treat the wounded regardless of all the enemy fire coming in at him and the others during the shoot-out. Unfortunately, the rumor going around was that the recommendation had been re-jected. This rankled a lot of the more experienced GIs, who griped that there seemed to be a two-tiered system for awarding medals. According to them, if Doc had been an officer he wouldn't have been nominated for a bronze in the first place. It would have been a minimum of a silver star because officers got more medals and higher medals than enlisted men for doing the same things.

One GI bitched that it was that way in all wars. His dad, who was an enlisted man, had helped an officer rescue people from a burning airplane that crashed on the deck of the carrier *Lexington* at Coral Sea. They both had performed in the same heroic fashion. Yet the officer got a medal for bravery and the enlisted man was left sucking the hind tit with no award or recognition of any type, not even a mimeographed certificate of achievement like they used to pass out in grammar school for minor accomplishments. I hadn't thought about it previously but it didn't surprise me. The system had probably been that way since before the Trojan War.

In my view, Doc should have received the medal and would have, had it been up to me. He had performed heroically under fire. His job, infantry medic, had risen to first place on my list of the worst jobs available in the combat zone. It had to be worse than serving in an armored vehicle or a helicopter. Those two had previously been first and second.

Easter Mass was said outside under the rubber trees in a section of the old Michelin plantation near division headquarters. There were a few wooden pews in front of a wooden altar. Behind the altar was a fifteen-foot white cross that served as an inspirational backdrop for the congregation. It was a nice setup compared to the one other Mass I had attended in Vietnam at some unnamed godforsaken place. There it had been said on the hood of a truck, without any pews or chairs for the congregation.

There hadn't been any announcement in our area that a Mass was going to be held. Huish had been walking by the area and had seen them setting up for the service. After returning to the line he casually mentioned it to us. Back in the World, I didn't get to Mass every Sunday, but like the parish

Easter eggs, as my mother used to call them, I managed to roll out and show up for the major holy days, like Easter and Christmas. So, figuring that the Lai Khe bunker line wouldn't cave in without me, I walked over and attended the service.

The sermon was short and insipid. How sad. For once I was actually listening, trying to glean some morsel of meaning from the priest's comments that I could apply to my current station in life. His words were neither comforting nor inspirational. GIs knelt in the dirt to receive communion. General absolution after the Mass was a real treat—being forgiven for your sins without having to actually admit and confess them to anyone. This was at least as good as being allowed to cheat on your taxes. Now, if I screwed up and got killed off, I could move on to the next world as a spirit in good standing. However, they would probably take away my rifle and grenades.

On my way back to the line, I crossed paths with Fairman. That was a mistake. He was hostile and read me the riot act for not getting permission to leave. My only defense was to play the religious angle. He didn't buy it and scolded me not to "wander off, fucking around."

Closer to the line, I encountered Cordova headed in the opposite direction. He was on his way into the village to get a cold soda pop at some girl's house and invited me to join him, which I did. This was genuine wandering off and bona fide fucking around.

We walked between the Quonset huts of division headquarters, then climbed over several dilapidated barbed-wire fences. They appeared to have been beaten into a state of disrepair by a steady stream of GIs over the years. A teenage girl named Sao (pronounced sow, like a female hog) greeted us in the backyard of one of the French colonial homes and led us inside. She knew Cordova by name and chitchatted with him while we drank Cokes from glasses full of actual ice. It was easy to listen to Sao, her voice was calm and pleasant. Unlike many Vietnamese, she didn't speak in that incredibly irritating, rapid-fire, high-pitched, squeaky way that made you want to start beating someone over the head with a golf club.

Most of the conversation was idle chatter. As we were leaving Sao asked, "How we soon see you again?"

"Not for a while," Cordova quipped. "The whole battalion is going to Phu Loi tomorrow. I don't know how long we'll be gone."

I almost choked. Whatever happened to "Loose lips sink ships"? When we got out of the yard, I asked him why he had done that and told him that we didn't need loudspeaker announcements about where we were going. He didn't see my point of view and wasn't concerned in the slightest. "Don't worry, Sao is okay," he said. Yeah right, I thought, like Chang and Tits in the barbershop were okay.

Thank God Cordova and I didn't have high-level security clearances and actually know important military stuff. Bob Reeves's security clearance was as high as they came, Top Secret Crypto. He needed that level to work on the division's secret codes. Below him was Top Secret and below that was Secret. Ordinary foot soldiers like Cordova and me had a sorry-ass level called Confidential. I guess for Cordova that meant only tell half of the people what you know. For me, it was now understandable why ordinary grunts like us weren't allowed to have a higher security clearance and know what was going on ahead of time. It was also understandable how the local people always knew where we were, even before we got there.

Back on the line, we found out that Cruz was gone. He and Fairman had not gotten along. Apparently, Cruz went off the deep end and threatened to kill Fairman somehow out in the field when he got the chance, maybe, he suggested, by accidentally shooting him during a firefight. We couldn't have this type of shit going on, so Cruz was transferred out. No one seemed to know where he went and it didn't matter to me.

The next day, we helicoptered into a desolate abandoned farming area north of Saigon. A search-and-destroy sweep of the area was unproductive. The best part of the day was making camp at about 1600 hours, which was earlier than normal for us. It was a comfortable time of day, not scorching but hot enough to dry out your clothes before the first hints of an evening chill arrived.

We set up for the night in a bone-dry, fallow rice paddy on the edge of the woods. The berm on the sides of the paddy was two to three feet high, providing good cover as well as concealment.

About two hundred fifty meters out from our camp across the flat farmland, six gooks walked out of the woods and casually traversed another dry rice paddy, moving from right to left out in front of us. They were oblivious to us, as were three other gooks moving from left to right to meet the larger group. Someone went to tell the CO while Gilbert and I set up the gun. Another gun crew came over and set up right next to us, hoping to get a piece of this turkey shoot. Soon everybody in town with a rifle crawled over to our berm with some ammo and picked out a firing position. I practiced sighting in on one of the guys toward the rear of the six-man group. My reasoning was that everyone else would probably target the first few guys in line and I wanted to have my own target if possible.

The two groups met up and stood out in the open ground talking for a few minutes before ambling off toward the far woodline. It was a hundred meters away from them and provided no cover. Captain Burke crouched as he jogged over to see this unusual sight. After a brief observation, he and Sergeant Fairman had an impromptu powwow about the situation. It was decided not to blow them away. We would let them go, then send a squad to track them to see if we could find larger fish to fry. Sergeant Smith and a squad were hastily organized and sent out. They returned shortly after losing the trail, which was to be expected. Following someone in the wild was almost impossible. It wasn't anywhere near as easy as those phony Indian scouts made it appear in cowboy movies.

Although we all wanted an instant victory with a one-sided wipeout, we weren't thinking clearly. Captain Burke was right. The situation was strange. We were in no way certain that these guys were really VC. We couldn't see weapons or any clear markers of enemy affiliation from two hundred fifty meters. The whole thing was suspicious, but if they turned out to be local civilians and we killed them, the damage to our side would be incalculable. It wasn't worth it.

No one grumbled about Burke's decision. We respected him. In his time as our CO, we had developed the feeling that he was a good leader who had his act together and knew what he was doing. We could survive with this guy. There was some concern that the VC may have spotted our tracking team and knew where we were if they wanted to start something with us after the sun went down. To preempt such an attempt, the 3rd Squad was being sent out as a blocking force to spend the night in the shallow depression of a farmer's furrows as a listening post, about seventy-five meters in front of the company's position.

Incredibly, the evening had started with dozens of our rifles zeroed in on a squad of suspected VC caught out in the open, and ended with us out in the open, after dark, hoping they wouldn't attack.

As soon as we got back in the next morning, Sharp called me in. Taking my M-16 and a bandolier of ammo, I followed him outside of our lager area. He had invited me to join him on a sniper patrol. The CO was uptight about the VC squad from the previous night. It was conceivable they knew where we were and had planted a sniper to kill a few of us when we left in the morning. Sharp and I were to walk completely around the company checking for snipers. If one was out there, he would probably shoot. We were the bait. I'm not sure why I was chosen for this dubious honor. Possibly it was because I was the tallest guy in the squad. Maybe Sharp knew that because I was at least a couple of inches taller than he was, I was a better target. Maybe he thought I was more gullible than the others in the squad. Maybe it was because if someone was going to get zapped, I was the one that he would miss the least.

If I had gotten more sleep the night before or had a cup of

coffee that morning, maybe I would have been alert enough to take the situation more seriously. It couldn't be described as good by any stretch of the imagination. We were wandering around Injun country like door-to-door salesmen peddling cannon fodder. I was the salesman and the product. My hope was that maybe, because Sharp looked more menacing than me and wore sergeant stripes, they would shoot him first. Then I could jump for cover while the others came to our rescue.

Twenty minutes later, we had come full circle with no threats to life or limb. We joined the others as they started through the local farms looking for suspects and checking civilian ID cards. I still wasn't awake enough yet to encounter anyone who might be a VC sympathizer or to be put in a situation where I might have to actually think.

An ancient lady on my side of the nearest rice paddy looked like a worthy opponent. How tough could she be when her age was more than her weight? Waving her over so that I could check her papers produced only a toothy, betel-nut-stained grin. This forced me to wave my arm more and point my rifle at her feet. I also gave her some tough-guy cop talk. She was going to have to come to me. There was no way I was going to walk through that rice paddy to her. It was too early in the day to have my boots fill up with that infected slime.

Her water buffalo, excited by the commotion, charged me. Someone had told me that those animals found the smell of white people extremely offensive. Pointing my rifle failed to intimidate the beast in the slightest, so I ran for my life. Jumping to safety in a nearby thicket caused me to fall backward into a bed of thorns, which pierced me from all angles.

The buffalo snorted and pranced about daring me to come out. Unleashing a torrent of high-pitched babble, the old lady took hold of the beast's tether, slapped him hard across the face, and led him away. She was still babbling when she passed control of the animal over to a ten-year-old who hopped on its back and rode off. There were thousands of these young kids that worked in the fileds all over the country, controlling the beasts of burden. We called them buffalo boys.

Before I could disengage myself from the thorns, Fairman, who had seen the event, walked by me. He still had the personality of a cold sore and his level of concern showed it.

"You kill that water buffalo and it'll come out of your paycheck," he warned as he passed without stopping.

"No, I'm not hurt, thanks for asking," was my reply, which he ignored.

The old lady walked back toward me just as I managed to untangle myself from the thornbushes. She smiled widely, held out her papers, and chirped along in words that I still couldn't understand. Waving her away, I screeched at her loudly. "Stop talking that cling-clang shit at me you shriveled-up old bitch and get the fuck away from me."

Later, on reflection, I was glad that she didn't understand English. Normally I didn't speak to people in that fashion, but I was suffering from a mild case of sleep-deprivation psychosis, precipitated by too many nights in a row of guard duty every other hour. This malady caused you to react with almost pathological hostility or rudeness if threatened or stressed. It was a transitory malady. The cure was sleep.

In lieu of sleep, which the army viewed as an unpardonable sin during daylight hours, my immediate goal was simply to exist until the sun went down. The afternoon wasn't very noxious except for the heat. It was brutal. We entered an area of canopied jungle so thick that not even a suggestion of breeze came our way. The ground, wet from recent rains, gave off moisture as the temperature rose. This raised the humidity as well as our perception of the heat.

Soon we had our third case in recent days of someone falling out, as the black GIs called it. That meant somebody had fainted. Potter, whose first name I didn't know, and another grunt had passed out from the sun a few days previously but came back healthy after spending one night in the rear. Now it was Ken Cain's turn. A quiet sort of person, he seemed more intelligent than the rest of us. He kept to himself and was, as a rule, not noticeable except for the fact that he took more photographs than anyone else.

Surprisingly, the majority of guys in the platoon didn't even have a camera and never took pictures. I couldn't understand this. How do you go halfway around the world and not take a camera, especially if there's going to be a good war to photograph? My mistake was bringing the camera and then not taking enough pictures. I waited for good things to photograph and ended up going home with way too few snapshots. What I should have done was take four or five pictures every day no matter what.

This was Cain's second fainting spell in the last week, which wasn't a good sign. Once you were overcome by heat exhaustion, you were more susceptible to recurrent bouts in the future. We didn't need that. At present, Cain was the center of attention as Doc poured canteens of water over him to reduce his core body temperature. The water soaked his clothes and puddled beneath his head. Between canteens, Doc fanned him with a ragged copy of *Stars and Stripes*. Periodically he tapped Cain's forehead to see if there was any discernible improvement in his mental status or some other sign that the treatment was working. Soon the patient stirred a bit and then groaned a little. When he opened his eyes, they were looking in different directions.

Overhead, a medevac helicopter bobbed and weaved while searching for a place to land. There wasn't a good site nearby, so they dropped us a stretcher, then flew off for a while. Sharp and Fairman perused the maps. Burke joined in, trying to decide which way to carry Cain. The delay seemed interminable in that heat. They did everything but form committees and subcommittees to study the matter. Eventually, we moved west with four of us at a time taking turns carrying the canvas litter with its heatstroked cargo.

After more than an hour of searching, we found a spot that was at present too thick for the medevac to land but thin enough for us to turn into a workable LZ with some effort. As usual, half the company set up a security perimeter surrounding the area while the rest of us flailed away with shovels and machetes.

Next, Fairman had someone pop a smoke grenade. After about half a minute, part of the purple cloud had drifted up above the jungle canopy and was now visible to the helicopter crew. This told them where we were. The chopper then hovered over us and lowered down two gasoline-powered chain saws on a rope. This really expedited the process of creating a landing zone. The saws were carried in the chopper for this type of situation. Soon Cain was airlifted away.

Eventually the weather changed, becoming a little cooler and a lot more tolerable. The heatstroke problem was resolved. This was fortunate for us, because the operation droned on for several more days with the Black Lions continuing to patrol in the Phu Loi area.

We found a number of small base camps and rice caches, which we destroyed. The Viet Cong in the region, members of the 9th VC Division, were as evanescent as ever, so we didn't see many of them. However, we did find an unpleasant surprise they had left for us in one of their camps. This consisted of several two-inch sections of hollow bamboo pole buried in the ground vertically in front of one of the rice caches. Only the uppermost tip of the device was visible in the dirt. There was a nail in the bottom of the bamboo and a rifle bullet had been placed on top of the nail inside the pole so that when someone stepped on it the bullet would be forced down on the nail which would set off the firing cap and shoot the bullet upward into the foot that had stepped on it. The gizmo was cheap and simple but might have been effective had any of the men stepped on one. Fortunately, no one did. The devices did cause a flare-up of my castration anxiety as I envisioned the bullet sailing right through my foot and then up into my crotch.

Two or three days after Cain left, Charlie Company was patrolling cautiously through dense foliage. The point men were having trouble chopping their way forward. The GIs behind them bunched up and at times came to a dead stop.

None of us minded the stops. We enjoyed the extra breaks.

At one of them, Sergeant Condor, who had been gabbing with his squad, left them and walked over to our squad. As he passed by me on the left, we heard a distinct metallic click. We looked at each other with befuddled expressions, as if expecting to get an explanation for the sound. We then shrugged our shoulders and began looking for the answer. We didn't look far. Condor's left boot was tangled in a booby-trap wire. Nearby was a Chinese grenade that hadn't gone off when the trip wire had been walked through and the grenade pin pulled. Maybe the explosives inside were wet. Maybe the blasting cap was defective. Something beyond my control had saved me from being blown apart. My brain was now in the middle of a serious vapor lock. It urged me to dart away quickly to get out of danger yet move slowly so that I didn't overlook and set off any nearby booby traps. Trying to appear calm, I nervously turned and walked away. Condor unsnagged his boot and collected the dud grenade. God or luck or something had intervened and kept me alive and healthy.

When I saw Condor again later in the afternoon, we were in a similar position. His squad was off to my right. At the time, our progress had been stalled again by dense foliage. The men were bunching up again. Sleepy, who was just ahead of me in line, turned and smiled awkwardly. Tiptoeing in place like a prima ballerina, he struggled to see beneath his feet, first one then the other. Nervously, he announced, "We're in a minefield." Despite the circumstances, his ever-present grin never left his face.

He was right. Dozens of half-buried, olive-drab mines poked up at us from beneath the dirt around our feet. Perhaps once covered, time and the elements had partially revealed them. They had been neatly placed like silver bells and cockleshells in precise little rows. We hadn't seen this type of mine before and weren't sure if it was antitank or antipersonnel. Nobody seemed to be sure of even what country they came from or during which war they had been planted. Incredibly, our rows of infantry had inadvertently walked between the rows of mines. We had waltzed in like a pack of Mr. Magoos, oblivious to the hazards, saved only by fate. We were unscathed in spite of ourselves, not because of ourselves.

Bad news travels fast. Soon everyone in the company was aware of our predicament and did an about-face. A hundred and fifty pairs of eyeballs were riveted to the ground as we attempted to extricate ourselves. We held our ground as the guy in line closest to the edge of the minefield walked completely out. The next guy in line then followed in his path, trying to step in exactly the same places and not discover any mines by the Braille method. We all exited safely. I don't know if anyone reported this encounter to division headquarters so that the minefield could be added to our maps of the area.

Shortly after vacating the minefield, we broke out of the jungle and spent most of the rest of the day in fairly open clearings between woodlines. Most of the time, open spaces made me feel like a target and induced considerable anxiety. This day, however, they were a welcome relief. I had overdosed on mines and booby traps in the morning and wanted to walk for a while where I could see the next bad thing in front of me before I stepped on it.

At several locations in the clearings, we had to change the route of our march whenever we encountered large plots of punji stakes. These were long bamboo spears stuck in the ground with about a foot and a half sticking out. The ends had been cut to sharp points. They were in rows about a foot apart, so trying to walk through them would tatter our pants and legs. Even worse, if shooting started it would be hard to get prone without piercing yourself. Of course, one persistent jungle legend I'd already heard several times held that whenever VC passed by punji stakes they would urinate or defecate on them to increase the chances of our getting a cut that would become infected.

Surprisingly, they were very appealing to me as souvenirs. For the longest time, I gazed wistfully at the first small cluster that we happened across. There were about five hundred of them. Memories of Sweet and Sour Tits and all his hokey, bullshit stories in jungle school flooded through my mind.

He had warned us about exploding punji stakes and other mementos taken as keepsakes. Maybe he had done his job well. Walking on by, I declined to tempt fate or challenge the punji stake gods. I left the bamboo skewers where I had found them.

APRIL

The next day started with a dangerous situation but ended on a lighter note. We were choppered out to a clearing just south of a section of the Cambodian border, in the lead slick of the first wave. My spot was on the left side, the pilot's side, with my legs hanging out of the always-open side door. The flight was longer than usual, maybe even half an hour. Periodically, I would stretch my legs by straightening my knees and holding my feet out for a time, then bring them back in, much like the movements made by a child on a swing.

This particular helicopter was some kind of a hybrid, part slick, part hog. A small pod containing about a dozen rocket tubes was mounted on each side. Those normally found on a hog carried about two dozen rockets. A normal slick had none.

During most of the flight, I didn't give the pods any thought. After thirty minutes of level flight, we began a gradual descent. Suddenly, the pilot lowered the front end dramatically and started a brief but precipitous dive. This caused me to retract from the doorway and hang on for dear life. Then, without warning, he fired off all the rockets on both sides. It rattled me. Just a few seconds earlier, my feet had been in front of the pod, directly in the path of the rockets. If the acute lowering of the helicopter's nose hadn't caught me off guard and caused me to pull back, my feet would have been in harm's way. They would have been sheared off at the ankles.

If he fired those rockets enough times without warning the door passengers, eventually someone would get hurt. Maybe he was a novice. Maybe he had just been lucky so far. Maybe he had the IQ of a toadstool. In any event, there was nothing that I could do or even say about it. As soon as we got near the ground, I had to exit the ship with alacrity and move away quickly.

The rockets had been fired just in case any bad guys were down there waiting for us. There weren't. We walked off the LZ without any hindrance. After several hours of a hot and somewhat languid march, we finally encountered something to write home about—about a half-dozen ten-by-twenty-foot houses, strung in a row, wooden skeletons with thatched roofs and walls. At first I thought it was strange that they were arranged in a linear formation rather than in a circle or square, like most villages. Soon, though, it dawned on me: In a row like this, the houses took maximum advantage of the concealment the jungle afforded. Most villages I'd seen had denuded at least some of the overhead foliage so that the sunshine could get in somewhere. Not this village. This village was hiding.

The house Sievering and I searched was full of wooden furniture, clothing, cooking utensils, and all the accoutrements of everyday life. Obviously, someone was still living there. There was nothing visible inside that appealed to me or would entice me to steal it. Given that we were part of an invading army, maybe it would be more accurate to speak of looting rather than stealing. Actually, I didn't see anyone take anything, even after word passed down the line to torch the place.

We weren't sure who lived there. They had all disappeared before we arrived. We didn't find any unhidden weapons or communist flags to tip us off. We hoped they were VC sympathizers. If they weren't, however, it didn't matter. This was an off-limits area, a free-fire zone. When we weren't patrolling this area, our cohorts were randomly firing artillery or dropping bombs there.

It was a tough policy for the local people. They had fished and farmed and grown up in places like this for hundreds of years. Then the authorities in Saigon suddenly make areas the size of Los Angeles County off-limits because of too much enemy activity. The idea was to try and decrease the problems of telling friend from foe. If you were found in a free-fire zone, you were not a friend trying to help us out. We hoped that the scorched-earth policy deprived the VC of safe sanctuaries and encouraged the non-VC to move to a resettlement area before someone got hurt. It was harsh.

Burning the village was fine with me. Although not a bona fide pyromaniac, I had enjoyed playing with matches and fire my whole life. In grammar school, I once accidentally set a neighbor's house on fire. Another time, it was an apartment building. Each instance was me playing with matches. Both the house and the apartment were substantially damaged but not burned to the ground. Thankfully, the Long Beach Fire Department showed up both times and squelched the flames.

The hootch that I had been in was as dry as a piece of crumpled-up old newspaper blowing around a desert. It would go up quickly when lit. This was going to be first-class fun, burning someone's house down, especially because it was legal. A few matches along the edge of the thatched roof did the trick. It burned furiously, as did all of the other dwellings. The heat was so intense that we had to back away to enjoy the spectacle without being incinerated ourselves. We watched for about fifteen minutes before leaving. Now we had to get away before dark.

Up ahead of me, Sharp suddenly left the line and skipped out about five meters into the jungle for the first of what would become many explosive, watery bowel movements. Soon he was out of toilet paper and began borrowing from others. Donations were made eagerly, with much unspoken sympathy and silent thanks that it was him, not us.

The attacks continued all day. Not wanting to be left behind, squatting with his pants down as we moved by, he began positioning himself more toward the front. That way he could step off into the jungle a few meters and finish his business before the end of the column had disappeared. Normally, as a matter of routine, we would cover the toilet paper with dirt or leaves to hide it. Sharp didn't have enough time to do this without falling behind and so, like Hansel and Gretel, left a series of markers outlining our path, only he wasn't leaving bread crumbs. We hoped none of the VC would spot the trail or follow it.

A mini-epidemic ensued. Stomachaches were as common as belly buttons. Many others joined Sharp doing the Oriental two-step by the side of the trail. The little C ration rolls of toilet paper became as valuable as rolls of dollar bills. Soon the tissue reserves dwindled to nothing and I began passing out my paperback book, *Travels with Charley*, a few pages at a time.

By midafternoon, about half of the company had become ill. In addition to diarrhea, some troops were suffering from nausea and stomach cramps. A quick glance down the line revealed pale soldiers who were getting ready to throw up and sweaty soldiers who had just finished throwing up. Veni, Vidi, Vomi.

It was too much—the microbes had brought us to our knees. Eventually, the brass at the top of the food chain figured out what was going on with us at the bottom of the food chain and rerouted us. That was smart because we weren't much of an effective fighting force anymore. We could barely march in a straight line and joked about being like this in Macy's Thanksgiving Day Parade in New York with everyone shitting all over the place. Wouldn't that be a spectacle to behold? We were to abandon our patrol and head for a night lager position in a safer area.

All along the way, we were attacked by hordes of land leeches. They were unusually repulsive little creatures that resembled common garden slugs or big elephant boogers that had turned crimson from glutting themselves on human blood. They left large hickeys on the skin where they had bitten, then migrated down into your lower pants or socks to rest until the next meal.

Periodically I'd stop, undo my leggings, take off my boots, and shake out my socks to evict them. The mottled red hickeys itched moderately but didn't hurt. Fortunately, land leeches were a localized phenomenon that we bumped into only occasionally. Most areas didn't have them. They were not ubiquitous like the mosquitoes. Thankfully, they weren't half as fearsome as water leeches, the type that attacked people crossing rivers or swamps in adventure movies and almost devoured Humphrey Bogart in *The African Queen*. Still they weren't something to be wished on your worst enemy and left me thinking that about the only shitty, unpleasant thing missing from this country that I could think of was alligators.

The gastrointestinal illness and leeches hampered our march enough so that it was dark by the time we stopped for the night. Still, we had to dig in. My foxhole was pathetic. At about a foot down, I hit tree roots several inches in diameter. Hacking them out with the machete created a bunch of sharp-tipped stubs sticking out into the hole. A lot of good it would do me. It was too shallow for a dwarf to hide in, and because of the stubs I couldn't even squat in it without injuring myself in an embarrassing location.

The chopping noise of the machete was loud enough to attract every VC in the province. As if that wasn't enough, the woodchips from the thick roots glowed a bright phosphorescent turquoise as they flew in all directions with each machete swing. It looked like sparks from a welder's torch. The chips continued to glow for a minute or so after landing on the ground. I'd never seen anything like it before and it made me feel even more conspicuous. Checking my watch in the moonlight, I saw that it was nearly 2200 hours. My tolerance for the situation had been expended. I was worn out and felt like puking. For me, that was the end of the digging. Smithers and Gilbert both agreed and ceased any attempts at further excavation for the night.

The next day, we were picked up by trucks and driven to a rock quarry near Saigon that was normally guarded by the ARVN. We temporarily took over their bunkers. The quarry itself was an insignificant entity that was of no importance to the VC. The sight of the place reminded me of a leaflet passed out back home by the American Communist Party. It claimed that we weren't in Vietnam to help anyone. We were there for self-serving purposes only, one of which was to gain control of the country's tungsten mines. There was even a map on the leaflet to show the location of the mines, as if that proved it. The memory made me chuckle.

While we were at the quarry, some guys barfed from one end, some guys had the Hershey squirts from the other end, and some guys did both. My main problem was intermittent stomach cramps. It felt like there was a small rodent inside my abdomen trying to claw its way out. It would claw for a while, then rest for a while. I stopped eating.

We didn't need a rocket scientist to figure out that some insidious parasite or undesirable microbe had lurked in the waters where we filled our canteens the other day. We had long ago been issued vials of tiny water purification tablets, iodine pills, to ward off such pestilence. Like a lot of guys, I never used them because they made a good canteen of refreshing water taste like radiator fluid. After the current miniplague ended, I still couldn't force myself to use the little pills and never did.

Sleepy walked past our bunker carrying a towel. He was pointing with his finger and said that there were some showers about a hundred meters away by a two-story guard tower. Our new platoon lieutenant had said it was okay for us to use them. Sleepy asked if any of us wanted to join him. "That's affirmative," Smithers and I said, almost in unison.

Lieutenant Anderson was new and inexperienced. At the moment, he was up in the guard tower with binoculars. He had been assigned to C Company only a couple of days before. I wasn't sure if he was a West Point graduate or one of those "ninety-day wonders" who simply went through three months of OCS (officers candidate school) after basic training. The prevailing early story on him was that he seemed to be a nice enough person. At least he hadn't bothered anyone in particular yet and didn't appear to have any glaring personality disorder. Best of all, he replaced Lieutenant Judson, the XO who sometimes acted as our platoon leader. None of us was sorry to see him go. As we approached the guard tower, we could see Anderson occasionally sweeping the horizon with his binoculars. A considerable amount of his viewing time seemed to be spent ogling someone down below him in the shower area next to the guard tower. We found out why when we got there.

The shower point turned out to be a twenty-by-forty-foot cement slab with several water nozzles and a couple of bars of soap at one end. It was ringed on all sides by a six-foot plywood privacy wall. There was no roof. Two Vietnamese girls about my age were showering when we walked in. Knowing that they could be watched from the tower, they hadn't stripped down all the way but were showering in T-shirts and panties.

The girls were a sight to behold. Two scantily clad teen-agers splashing water on each other as well as all over the place. They were playful, like a couple of dolphins frolicking in the surf. Together they let out a chorus of giggles when we entered. The laughter brought us to a dead stop. Collectively, our eyes bulged out of their sockets. Smithers was the first to speak. "Hot dog," he said loudly to no one in particular.

"What'll we do now?" Sleepy asked while petting the girls with his eyeballs, up one side and down the other.

"Christ if I know," I said quietly, almost under my breath, while trying hard not to appear too ruffled by the situation.

"Come on, they won't bite," urged Smithers, who already had about half of his clothes off.

"Yeah, I can't pass up a shower," Sleepy said. "No way in hell." He was also now taking off his clothes.

I wasn't used to coed bathing and found the situation awk-ward. My battle plan was to talk myself into remaining calm, ignoring the girls, taking off my clothes, and showering in front of them. The conversation was held quietly, without moving my lips, so that the others wouldn't know I was talk-ing to myself. The girls did figure out that I wasn't as cool and casual as I was pretending to be when they saw me take off my clothes, turn on a shower nozzle, and walk under it while still wearing my helmet. What an idiot, even my own guys were laughing at me at this point. The entire situation was a little embarrassing but it surely wasn't enough to derail the event. I wouldn't have passed up a chance to get clean if it had meant taking a bubble bath with Ho Chi Minh's mother.

The young ladies who had initially giggled and then boldly ignored us while continuing their wet T-shirt contest decided to bail out. They moved to the dry end of the cement slab to towel off. Their drying process was dragged out a bit. They had been ogled as the price for using the round-eyes' shower. Now they were going to get an eyeful of us. It was part of the Americanization of Oriental modesty in Vietnam.

Back on the line, we relaxed inside our bunker, relishing the sudden cleanliness that made us all feel good. A much-appreciated breeze blew through the gunports, cooling us off and increasing our sense of well-being. I was literally trying hard not to sweat, hoping to preserve my un-grimy state as long as possible.

We had almost dozed off when a gray-haired local woman carrying a rumpled brown paper bag stooped over at the doorway and walked in, followed by a teenage girl. She squatted in the corner in such a way that her feet were flat on the ground and her butt was on her heels. Only malnourished, skinny, Third World people could squat that way. Like all of the people in Nam this mama-san was rail thin. There just weren't any fat people in Vietnam.

The story of her life was probably a litany of woe. She looked old, too old to be the mother of a teenager. Her face was brown and rough, like an old saddle beaten for years by the sun. A myriad of fine lines fanned out from the corner of her eyes, hinting at her true age like the rings of a tree. She had lost some of her teeth. She didn't look contagious or skuzzy, but, as the farm people say, she looked like she had been "rode hard and put away wet."

The old woman launched into a monologue in broken English about the inexpensive sexual pleasures that the girl, who was purportedly her daughter, could provide. She was, of course, a virgin, and was available for the bargain-basement price of seven hundred piasters each, about six dollars, should any or all of us care to screw her on the spot. The old lady promised that we would be purchasing really good boom-boom.

The girl was as pretty as could be, with shiny black hair, a flawless complexion, and teeth that sparkled. Her looks were matched by her hustler's mentality, which she used to promote the merchandise by plopping down in the dirt between Smithers's legs with her back to him, then snuggling up real close. Although young enough to still be innocent, this gal was clearly no nun. Smithers reached around under her sleeveless white silk blouse with both hands and played with her breasts. They were quite ample by Vietnamese standards and stood straight out without the aid of a bra. Smithers softly twirled her nipples like he was fine-tuning a radio dial to get better reception. She didn't seem to mind and laughed playfully but didn't speak a word to us in English or Vietnamese.

When none among us proved daring enough or uninhibited enough to have sex with the girl under these circumstances, they left, moving on down the line to try their sales pitch on the next group of GIs. Almost as an afterthought, the old woman stuck her head back in the bunker and held out the paper bag for us to inspect. Inside were a couple of small tomatoes and some slightly wilted lettuce for sale. As an added bonus, there was a small glass jar of fish sauce, called nuoc mam, to dip the produce in. What a deal: we could buy the old lady's daughter or the stuff she grew in her garden, or both.

Nuoc mam was a common Vietnamese sauce. It was made from fish that were ground into liquid, then left to ferment in the heat of the day without any refrigeration. It was as common at Vietnamese meals as mustard or ketchup was back in the United States. Most round-eyes, myself included, thought that the taste of nuoc mam would make a maggot gag. We decided not to buy anything from the old lady.

Despite having spent the night alone, successfully protecting my celebrity status as the only GI during the entire Vietnam War to not get laid, I felt much better when the sun came up. The evil spirits inhabiting my gut for the last two days had mysteriously fled. Several cups of ninety-weight coffee went down without so much as a whimper from my intestines. I smoked ruthlessly without fear that the nicotine would set off stomach cramps and spasms of gut pain.

Breakfast, however, was a bust. The higher-ups had arranged for us to get hot chow and even though I felt quite well at the moment, my appetite was missing in action. Like most of the company, I just stared at my plate. It stared back, scrambled eggs and white doughy biscuits speckled with protein bug dots. On most days, one of us would have devoured the other. Today, was a tie. After a short time, when nothing crawled off my plate to escape, I jettisoned the whole mess.

After breakfast, the long-awaited first normal bowel movement in several days was also a bust. Like millions of Americans who arise each day and judge the quality of their lives by the normalcy of their bowel movements, I too believed that on this very morning a good solid crap was in order. It would provide proof positive that the bull-piss gastroenteritis we were all experiencing was gone forever. It might also signal a change for the better in my overall karma. Lord knows, I could have used that.

Unfortunately for my bowel-fixated psyche of the moment, the only facilities available consisted of some long wooden two-by-fours laid out across the top of some sawhorses. The boards over the sawhorses formed a large tic-tac-toe game. A hole to crap in had been dug in the ground under the center square.

It seems that the local quarryman had complained to the CO about how the infantry had moved in and were shitting everywhere, planting an astonishing number of gooey land mines in every conceivable nook and cranny. Tic-tac-toe over a hole was a way to localize the problem.

In grammar school, commode stalls without doors were funny, even hilarious. In high school, which was rife with self-consciousness and adolescent anxiety, they became distinctly unfunny and as such were easily rejected even though this might precipitate an episode of fatal constipation. My feelings hadn't changed much since high school, at least not on this subject. Crapping in public was as uncivilized as war itself. Doing so from astride wooden planks over a crater, like some hotshot air force bombardier as a line of gawkers looked on was hard to accept. With everyone staring at me, I developed a sudden case of stage fright, which locked up my bowels like they were full of cement.

The boards stretched and groaned as I strained. The only thing more life-threatening to my self-esteem than taking a dump on this contraption in public was sitting on this scaffolding, in full view of everyone and producing nothing. Minutes flew by like fortnights. The line grew with fidgety men that shifted from foot to foot as I failed to produce yet refused to get off the throne. John Wayne never had to do this in any movie that I ever saw. My straining progressed to a slight quaking and one of the boards slipped a little. Staring down into the murky abyss that had been produced by those before me that morning, I planned my abdication. A few more quakes and the wooden contraption might collapse, and I would disappear into the sump below like a tanker at sea going down without an oil slick. I was certain there wouldn't be many volunteers jumping in to rescue me. Accordingly, with appropriate fanfare, I produced a large wad of toilet paper and ceremoniously wiped my ass. If they hadn't seen my turd drop, they must have blinked and missed it.

Once off the main stage with my pants up, I intentionally lingered a bit while buttoning my fly just to demonstrate that I wasn't embarrassed or intimidated. I was an 11-Bravo, a foot soldier. This type of stuff didn't bother me.

Our four-day break at the quarry was over. We had to go back to the field. While we were packing up for a helicopter assault, I noticed that Sergeant Sharp had a passel of grenades with broken spoons next to his gear. If you bent and unbent the spoon part putting it on and off your web gear enough times, it would eventually break off. Then they were hard to hook on your belt and had to go inside a backpack or pocket or something. He asked me to carry some of them, which I agreed to do. They could be disposed of later at the company armory back at Lai Khe. He also suggested that they might come in handy before we got back. His simple observation later proved to be prophetic.

The addition of the grenades put me at the zenith of my experience as a military beast of burden. I was now carrying nine fragmentation grenades, one smoke grenade, one tear gas grenade, a helmet, a .45-caliber pistol, four clips of pistol ammo, an M-16 rifle, three hundred rounds of rifle ammo, a claymore mine with detonator, four quart canteens of water, four boxes of C rations, eight hundred rounds of machine-gun bullets, a heavy bowie-like knife and a shovel, plus a poncho and other personal items such as my current book, camera, journal, toiletries, and an unopened three-pack of prophylactics. Trip flares were no longer eligible to ride in my backpack. After checking the weights listed on the containers that all this stuff came in, my estimate of the gross tonnage was that it had to weigh about eighty-five pounds. I weighed only a hundred fifty myself.

The story that foot soldiers sometimes carried backbreaking loads of gear was no jungle legend. Those World War II and Korean War guys hadn't been fibbing.

The smoke grenade part of the load that I carried was about the size and shape of a can of beer. The top surface was painted the same color as the smoke it was supposed to produce. Unlike the fragmentation grenades, which fit most comfortably on your belt, most of us hooked our smoke onto the front of our chests at about the height of our shirt pockets. From that position, you ended up glancing at its painted top too many times a day to count. I liked seeing yellow there. White was too bland. Red wasn't available. There was already more green in my life than I needed and purple was too psychotic for my tastes; it agitated me.

Because of this, I always carried yellow. Besides, when in bloom, yellow smoke was more pleasing to the eye than any of the other colors. It didn't matter if it was being used to poison someone's drinking water or to mark the spot where jets could drop napalm on the little people, yellow smoke was just plain more pleasant to watch. I never carried any other color.

I carried the big hunting knife for cutting and chopping. A lot of guys did. They were more useful than bayonets, which were designed more for sticking and stabbing. In fact, bayonets were not required items in Charlie Company, as smoke grenades and claymores were. Although bayonets had not been relegated to the scrap heap of history, most guys didn't carry one.

I'm sure that it would have been different had we expected or worried about the possibility of getting involved in hand-to-hand combat. So far, that type of fighting had not been very common in this war and we knew it. For this, I was thankful. I had never won a fight in my life and didn't consider myself to be much of a brawler. However, I had fought David Fleming to a draw in the seventh grade before Father Larry broke it up. (Most of the spectators thought David had won.)

Another reason not to worry about hand-to-hand fighting was that the Vietnamese, unlike the Chinese or North Koreans, were not billed as a society of martial arts experts. Those people needed to be feared. They could kill two or three guys at one time with their bare hands. The VC also weren't the size of overweight Sumo wrestlers. The average adult male stood five feet two inches and weighed 112 pounds. As a six-foot, 150-pound string bean, I had thirty-eight pounds on my potential opponents. The statistics were comforting. I was glad the Vietnamese were small. Had our opponents been 190-pound German boys, for example, fear at the mere possibility of hand-to-hand fighting would have had me crapping eight balls on every ambush patrol. With things the way they were, this matter wasn't a source of concern for me. It didn't worry me or induce tension headaches like a lot of other things did for me in Vietnam, which was good.

For our return to the field, we were sent out by helicopter. As a rule of thumb, if the landing zone is already on fire when you get there, that's not a good sign. We could see flames as our helicopters made their final descent and a lot of smoke on and around the LZ, so much that it was difficult to gauge what exactly was going on down there.

Closer to the ground, all of the door gunners opened up. This was routine. They shot into the vegetation adjacent to the LZ. The shooting continued from about a hundred meters out until we touched down. They stopped when we jumped out and were in front of them. This type of suppressive fire was done in case there were enemy soldiers below, waiting to ambush us.

The door gunner on my side was a little too nonchalant for my taste. Without a specific target to go after, he was supposed to be ripping the woodline, shooting at any shrub or bush that might conceal the enemy. Instead, he was like a child playing with a garden hose, shooting at small puddles just to see them splash. None that he shot at were large enough to hide a salamander. It pissed me off. I thought it was strange that he wasn't taking our circumstances more seriously, but then again he didn't have to get out when we landed.

Phantom fighters were dropping bombs in the jungle just off the LZ when we arrived. Great clouds of dark smoke rolled down the embankment toward us, obscuring the view ahead of us. Just at the top of the embankment, behind the smoke, I could see a silhouette about five feet high and two feet wide. At first it startled the shit out of me. I thought it was a VC. Before I could shoot, the smoke thinned out a little and transmogrified the fearsome figure into a sheared-off tree trunk. Laughing with relief, I put a couple of slugs in the center of where his heart would have been had it really been a VC. It bled glistening white sap. Getting closer, I put a couple of more slugs in just for fun, pretending that it was a VC. It bled more sap.

Just as I got off the LZ and into the jungle a little ways, a five-hundred-pound bomb landed out in front of me. The blast blew me back a couple of steps and knocked me off balance. The explosions were closer than ever and very powerful. Large sheared-off tree limbs sailed overhead. Mountains of dirt that had been blown skyward rained down on us. Suddenly, right after another blast, a foot-thick section of tree trunk about five feet long cartwheeled by me at a high rate of speed and disappeared onto the landing zone behind me. It would have destroyed any helicopter it collided with and done far worse to any GI on foot. The air strike was hazardous as well as daunting.

Everyone was diving to the ground or jumping behind trees to avoid the shrapnel and flying debris as more Phantoms dumped their loads. None of the men around me looked familiar. God only knows what platoon they belonged to, but it wasn't mine. Most of the 3rd Squad was off to my right. Fairman and Spangler, who was serving as the platoon radioman for the day, were even farther away on my left.

Another bomb exploded as Fairman marched by without even flinching. His face was flushed. He was talking to himself through clenched teeth and looked madder than hell. You could have fried an egg on his forehead. The bombing was all right, but the platoon becoming so strung out and disjointed really had him seething.

Another Phantom darted overhead. As I turned to jump behind a tree, the jungle in front of me exploded. A chunk of shrapnel the size of a waffle slammed into my helmet about an inch above my right eye. It weighed around a third of a pound. The impact knocked me down and stupid for a few seconds. It felt like I had been cracked in the noggin with a Louisville Slugger.

The steel pot had saved my life or, at the very least, prevented me from an unwanted lobotomy. Before today it hadn't been a lifesaver but had been more of a utility tool, sort of like a Swiss Army helmet. I used it as a stool every day, often as a washbasin, and more than once as a shovel when there weren't enough real ones to go around. We didn't have to use our helmets to make coffee or cook hot chow like guys had done in previous wars. That, however, was only because we had a formfitting cooking cup on the bottom half of our canteens for the purpose. This was a blessing. There was no telling how many soldiers had worn this particular armored hat before I did. Any notion of eating out of it induced visions of someone else's dandruff in my mouth and me getting some really strange and repugnant medical condition such as throat lice.

The area just above my right eyebrow was beginning to swell as I reached to pick up the shrapnel for a souvenir. Like all of our ordnance, it was made to cut or tear flesh. Our bombs and artillery shells were designed to break up with jagged edges. This piece had sharp spurs on all sides, like the teeth on a buzz saw. It looked angry just lying there. It was also hot and burned the hell out of my fingers in an attempt to escape. Using a dirty sock as a pot holder, I scooped it up, juggled it like a hot potato, and ran to catch up with Fairman.

Along the way, another bomb that was too close exploded and a chunk of shrapnel bounced off my left ankle. It hurt bad enough to make me hop around on one foot for a few steps, but did no real damage. Fortuitously, I was wearing leather boots instead of the skimpy canvas ones that day.

Our love-hate relationship with the air force continued. After cursing them and their bombs for being too close that morning, we saluted them with gratitude afterward when we found that whatever resistance had initially been there was now gone, either blown away or scared away. We were able to regroup and search the area without opposition. The region was riddled with numerous short tunnels and slit trenches with well-camouflaged tops, which we invaded and looted. There were undoubtedly countless others we missed.

The brass always considered weapons of any type to be the primo enemy equipment that could be captured. From that standpoint, our haul was a good one. There was the usual assortment of Chinese assault rifles, Russian AK-47s, plus U.S. Army rifles from World War II through the current conflict. Surprisingly, what we found included a matching set of precision-made, Belgian shotguns inside a nice leather carrying case. They were covered with a light layer of Cosmoline grease and did not appear to have even a scintilla of rust on them anywhere. Their fine wooden stocks were as smooth as silk. Maybe they had been made for a European aristocrat to hunt with on his estate. It was difficult to imagine what odd and circuitous route had brought them, in mint condition, to a muddy trench in Indochina.

It was easier to understand how the bulky Russian machine gun got there. It had a round flat pancake-shaped magazine on top. What a dinosaur. I'd seen these only in World War I movies. They were almost completely gone by World War II.

Because we had no specifically designated tunnel rats in our unit, the searching was done by enlisted men on a voluntary basis. If you wanted to go down, you did, if you didn't, you skipped it. Surprisingly, there was no shortage of volunteers. This was probably related to the fact that there was no shortage of kids in the unit who didn't know any better. If anyone had gotten shot or blown up down there, the pool of volunteers would have dried up rather quickly. I'm not sure how the brass would have coped with that, but you can bet your backpack that they wouldn't have gone down themselves.

About 1300 hours, 3rd Squad found a tunnel opening about three feet in diameter. Little niches or footholds were scooped out of its sides to facilitate climbing in and out. After dumping my helmet and other gear, I cautiously descended for about thirty or forty feet with my pistol and a borrowed flashlight that wasn't very bright. Toward the bottom, where the foot niches ran out, I could see that the shaft had been excavated and widened on one side below me as the vertical drop ended. From my perch on the last foot niche, I couldn't see around the corner below. I could have simply dropped the rest of the way down, because it was only about five feet. This scared me, however. In the center of the surface below me was a round, shiny, metallic device just barely visible beneath a thin layer of dirt. My thought was that it probably bore me ill will. I could visualize myself being blown skyward out of the shaft like the Great Garbanzo shot into the stratosphere from the Ringling Brothers circus cannon.

To make matters worse—not just unfavorable, but actually intolerable—the atmosphere down there was oxygen-depleted. It made me wonder if a grenade had been thrown down earlier in the day. Standing on the bottom footrests observing, not exerting myself, I became short of breath and began gasping for air. It was time to return to the surface.

Back up top, Fairman bitched that I hadn't gone all the way down. Explaining about the possible exploding device and definite lack of oxygen, I suggested that maybe someone else should give it a try. There were no volunteers. It pissed me off that Fairman would let me do a job that nobody else wanted to do, then gripe about the way I had done it.

As we prepared to leave, I pulled a grenade off of my belt. Pointing at it and then the hole, I asked Sharp in sign language if I could throw it down there. He nodded that I could. I didn't ask aloud for fear that Fairman would overhear and veto the plan just to put the kibosh on my fun. Memories of blowing the claymore in jungle school on the basis of a nod and not a spoken command were still with me, but this situation was different.

Ceremoniously holding out the pineapple so that everyone could see it and back away, I walked over to the edge of the hole. After looking down one more time, I stepped back a few feet before pulling the pin. This was to help me overcome a sudden and irrational fear that I might somehow fall in after dropping the grenade. I didn't want to do that. After pulling the pin, I opened my hand and let the grenade gently roll off my fingertips and down into the hole. Then I turned and walked away as calmly as if I had just dropped a letter in a curbside mailbox back home. Unfortunately, I forgot to yell "fire in the hole," which we were always supposed to do as a warning when we were setting off a controlled explosion of any type. The phrase was supposed to be repeated, loudly, a couple of times for all demolition efforts, not just for explosions in a hole like this one. It was also yelled if you were blowing up something else, such as a hootch or a hut or a bridge. None of us knew its origins. Fortunately, Sharp, who was still overseeing everything, noted my omission and shouted for me.

I didn't hear any secondary explosion after the grenade

went off. With luck, the shaft had just been a dry water well and I hadn't been tricked into missing something more important around the corner down there.

The next day we again found a lot of trenches and hiding places. The weapons we captured were a little heavier and included Chinese mortar tubes, claymore mines, and Bren guns, a light machine gun used by the British army. We lugged them to a clearing along with other booty, like radios and batteries, to be flown out by helicopter. The entire haul was impressive.

Unfortunately, the local VC had regrouped from the day before to raise the price we were paying for real estate. The quality of the Viet Cong units opposing us varied considerably. Like the American units, some VC groups were tough and could inflict a lot of damage, but other units weren't so impressive. The Black Lions thought that the Phu Loi unit was first-rate. We called them the Phantom Battalion because they seemed to cause problems then melt away before we could inflict any punishment. They had a lot of savvy and had to be treated with respect, or at least as a potential threat. We often referred to the Viet Cong as VC or Charlie, but in certain areas—such as Phu Loi—we called them Sir Charles. They always made the area decidedly nasty for us.

That day, as we rummaged around the area confiscating weapons, we were harassed by a series of snipers. Two Black Lions were shot and we had to hole up for a while, then change course to a clearing so that we could evacuate them. The wounds weren't life-threatening. Either one or two snipers were killed, but that part of the story wasn't clear. Our company was spread out in the jungle and none of the shooting involved my squad directly. My only involvement was having to jump for cover every once in a while when we heard shots but didn't know where they came from or went to. Though we were all fearful of bullets with our names on them, we were also aware of the infantryman's adage to be wary of those fired at "to whom it may concern."

In spite of the increased asking price, we again had managed to collect a formidable array of weapons. The brass were pleased and ordered hot chow to be sent out for our evening meal. From the edge of the landing space in the center of our lager area we heard the rotors, then saw a slick headed our way carrying Jones the cook and multiple containers of hot food.

POP, POP, POP! A sniper unleashed a short volley of shots, one of which nailed Jones in the left elbow. The landing was aborted so that the chopper could fly Jones back to Lai Khe. Unfortunately, our food went with him, which left us standing there thinking once again that in this area the appropriate title for the enemy was indeed Sir Charles.

At dawn it was back-to-base-camp time. We started out on a ninety-minute march to rendezvous with the Yellow Jackets for the airlift to Lai Khe. The march was uneventful for the first hour. Then, up ahead the troops began to bunch up and come to a stop. Half a dozen GIs were standing in a semicircle watching a canvas satchel on the ground. Purple smoke flowed out of it and drifted skyward, mesmerizing the onlookers like a nighttime campfire.

"What's going on?" Sleepy asked.

"A tree branch pulled the pin out of my smoke grenade," MacChesnay explained, "Now it's too hot to carry."

"What else is in that bag?" Sharp asked abruptly.

"Grenades," said MacChesnay, as cool as could be.

The small crowd scattered for cover. Activated smoke grenades get too hot to handle and possibly hot enough to make a fragmentation grenade explode. After a few seconds, MacChesnay's time-delayed brain finally told him to stop standing there like a cigar store Indian and move away. Before this episode, I had thought of him simply as having a room temperature IQ. Now he appeared dumber than a soap dish, even dangerous.

Eventually, the smoke grenade burned itself to death and went out without igniting anything else in the bag. MacChesnay reclaimed the scorched canvas container and we moved on toward the helicopters. We were fortunate. The episode demonstrated once again that we had as much potential to kill ourselves as the Viet Cong did. That's what happens when you pass out wagonloads of lethal ordnance to a bunch of teenagers. It lent credence to the witticism of the cartoon character Pogo: "We have met the enemy and it is us."

We were also fortunate that the tree branch hadn't pulled the pin out of one of his fragmentation grenades instead. That was a frequently heard jungle legend that I'm sure had happened more than once. Later in the year it was true of a Black Lion in the newly formed Delta Company. A Delta Company grunt who witnessed the event told me that one side of the dead GI was so badly ripped up that he looked like he'd been half eaten by a shark.

Lai Khe was about as placid as usual and as such always an enjoyable place to call home and return to after an operation. Even on the hottest days you could count on some degree of breeze being trapped beneath the canopy of the tall rubber trees and creating a wind tunnel effect to cool you off nicely. Showers, a change of clothes, and a mess hall meal were like being away at a resort for a weekend holiday.

For the GIs who rarely left Lai Khe, those who spent their year working in the PX or maintaining the helicopters, it wasn't such a wonderful place. For them, it was dirty and boring, a place you couldn't wait to leave. For us, it was clean and fun and even the food was good. It was a place where you could pretend that the war wasn't very bad, a place you could let your anxiety level drop a notch or two. All things are relative.

Standing out in front of the PX, watching the various people and vehicles come and go was about as close to real entertainment as I could come up with that afternoon. So that's what I did for a while. Besides, the last thing I wanted to do was hang around the company area long enough for someone to decide that I wasn't being productive and put me on a pseudo-work detail.

Herbert Beck, my friend from infantry training in Georgia and now in Alpha Company, wandered up and hollered from ten meters away that he couldn't believe that I was still alive. His voice was instantly identifiable and very welcome. He too had fled his company area to avoid the dreaded four-letter word *work*. Herb complained bitterly about a national shortage of cold soda pop and suggested that we venture into the village to find some. We did this while swapping war stories.

Not only was there a shortage of cold soda pop but also an acute shortage of good brands. Sometimes, orange was the only available flavor with not much Coke or Pepsi to be found. Only rarely was there grape soda. It was always too tart for me, so I only drank it in emergencies.

Sometimes the decrease in soda pop selection was accompanied by a decrease in the variety and quantity of beer. Often the selection was Hamm's or nothing. In theory this phenomenon was explained by a jungle legend that I had first heard in one of Sergeant Lasagna's jungle school classes. He explained that when attempting to blow up vehicles on Thunder Road in the supply convoy headed for Lai Khe, the enemy would always try to bag the beer truck to help flatten our morale. I wasn't convinced of the merits of the theory. It didn't seem plausible.

On the way out of the village, we ruminated on a number of topics. We agreed on several truisms that every GI this side of the North Pole knew, even if the concepts had eluded all members of the Joint Chiefs of Staff in Washington, D.C.: Some of the ARVN units were worthless, we couldn't win with them, we needed more B-52s, we should bomb the enemy around the clock, and when we ran out of bombs we ought to drop ARVNs.

Up ahead, Colonel Somebody's chauffeured jeep came buzzing around the corner and bore down on us at a brisk pace. Beck and I were at first oblivious to the vehicle as we walked along grousing and laughing. As it passed us, Colonel Somebody stood up, took hold of the top of the windshield with one hand, leaned way out, and gave us a grossly exaggerated salute.

"Good morning, gentlemen," he bellowed way too loudly. He was miffed, apparently, that we hadn't stopped, come to attention, and delivered his royal nothingness a snappy salute.

His antics stopped us dead in our tracks. We turned and stared like a couple of slack-jawed hillbillies as he disappeared down the road. Our eyes wouldn't have opened any wider had it been Lady Godiva, nude, riding in that jeep.

"Why, you motherfucker," Beck yelled. "Did you see that cocksucker?"

He was so loud, that at first I was afraid that the colonel would hear him and come back to really fuck with us. "Forget it," I suggested. "He's just an asshole in a bad mood. He's not worth worrying about." Beck wasn't buying it. He was beside himself exploding with contempt.

"No man, this is bullshit. It's bullshit, just plain bullshit."

Out of the corner of my eye, I looked back over my shoulder to make sure that the colonel was still driving away from us. To my relief, he was. Maybe he had been concerned about the lack of military formality back in the base camp. In the States, proper etiquette was a simpler matter for us peons. As a rule, if it moved, you saluted. If it didn't move, you cleaned, polished, or painted it. In combat areas, officers were to be treated with the usual degree of respect sans all the visual pomp and circumstance. Saluting was curtailed in general to keep from tipping off the enemy, especially snipers, as to who the officers were. Out in the field saluting was virtually eliminated. The colonel should have known all about this. Hell, they were probably already teaching it at West Point by the time one of Napoleon's sharpshooters killed Admiral Nelson at Trafalgar—the man in the gaudy uniform everyone else was saluting.

From my point of view, you didn't need salutes to identify the officers. They were the ones who weren't carrying as much stuff as the rest of us. In any event, it was disconcerting to go through what we did out in the bush and then have this insecure dolt, with a psychological case of the short-dick syndrome, serve us a ration of crap over something so trivial. Maybe he wouldn't have done it had he known we were infantry and not rear echelon. In base camp we didn't carry any weapons or other accoutrements of war that would clue anyone in that we were ground pounders. Olive-drab fatigues and a baseball cap was it, just like everyone else. We didn't have a CIB patch on our shirts at the moment to distinguish from the REMF.

Herb and I said our good-byes as promises to get together the next time both of our units were at Lai Khe. We had refined the process of our mutual pep talks. Rather than discuss the probability of survival, we spoke of future meetings as a fait accompli. Our confidence was growing.

I never saw Herb again. He didn't get killed, but the next time at Lai Khe I was told that he was under arrest for allegedly punching an officer for unknown reasons. I didn't hear whether he was court-martialed or how his case turned out.

Bitter disappointment enveloped me as I walked between the rubber trees and approached the barracks. There were trucks in the company street, and men swarming on and around them. The sight was about as welcome as a turd in the punch bowl. An afternoon off was now out of the question. Something bad was happening, and I was about to be invited to join the fun. My pace quickened a bit, because I knew that wherever the hell they were going, I'd sure better be ready to go with them.

The activity was a few kilometers north up Thunder Road. Apparently a handful of VC were being pursued by three tanks named Bloody Mary, Barfly, and Beer Can. I wasn't sure which battalion or regiment the tanks belonged to, but they were obviously part of a Bravo Company from somewhere. One had thrown a track and was unable to continue. The hunters became the hunted as the VC circled cautiously around the vehicles like ants sizing up a wounded beetle. Periodically they moved close enough to get off a potshot or two before being driven back by machine-gun fire. Our job was to go out on foot and roust the snipers so that the tank guys could repair their vehicles in peace and head back to Lai Khe.

Our convoy moved at a furious pace. There was no slowing for bumps or small potholes as we raced past the usual broken wheels and mangled parts of vehicles that littered this highway. The lead vehicle swerved erratically to miss oxcarts or craters that looked large enough to swallow a truck. Without arranged security, this was no time for slow or timid driving. The tailgating was ferocious. The trailing vehicles couldn't see past the lead vehicle's dust. The only hope was to stay close and snake along behind. By the time we stopped, I was so seasick that it would have been more appealing to get out and face an entire division of Viet Cong regulars than to go another foot in those trucks.

Luckily, all of the action was taking place about a hundred fifty meters away from the road, so we had a chance to walk for a few minutes and get our land legs back, rather than jump right into the thick of things. Locating the tanks was easy. We walked toward the gunfire while Fairman made radio contact with the tankers and arranged a cease-fire in our direction. Because the VC didn't catch on to our presence right away, we were able to get right up next to the tanks before they took their first shots at us. For the better part of an hour, we crouched in the jungle surrounding the crippled Bloody Mary. The vegetation in the area was so thick that whenever a shot was fired we could hear the pop but not see the shooter or even a muzzle flash. We wondered how they could see us. Maybe they couldn't. We retaliated by spraying lead back in the general direction of the shot.

All the while, Bloody Mary, with one track on and one track off, jerked forward, then rocked backward and spun wildly in small circles as the driver tried to direct it onto a new section of track that the crew had laid out. After thrashing about for half an hour like an elephant on LSD, the tank moved forward, its track reattached. All the tanks and all the men immediately headed back toward Thunder Road.

The evening sky was darkening as we met up with the trucks that had been sent out to retrieve us. We were surprised to see that not as many were sent to pick us up as it had taken to deliver us in the first place. We joked that they didn't expect all of us to be coming back. Half of the 1st Platoon, including my squad, was chosen to stay behind and be picked up later.

The sun was going down, darkness was coming, the trucks were gone, and we were alone in hostile territory. The cavalry to the rescue. Just as we were starting to get nervous, the three tanks reappeared. They had rumbled away as the trucks started loading up. When they saw us get stranded, they did a U-turn and came back for us. There were about half a dozen of us hanging on each tank as we started back. My seat was on the left front fender of Barfly. I'd never ridden on a tank before and thought it was really groovy. I took a picture of the tank driver whose turret was just below me. I then passed my camera up to the tank commander in his turret so that he could take a picture of Gilbert and me from above. Never in my life had I seen anything this large and heavy move so fast. Maybe it needed new shock absorbers, because the ride was rough. We were bouncing up and down quite a bit and hanging on for dear life while trying not to get our boots or fatigue pants caught up in the tread on our side. It was certainly more exciting than any class A ride at Disneyland I'd ever ridden. We raced back to Lai Khe hot on the heels of the trucks, a trail of dust rising behind us. We looked and felt very much like a wagon train trying to reach Fort Apache before nightfall. It was exciting. It was fun.

Unfortunately, we not only managed to reach Lai Khe before the evening was over but made it all the way back to the company area as well, where we were rewarded for rescuing the tanks by being sent out on ambush. It was really dark when we crossed the river. We had actually stalled a bit before crossing, hoping that we would get a last-minute reprieve from the brass because of the darkness. It didn't happen. I had noticed going out that it was already too damn dark to see my cannonballs in the weeds. This struck me as a bad omen. I generally checked them before crossing the river. They were like family pets, familiar things that were always in place, a symbol of the safe confines of the base camp that would inevitably be there to greet and protect me.

Thank God that Sharp was leading the patrol. He had no intention of going very far into Indian territory at night. We didn't really know how far out he had been told to take us.

However, after wading across the river, he stopped and picked an ambush site before our clothes stopped dripping. It was the shortest ambush patrol in recorded history. Maybe we went the requested distance, but I doubt it.

There was a downside. We didn't outdistance the squadrons of mosquitoes that usually jumped us by the river but fell by the wayside as we marched. The first wave hit us with a vengeance and continued all night long. Normally, I didn't use insect repellent because it was too greasy and sticky. That night was an exception. It went everywhere—on my face, in my hair, in my ears. The fumes burned my nose. I did everything imaginable with the oily liquid except drink it. The stuff didn't work well at all and at times seemed to have a reverse effect. It was like trying to drive away flies with chocolate syrup.

By mid-evening we were being pelted at times by a light, intermittent rain. Later it got heavier and soaked us. Although a driving rain and being completely drenched didn't bother me much during the day, they were more problematic at night. Nodding off was difficult, like trying to sleep in the shower. The rain was chilly, if not downright cold, and helped convince me for the moment that everything about the Nam was fucked up and maybe not worth fighting for. However, there was one minuscule advantage to the rain. While it was falling it drove most of the mosquitoes away from the human chow line and into hiding on the bottom side of leaves.

Whenever the rain abated, the mosquitoes returned. Adding insult to injury, every mosquito, no matter where they were going to bite, first paid homage to your ears for a while. There was no way that you could sleep through their attack. About 0100 hours, I covered my face and neck with empty sandbags and put each hand inside one as well, as if I were wearing oversized mittens. I must have looked like a partially wrapped dead body accidentally been left behind after a battle. There was, however, a small period of sleep to be had, because eventually I passed out from either fatigue or loss of blood. All things considered, it was truly a world-class miserable night to remember.

In the chow hall the next morning, they served the usual breakfast foods—eggs (always scrambled), bacon or sausage, toast or biscuits with bugs, oatmeal, fruit juice, coffee, and the dreaded reconstituted milk. This day they had added sliced beets in beet juice to the menu. We were already being served beets at half the lunches and dinners at Lai Khe. Now they were invading the breakfast menu. I was so sick of them that the sight killed my appetite and I left without eating any breakfast. Maybe we were supporting local farmers. Maybe the beets came from some powerful congressman's district back home. It didn't matter. Weight loss or no weight loss, I just couldn't eat them anymore, or even look at them, for that matter.

Inside our hootch, I sat on my footlocker for a few minutes to rest before changing out of my wet and greasy fatigues. A few bunks away, someone's transistor radio played softly. *The Chris Noel Show* was just beginning. Chris was a gorgeous, leggy blonde who did a radio show on Armed Forces Radio. She might have been part angel. When not doing her radio work, she choppered out to isolated firebases or distant outposts to cheer up the troops. She wore tantalizing outfits such as a short miniskirt and knee-high leather boots.

Everyone was in love with her. She started her shows by saying, "This is *The Chris Noel Show* and you've got a date with Chris." Every day thousands of servicemen listened to her opening words and then considered the possibility that maybe she was speaking specifically to them. I did likewise and wished that it were true.

Jamison's M-16 suddenly roared and blew a big hole in his foot.

"Goddamn it, who put a bullet in my gun?" he yelled loudly as if anyone had any reason to fool with his weapon. It was obvious to all of us that he had failed to remove a bullet from the chamber and now wanted to shift the blame. Within seconds, he was on the floor groaning and holding his leg. With his boot removed there was a shiny, white thing visible on the bottom of his foot. It was either a bone sticking out or a tendon hanging out. The sight of it made me want to puke. It also made my foot hurt. I almost developed a limp. Soon a jeep arrived and carted him off to the aid station, where he was diagnosed as having a too-badly-damaged foot and was sent stateside.

I never much cared for the guy. He impressed me as a pompous ass with no ability to think for himself. Still, he deserved a better fate. The military doesn't understand self-inflicted wounds, accidental or otherwise. They never have and probably never will. They interpret each one as a personal affront. Accordingly, they sent all manner of psychologists and psychiatrists to talk with Jamison before he left and to persuade him to sign a statement admitting that he had shot himself on purpose. For once, he declined to keep his mouth shut and do as instructed. He refused to sign. I was happy for him that he had made the right decision.

These accidental shootings weren't all that unpredictable. A few weeks earlier, a truck full of Alpha Company guys at Lai Khe hit a bump in the road. One fellow's rifle went off, shooting him in the abdomen, not once but twice. After that came a rule that if you entered Lai Khe by truck you were supposed to unload your rifle as soon as you passed through the gates.

Another safety measure was implemented to help prevent similar self-inflicted mishaps. When we came out of the field by helicopter, we were sometimes made to get into platoon formation right on the airstrip. When everyone was lined up, we all unloaded our rifles, then, after pointing them into the sky, we cocked and fired them to check for live rounds in the chamber. We repeated this sequence to be doubly sure. Afterward, we could leave the formation and walk back to the company area.

With Jamison's departure, the excitement died down and I resumed sitting on my footlocker in a vegetative mode. A small band of flies practiced takeoffs and landings on the bloodstained floorboards. There was no attempt to clean up the mess. No one cared. It wasn't like we were staying at The Ritz. The only attempt at housekeeping had consisted of throwing the perforated boot out the front door into the company street.

Suddenly the back door clattered open and in walked Fairman. He walked straight down the center aisle talking nonstop like a ticker tape machine. We were informed that the break was over, we should all feel refreshed and well rested after several days off and be ready in full gear to leave by helicopter at 1100 hours for an extended stay in the bush. Still jabbering away, he went out the front door, stepped over the bloody boot, and moved on to the next hut.

The choppers took us back to the encampment at the base of Black Widow Mountain in Tay Ninh Province. In our absence, the camp had changed dramatically. It was much larger, with tarmac roads, numerous structures, an ammo dump, expanded runways, and a lot of armored vehicles and artillery pieces scattered about seemingly everywhere.

One thing hadn't changed. The local VC were still present and just as unfriendly as they had been, hitting us with a short mortar attack just as we were disembarking from the helicopters. The frenzy of activity that ensued included the choppers lifting off rapidly to safety, leaving us crouching beside the runway. Most of the shells were about two hundred meters away. Afterward, it appeared to have been a fairly unproductive attack. There were a few holes in the ground but we didn't see any direct hits on structures or vehicles. Three or four local support personnel, none of them Black Lions, had been wounded by shrapnel. Of course, if you were one of them, it had been the worst attack since Pearl Harbor.

Our battalion lager area out in the jungle was pretty much as we had left it except that there was a substantial increase in the trash lying around. Our worn-out, overused ambush site just up the road was also still there. The brass were infatuated with that spot. They must have thought that it was the most likely location for VC headed toward our battalion to pass. As luck would have it, 3rd Squad was selected to set up an ambush there once again on our very first night back.

God only knows why, but for some reason Sergeant Carter

led our ambush patrol while Sergeant Sharp stayed back at the NDP with Carter's squad. Maybe Carter had lost a political bet of some kind. Anyway, he was unique. He didn't pull an hour on, an hour off like other squad leaders on ambush. Carter instead had three positions of three men forming a straight line parallel to the road, which was the ambush site. He then took a position, by himself, a little behind this line of men to guard their rear. There, he remained awake all night at his solitary position. He was in his mid-thirties and probably had a wife and children at home he wanted to see again. The married guys always acted like they had more to lose than us single guys. My guess was that he simply didn't trust a bunch of teenagers to not nod off at the wrong time. This way, if he stayed awake all night he didn't have to worry about VC showing up when everyone was asleep.

The first half of the ambush was exceedingly unusual. A group of half a dozen M-60 tanks drove down the road in front of us. When they passed by, we could feel the earth beneath us vibrating. Each tank had a multimillion candle-power klieg light mounted over the cannon and aimed down the road. They were just like the searchlights used to spot enemy planes in World War II except that they were square, not round, and smaller. The tanks scared us at first. We didn't know they were going to be out there. Nighttime patrols by columns of armored vehicles were unusual. What was disconcerting was that maybe they didn't know we were out there. We didn't want them to see movement and start blasting us. It would be even worse if they got in front of us and decided to suddenly turn in our direction and drive off into the jungle. We'd be squashed flat. They made several trips down and then later back up the road, which was fun to watch and made the evening go faster. When they were near us, there was so much noise that we could cough, fart out loud, or even talk in a normal voice without fear of being detected. Close to midnight, they went by for the last time.

The early morning hours came and went, one by one, with Sergeant Carter maintaining his lonely vigil behind us. Had he noticed that there was less than the usual amount of muffled yawns, sighs of boredom, and muscle stretching he might have realized that every one of us was asleep. He was, however, aware of a solitary figure, a lone VC, walking down the road toward us. He waited for someone to open fire. No one did.

"Shoot! Shoot! Goddamn it, somebody shoot!" he yelled in exasperation.

Deep in slumber, I had no idea what was happening. It was my turn to be asleep and I was doing my job effectively. Somebody sprayed half a clip of M-16 fire at the passerby and he took off like a jackrabbit, crashing through the brush on the other side of the road. He ran right out of his Ho Chi Minh sandals, which we found on the road when the sun came up. After the rifle shots, Cordova stood up and pitched a couple of grenades at the guy. In the morning, there was a difference of opinion about whether or not we found blood. Some believed that a few minuscule, brown specks on a couple of stones in the road were of human origin. I didn't buy it. To me, they looked like little piles of fly shit. The tiebreaking vote, Sergeant Carter, was still so peeved at us that he wouldn't even walk over and look.

For the trip back to the NDP, we crossed the road and entered the jungle on the other side so that we could travel a different route. There we spotted easily identifiable blood splashes. Something had indeed punctured our unwelcome nighttime visitor. Good! It would be most helpful to us if he had been severely maimed or, better yet, if his wounds became infected so that he used up weeks of valuable Viet Cong manpower and hard-to-get medical supplies before dying.

Our ambush patrol had been an opportunity lost. Even those of us who weren't supposed to be awake and on guard shared in the collective guilt of our failure to capitalize on the situation and kill this guy. We knew that Fairman would have acrid comments for each of us. Upon our return to the lager area, we immediately broke up and scattered in all directions before he could confront us as a group. Then, not surprisingly, when approached individually, each of us swore on a Bible that it had been our turn to sleep and blamed someone else. The matter soon evaporated.

In the morning, our company was helicoptered out on a sweep. We seemed to be close to something all day long but never could cash in. During our first hour out, the lead platoon found four unmarked graves of undetermined age. Thank God somebody else found them so that they had to do the search for weapons. We didn't need a county coroner to tell us that the homicides might have been from the not-too-distant past, but they were certainly not new. Putrefaction was in high gear: We were dealing with serious worm chow. The smell of the decomposing bodies was hard to describe and impossible to forget. After a few minutes, the stench of eau de cadaver made my nose run in self-defense.

As the graves were searched, I spent most of an hour leaning against a dead tree. All its leaves were gone so there wasn't much shade. The trunk, however, was eighteen inches thick and did block a lot of the sun. Eventually the section of bark that I was leaning on began to crumble. A one-by-two-foot piece sloughed off and fell to the ground. This exposed dozens of disgusting chartreuse-colored scorpions scurrying in all directions to find a new hiding place on the tree. They had been right next to my face. The scene made my skin crawl.

Later in the day, we stopped for whatever reason while 3rd Squad's part of the column was in an old graveyard with dozens of little cement headstones. They were small, only about a foot and a half high. We used the gravestones as little stools while we waited and sat down for a rest. Luckily we were surrounded by thick foliage and no one could see us.

Whenever we traversed a cemetery we talked about stopping there for the night. The jungle legend was that the VC wouldn't dare attack into a graveyard because it would be disrespecting their ancestors. I didn't buy it. The Viet Cong often killed or maimed women and children with bombs in marketplaces or on crowded streets to get what they wanted. The leaders and operatives of the NLF (National Liberation Front), the communists' political organization in South Vietnam, didn't seem to have much of a conscience. They were a pack of morally bankrupt butchers and a few dead bodies in a burial site wouldn't stand in their way. Besides, I didn't want to stop for the night without digging in, and I damn sure didn't want to dig in places where it would uproot femurs and clavicles and other unsavory things. That would be at the very least unsightly.

If it were up to me, we wouldn't tarry in this place. The only good thing about the idea was the little headstone stools for sitting. There were also some edible, spicy peppers that some of the guys found growing around the graves and harvested as condiments for a C rats meal in the near future. This didn't help me. We always seemed to find them near graveyards, as if they got some special nutrient from the nearby soil. I wasn't eating anything that had grown plump on human compost.

Nearby, when we resumed our march, we found the remains of what must have been a temple. My guess was that it had originally been about the size of a small one-bedroom ranch house. Now it was a heap of rubble not three feet high, done in by bombs or artillery.

To my amazement, about forty meters past the temple site was a ceramic Buddha's head. It was the size of a softball, and had been cleanly decapitated at the neck without much damage to the face. The amazing thing was that no one else saw it or had bothered to pick it up. It went right into my rucksack as a souvenir.

Some days were kind of dry. You didn't sweat much, even though the heat was stifling. Other days were hot and wet with perspiration. That day was a wet day. My clothes were soaked. The sweat from my forehead ran down my long nose and dripped off the end like a slowly leaking faucet. Sometimes, turning my head quickly caused large drops to fly off and hit the Old Gold cigarette in my lips. Enough hits would cause it to go out or even fall apart. The best thing about wet days was that if you happened to stop in the shade and then get hit by an unexpected breeze you felt as if you'd stepped into a meat locker for a few seconds. What ecstasy. It was more refreshing than a nap.

Up ahead in a clearing, our parade had come to a halt. The front of the company had crossed paths with a shirtless Viet Cong hobbling along using a tree branch as a crutch. His shirt was wrapped around his right lower leg where his foot should have been. God only knows how he lost it, probably something he stepped on. Even more of a mystery was why he hadn't bled to death, how could he tolerate the pain, and where he had hidden his weapon.

We wouldn't get the answers to any of these questions. As usual, we didn't have an interpreter with us. Not wanting to be interrogated, this guy would rather eat ground glass than admit he spoke any English. It was exceedingly rare to encounter any young adults who didn't know at least some English words. However, we couldn't prove anything and this guy was clamming up like a Mexican pulled over by the California Highway Patrol.

Of course, the bastard had a Chieu Hoi ticket on him. They all did. Chieu Hoi tickets were three-by-six-inch, brightly colored flyers that our psychological operations people dropped out of airplanes by the millions all over Vietnam. "Safe-conduct pass to be honored by all Vietnamese government agencies and allied forces" was printed on them in English. The rest of the text was several paragraphs of gobbledygook in Vietnamese. If you were a VC and wanted to defect to our side, these papers were supposed to be a guarantee of humane treatment, no rough stuff. Some had a photograph of a smiling ARVN soldier with his arm around a VC soldier, who of course was also smiling. It made you wonder how the ARVN had treated POWs in the past. Another version had a childish drawing of a VC at a fork in the road. One side led to a peaceful village. The other led to a place where bombs were falling. How subtle.

A lot of the VC carried a Chieu Hoi ticket and started waving it around whenever they were unable to continue on or were otherwise trapped like a rat. We all believed that the program was incredibly stupid. Why give these guys a get-out-of-jail-free-card and better treatment than other captured VC? The flip side of the safe conduct pass should have read, "If I don't start waving this pass around until after I'm completely surrounded or captured, please kill me." Soon a dust-off flew in and carted our one-footed friend away to a hospital.

The Viet Cong also tried their hand at psyops (psychological operations) with little flyers about the size of an index card that they scattered around our military installations. These were quite simple—black type on light brown paper with no colors, drawings, or photographs. A common headline was "What's in it for you, GI?" in boldface type. This was followed by a simple message such as, "Combat pay and a Purple Heart if you're one of the lucky ones. Combat pay doesn't do much good when you go home in a box."

My personal favorite was a jab at Secretary of Defense Robert McNamara: "McNamara says Americans will have to learn to accept casualties. And that means you, brother, you won't find him sweating in the jungle or going home in a coffin." It was funny but true. I wondered if McNamara ever heard about the flyers. What defense department employee would be stupid enough to bring it to his attention and risk being reassigned to some military base in the Aleutian Islands for the rest of his life?

Not long after the wounded VC was evacuated, we rendezvoused with some trucks and were transported back to Reno site inside our base at Phu Loi. To our surprise, no specific duties were assigned for the day. Most of the squad and I wandered over to a nearby vehicle maintenance unit and asked to use their showers. Sergeant Dickhead, a slightly corpulent man with thinning hair, refused admantly. He said that there were too many of us and he didn't want to take a chance on running low on bathing water. We couldn't use their facilities even if we took really quick showers, which we had offered to do.

I didn't like the sergeant. As far as I could see, there wasn't a single molecule of dirt visible anywhere on his fatigues. They appeared, in fact, to have been recently starched and pressed. In my book, this instantly classified him as a pussy on the social scale of American servicemen in Vietnam. He deserved our contempt.

On our way back to the company, not far from Sergeant Dickhead's office, we came across a cement trough about thirty feet long, ten feet wide, and a foot or two deep. The center was full of water and there were ramps at both ends so that vehicles could enter and exit. It was a drive-in car wash for trucks and jeeps. The water appeared to be dirtier than shower water but cleaner than we were. After stripping down a bit by removing our boots and some fatigues, we waded through the trough in varying states of undress. Using my hands as a washcloth helped to remove the visible filth as well as freshen up some of the more smelly areas, like my armpits and crotch.

Several REMF types passing by stopped to gawk at us. We were giddy with laughter and made a lot of loud, chopping comments about that well-known pathetic loser, Sergeant Dickhead. You could tell that we were using his car wash as much to piss him off as we were to get cleaned up and hoped that he was watching us. After our bath, we dripped our way back to Reno site. We were almost dry by the time we got there.

Inactivity ruled the day. Nothing was happening. Then Smithers walked up and delivered the astonishing news. The army had decided it was going to truck any of us who wanted the afternoon off into Phu Loi village for recreation. I was skeptical. Once in a while, you got some hours off, but being taken somewhere to have fun was unbelievable. It was like your dad taking you to an amusement park instead of just telling you to go outside and play. Best of all, if they were turning us loose in the gin mills of Phu Loi, they didn't expect us to go out on patrol that night. Alcohol and ambush don't mix.

Soon, a deuce-and-a-half arrived to transport us to the village. Almost the entire platoon climbed on board. None of us were too thrilled about not being allowed to take any weapons. It didn't feel right. We became more comfortable with the idea when we realized that the main drag was less than a mile from Reno site and was teeming with unarmed support personnel. If the REMF types felt safe here, the place had to be secure. Plus, there was a smattering of MPs with sidearms here and there.

The place was safe all right, safe and vulgar. From the back of the truck, we saw bars and houses of ill repute as soon as we got on the main street. Two girls leaned casually against the wall outside the first cheap whorehouse we passed. One was talking with a GI who had his hand between her legs and was sampling her pussy in full view of everyone. The girl was chatting with him as calmly and nonchalantly as if she were selling produce and he were examining a piece of fruit to see if it was ripe. The other girl looked up at us as we drove by. Her face was layered with enough makeup to repair the rutted street we were driving on. Black lines of mascara attempted to round out her eyes.

The local establishments were geared for the Americans and had enchanting Oriental names like Chicago Club and Dodge City Steakhouse.

While the others started checking out the bars, Cain and I walked off down a side street away from the main drag just to see what we would be missing after the drinking started. We found ourselves in more of a neighborhood area than the business district on Main Street. Children ran naked, dogs ran wild, and gutter sewage ran freely. The houses were more brick and mortar than bamboo. The scent of garbage thrown out the front door right on the ground was strong. It had a rotten urban smell to it somehow different from the rural dung smell.

Maybe they weren't used to Americans here because nobody tried to sell us anything. We were approached by a cadaverously thin, elderly man who walked with a cane. He had a cough like a cheap party horn. He palavered at us in Vietnamese and forced us to retreat down the street farther away from the business district. We weren't sure what was ailing the old guy but didn't want it hacked on us.

The number of dogs surprised me. Everyone said the Vietnamese ate dogs like we ate cattle. A disproportionate share of the dogs did seem to be puppies. Maybe they were waiting for them to get plumper or preferred older dogs. I wondered if the various breeds tasted different. Could you tell the difference between a poodle and a greyhound, or did they all taste like chicken? ("Oh waiter, could you bring me some more beagle?") Maybe it was just another jungle legend.

Up the street was a fish market with items for sale that actually looked pretty good. Maybe that was because I grew up in California, enjoyed seafood of all types, but hadn't seen so much as a tuna sandwich since arriving in this country.

We found a Buddhist temple, then stood around like tourists, mulling over whether to venture inside. The exterior of the building had been tortured by wind and rain. The last chip of paint on the outside had long since been peeled away by the sun. Shrapnel marks pocked the walls in many spots. One corner of the building had been severely damaged by what appeared to have been some type of explosion. There were no signs of repair. We wondered if the locals would mind a couple of round-eyes clomping through their holy place. Hell, we had probably been the ones who had blown up that corner.

After several minutes, we entered quietly, trying not to disturb the gods with the sound of our boots crunching through the sand covering the unswept, marble floor. A chorus of snores greeted us from half a platoon of ARVN soldiers asleep inside. They were lying all over the place, along with their rifles. All around them were half-empty soda pop and beer bottles. One or two awoke for a moment and eyeballed us curiously. Apparently this communal nap was their contribution to the war effort for the afternoon. After snooping around for a few minutes to see what the inside of the temple looked like, we left to rejoin the rest of our platoon.

Almost everyone in our platoon had ended up inside the Chicago Club, tossing down beer. Like a pack of teenagers running amuck without their parents, they had chosen the most garish, seedy bar imaginable and available. Sloppily painted renditions of bigger-than-life, nude women with gargantuan breasts and erect nipples covered the front windows. A string of red and green lightbulbs blinked on and off over the doorway and windows. Inside, scantily clad young prostitutes with thickly painted faces hustled the GIs for drinks at a hectic pace. In terms of sleaze, this place was off the charts. The whole scene would have made a Las Vegas pimp blush.

Once inside, I hadn't had enough time to suck the suds off the top of my first beer when a couple of MPs barged in and started ordering people out. We wondered why the military police would be rousting everyone. It didn't seem like anything conceivable could be illegal in this place. One of them tapped me on the shoulder, asked if I was with the 2/28, then told me to go outside and load up on the deuce-and-a-half. He walked away without waiting for a response.

Outside, the truck driver, whose red hair was so bright he looked like his head was on fire, yawned and revealed a big gob of chewing tobacco in his mouth. He then informed me that a sniper was shooting at a village chief in a small hamlet just up the road. We were being sent out to "rectify" the situation, he said with a half smile, half smirk. This type of activity was not at all unusual in South Vietnam: The Viet Cong had a liberal murder policy for dealing with civilians that they didn't like.

First, we returned to Reno site for our weapons and other gear. The trucks idled nearby as we retrieved our belongings and climbed back on board. We drove back through Phu Loi, then turned off on a smaller road. In another minute or two, the trucks stopped. We were let out next to a wide ditch that ran perpendicular to the main road going in and out of the village. Our position was about seventy-five meters from the main gate and the nearest huts.

We took cover in the ditch and watched as a number of peasants fled down the road toward us and away from their homes inside the village. One or two looked worried but most seemed unfazed. They were used to it. It was just another day's event when you lived in the rustic village of Buffalo Turd, South Vietnam.

Behind us, a unit of ARVN soldiers occupied a concrete blockhouse surrounded by a Cyclone fence and concertina wire. An ungodly cacophony of Vietnamese rock music blared out at us from inside. There wasn't much activity to be seen. The guys inside listening to the music weren't interested enough to come out and see what was going on. The one sentry on duty outside sat in a chair under the shade of a large beach umbrella and sipped at a bottle of orange soda pop. He might have wondered how we were going to get into the village, but it didn't really matter because the one thing he knew for certain was that he wasn't going in after that sniper. We were. When I turned and made eye contact with him, he held up his bottle of orange soda like he was going to toast me, then he put his head back and laughed out loud.

He made me mad. I wanted to flip him off but wasn't sure that they knew what it meant in this part of the world. There's a saying that if you do an Oriental's job once, he thanks you. If you do it a second time, you've inherited the job. This guy acted as if we had done his job a thousand times before. We probably had.

Fairman asked for a couple of us to go up on the road and check IDs on the people fleeing the village. Tynes and I volunteered. Most people just flashed their ID cards and walked by like factory workers at the beginning of a shift. There weren't any overtly suspicious villagers. Still, it wasn't as easy as I thought. No one spoke English, everyone looked alike, and the IDs they were flashing could have been Korean baseball cards for all I knew. I wasn't familiar with them and had not been told what to look for.

A couple of the people coming toward us were on bicycles. The VC had been using bicycle bombs to terrorize citizens and soldiers alike for years. The frames were packed with dynamite or gunpowder then detonated in crowded places where American soldiers, and often Vietnamese women and children, would be killed. One of the national news magazines back in the States had previously reported that the ever-ingenious VC were able to grind up the white, rubber soles of American tennis shoes and somehow use them as explosives, maybe even in bicycle bombs. The article said that they were killing us with PF Flyers, the ones guaranteed to make us "run faster, jump higher." This story was harder to believe than most jungle legends. Anyway, I thought about the approaching bicycles for a few seconds, then dismissed them as not being a real threat because I had never heard of a bicycle bomb being used kamikaze style.

One middle-aged man suddenly hopped down from his oxcart after we stopped him. I quickly backpedaled a few steps while listening to his incomprehensible chatter. The fear and alarm on my face didn't worry him or slow him down, so I pointed my rifle at his head. He stopped walking and talking, perhaps realizing that I was jittery and might shoot his face off. Tynes searched through the load of bamboo poles on the cart without finding any weapons or the boogeyman. We let the man pass. I was now sweating. Behind us, the ARVN guard with the orange soda pop was laughing at me again.

Instead of moving directly down the road to the village, we approached at an angle toward the left front. We fanned out well and got good distance between us before tiptoeing across a narrow wooden plank a little less than a foot wide that spanned a small stream. The plank was about ten feet above the water. If the village kids could cross over without falling in, so could we.

A few feet from the crossing point, a wooden waterwheel turned slowly to irrigate a delightful little cucumber garden. The entire scene was strangely idyllic, considering the circumstances. As incongruous as it seems, we approached the first row of huts with one eye out for a sniper we wanted to kill and the other eye on farmer Nguyen's cucumbers that we didn't want to step on. The villagers had all long since disappeared inside of their huts. Most had no doors, just tattered rags tacked up to ward off the incessant barrage of dust and insects.

As we moved in among the huts, a small boy clad only in a turquoise T-shirt peered out a doorway until jerked back by an adult hand. The quiet, seemingly deserted enclave, with no one visible outside, presented an ominous scene. I felt like Gary Cooper walking down Main Street in *High Noon*. It was way too quiet. This place was trouble waiting to happen and we all knew it. The villagers weren't hiding indoors for nothing. What they knew was that the sniper had not fled as we approached the village and started checking identification papers out by the ditch. He was still there, hiding, waiting to make his move against us.

POP, POP, POP! With more guts and bravado than we could possibly imagine, the sniper stood up from behind a small earthen wall that separated a garden area from the huts where we were standing. He cut loose on 3rd Squad with half a dozen shots fired in rapid succession from very close range, about fifteen meters. His weapon was an M-1 carbine. The fact that none of us was hit was miraculous. All the bullets struck the ground around us, creating little explosions in the dirt, which forced everyone in the squad to do the dive-and-roll. A little farther back in line a couple GIs in the 4th Squad did the turn-and-fire instead of the dive-and-roll. A burst of bullets caught the would-be assassin in the left face and blew off the right side of his head. The episode was over. It had ended in the length of time it had taken the gook's heart to pump its last beat.

Fairman put most of us at guard positions around the village to secure it, then had the leftover soldiers search the huts. He gave me a guard spot right next to the deceased. I'm sure he did it on purpose. Soon peasants emerged to stare at me, the dead guy, and the bad stuff on the ground between us. We watched them and knew that there weren't any more shooters in the village that day. These people weren't stupid. When they reappeared in public, we knew that the hostilities were over for the moment.

A small pile of brass shell casings lay next to the body. I played with them and juggled them in my hand for a while, trying not to look directly at my companion for too long until I sort of got used to it and could stare a bit. The bad stuff on the ground was part of the poor fellow's brain. He lay on his left side. The hole in his skull was so large that flies could zoom in and sail around in small circles inside his head without even landing if they chose.

When I asked him if he was sorry that he had shot at us, he didn't answer. He didn't respond to any of my comments or questions. There was no shade at my spot. It was very hot. It was very boring. After about ninety minutes, orders came to abandon the village and move out. Before leaving, I said good-bye to the dead man. My guess was that the villagers would get tired of the body and bury it. At the very least, they would drag it away from their vegetable garden and dump it out of sniffing distance.

Just as there were certain Viet Cong elements composed of superior fighters who deserved to be respected and called Sir Charles, there were also independent, reckless, disorganized ones, like this guy. He was a foolish dope. One guy with a carbine doesn't shoot at a forty-man column bristling with weapons. He deserved to die.

Magically, the trucks appeared to take us back. We had just reached the outskirts of Phu Loi when Irving, who was toting the captured M-1 carbine, hit the trigger and accidentally fired a shot at the sun. Apparently, he hadn't bothered to unload the gun or even put the safety on. How dumb was that? Only by the grace of God was no one seriously injured. The shot made everyone flinch or duck for cover, then hurl all manner of slurs and insults at Irving when we realized what had happened. The veins of Fairman's temples bulged out. He was so mad it looked like he was either going to slug Irving or blow an aneurysm.

We were taken back to Reno site and not returned to the seedy bars of Phu Loi. While we were waiting there a bunch of small-arms fire suddenly erupted on the perimeter about a hundred twenty-five meters away. It was an ARVN group on our side of the fence, shooting at something outside the fence. We couldn't see clearly what was happening at that distance so we scrambled to put our helmets on and crouched behind the sandbag walls. We were certainly close enough to get hit if anyone was shooting back into the base. About two dozen guys were doing the firing from our side of the fence.

After about five or six minutes, the firefight ended. It turned out to be just one more in a string of numerous incomprehensible events in Vietnam we were interested in but would never have explained to us.

That night we slept at Reno site. Only one guy stood on guard every hour for the whole platoon. My name wasn't selected, so I got to sleep all night. This was an exceptional treat when we weren't back at Lai Khe. The day's events had been exciting and I wrote about them in my diary for a while after the moon came out. I decided that night to refer to my opus as the Orange Soda Pop Journal because I was hot under the collar about the ARVN drinking orange soda pop while laughing at me for doing his job.

I put the mental movie screen inside my head on rewind and tried to see if any of the ARVN soldiers lollygagging in the temple had been drinking orange soda pop. I couldn't tell. Why didn't they wake those guys up and send them after the sniper? To me, the episode was emblematic of one of the major problems we had in trying to win this war.

I decided to write President Johnson a letter saying that we couldn't win the war with these allies. The letter would be pleasant, and I'd ask for his autograph so he would know that I was a friend offering sincere advice and not just some antiwar guy bitching. Maybe he would listen to a foot soldier who had been there. Of course, this would have to wait until I was out of Vietnam and not a target for any retaliation. I wasn't crazy. If I sent the letter before getting shipped stateside, my next mission might involve me by myself in a parachute over North Vietnam.

The next day, we were held in reserve at Reno site. They weren't going to let us go back into Phu Loi and told us so up front. In anticipation of nothing to do, when we visited the PX in the morning, I bought two paperbacks from a limited selection. I finished the first one, *Bougainville*, that day. During the World War II island battle described in the book, one of President Johnson's current cabinet members, Secretary of Agriculture Orville Freeman, had been shot in the mouth.

That sounded grisly and it stuck in my memory bank. I'd never seen that in the movies.

Not wanting to carry the no-longer-needed deadweight around, I offered the book to anyone who wanted it. Sievering thought it was unusual to finish a book in one sitting and started calling me Professor.

Maybe I looked like a guy who needed a nickname, even though none of them stuck with me. Tynes and Huish had called me Gung-Ho for a while after I went down in that tunnel. Ortiz called me Choo-Choo after my beverage powder. I would have liked a nickname if it had been something rugged and macho like Killer or Buckshot. None of these were. Gung-Ho, Choo-Choo, and Professor all sounded like characters from a Saturday morning cartoon show.

In my trips to Neverland I would be called Hitman. This wasn't possible yet because so far I hadn't hit a damn thing. If the brass in Saigon became aware of my prowess and decided to use me on secret operations they would change my nickname to a code name. I'd be The Kansas City Hitman, because that's where I was born. I wanted to be special.

One of our company's lieutenants had been bounced to the rear. Apparently he had not been doing well out in the field and the CO was afraid he was going to get someone killed. Being a no-nonsense leader, the CO complained to division-level brass and got the guy transferred to the rear. This was done hush-hush. I was flabbergasted when I found out about it. The thought had never even occurred to me that an officer could get kicked out of a war.

A new officer was on the scene. Lieutenant Billy Murphy had been brought in to shape up one of the platoons that was floundering. Some guys in 1st Platoon believed that we were getting more than our share of squad patrols and night ambush because at times this other platoon wasn't ready or reliable.

One of the first things Murphy did was catch a squad leader drinking on ambush patrol. Instead of smoothing it over he had the sergeant court-martialed. The sentence was six months in LBJ—the Long Binh Jail—and everybody in the platoon knew that it was time to shape up. It wasn't clear if the jail time was going to be counted as part of his twelve months of Vietnam time or not.

The next day, we walked out a kilometer or so before starting a cloverleaf pattern. It took our platoon, without incident, to a place where the jungle met up with some rice paddies. There we found four one-room houses next to a shallow stream. The house that I searched had an old automobile battery and some empty soda pop bottles on the floor, but not much else to indicate current occupancy. The house itself was well maintained, as if it were owned and used, which shouldn't have been, given that we were in a free-fire zone. No one was supposed to be in the area.

Suddenly, Spangler saw a VC off to his left about ten meters, took a shot at him, but missed. The gook ran for his life as someone else fired a couple of shots in his direction. Now we knew that they were here and they knew we were.

A claymore mine exploded in front of one of the other platoons, which was about fifty meters away. The blast shredded two or three GIs and a shoot-out ensued with a platoon or more of VC. Every radio in existence went off and our platoon moved toward the fighting on the double. We started out moving at a brisk pace in an upright position. As we got closer, the firing got louder, with some bullets flying out our way. Our progress slowed as we began crouching or stooping as we moved.

As we reached them, I began to notice equipment littering the area everywhere. Sergeant Smith, who was crouching by a tree, looked up at me and said, "Get rid of that shovel." There was a certain irritation in his voice. The situation was huge, it was beyond serious, and I hadn't figured it out yet. If I had, my shovel would have been jettisoned by now and I'd be holding my rifle in the firing position with both hands, which is exactly what I did next.

As we moved forward, Gilbert and I passed through our casualties, which was a dreadful sight to see. We were then directed to set up the M-60 between the wounded behind us and the VC in front of us. There were so many shots going off and coming at us from all directions that it was hard to concentrate. Leaves and branches were being clipped off of bushes, small clouds of dirt popped up from the ground all around us, and pieces of bark were being blown off of nearby trees.

About fifteen meters past the wounded, we got down on the ground in the prone position and loaded up the gun. Gilbert started firing in three- to five-round bursts at the thick jungle in front of us. We couldn't see anything behind it, just occasional flashes and the movement of foliage as bullets flew out at us. Every once in a while a tracer sailed out. One of my duties was to open up the ammo belts, hook them together into one giant belt, and feed them into the gun so that it didn't go empty. When I wasn't helping to hook up the belts and feed the machine gun, I blasted away with my M-16. As the other guys came up behind us, they dropped their ammo belts next to us before peeling off to the right or left to find a position on the line.

After firing about six hundred rounds out in front of us, our barrel was glowing red-hot and threatening to melt. The gun was so hot that it was igniting the shells and firing them without the trigger being pulled. This was a runaway gun. Gilbert opened the breech and knocked the belt out. He then hollered at me that we needed to change the barrel.

To hear each other above the noise of all the shooting going on around us, we couldn't speak from a normal distance. We had to get our noses about three or four inches apart, like the two stars in a movie. As we spoke a bullet sailed through our conversation, right between our faces, and sheared off a twig sticking up between us. It was scary and sobering.

The sound of the bullet was unmistakable. When they passed within a few inches of your ear, they often cracked loudly, much like the snap of the cheap leather bullwhip your parents bought you as a child at the rodeo and then took away from you after you hit your sister with it. It was hard to forget that sound.

Prone, Gilbert dug through his gear for the extra barrel. Removing the hot one was easy—just flip a release lever and then yank it out by the cooler bipod part. The gun crews were issued a pair of thick, heavy asbestos gloves for this infrequent need. No one carried them. They were burdensome, probably the result of some Defense Department pork barrel purchase organized by a general who hadn't changed a machine-gun barrel in decades, if ever. I pitched the glowing barrel into some nearby weeds, which immediately started smoldering. Like we really needed more smoke in our faces at that point.

Behind me, a long, loud burst of M-16 fire rang out. Seemingly too close for comfort, it startled the hell out of me. Lopez and Lieutenant Anderson had moved up to within five meters of us and opened up. Lopez smiled broadly at my alarm and screamed, "Don't worry, I won't hit you."

Not far from Lopez lay some of the initially wounded. Willis was on his back, eyes closed, motionless. Dark red bubbles were coming out of a hole in his upper chest. Another guy, Glenn, the one whose wife had been killed in the auto accident just before he came to Vietnam, was lying not far from Willis. The nature of his wounds wasn't readily apparent, but he did appear to be unconscious, though not dead. A little way away was the worst-looking guy. He had been chewed up by a claymore that had blown off all his clothes. Both of his legs had been broken and punctured in multiple sites. There were also cuts on his chest and an obviously broken arm. He was kind of greenish-looking for a white guy. The sight was sickening. As Doc Baldwin worked to stop some of his bleeding, the patient writhed a bit in pain, then passed out for a while before briefly regaining consciousness and repeating the cycle.

While the gun was being rebarreled, I went through magazines of M-16 ammo in two- to three-round bursts. With all the smoke, the visibility was actually worse now than earlier. I fired at the jungle, not at distinct targets or images. Once or twice, I thought I saw movement and let fly with a five- or ten-round burst.

Soon the machine gun was back on rock and roll. On my knees and bent over, I faced Gilbert while feeding in a five-hundred-round belt I had hooked together. Gilbert was firing more slowly now, to conserve the new barrel. The old one had not actually melted or warped, which meant we could have used it again, in a pinch, after it cooled down.

Like an octopus contracting and disappearing into a subtle depression or slight crevice on the ocean floor, I tried to crouch and make myself as small as possible, hoping to vanish from sight. It's amazing how small you can get when people are shooting at you, but it's never small enough.

WHAMMO! A piece of ricochet bullet that had struck the ground right in front of me, bounced up, sliced through my boot, and disappeared inside my left foot just below the ankle. It made a small hole that bled a little but hurt a ton. I'd been shot in the foot. The pain was so bad that it took my breath away and made my eyes water. I groaned.

From watching war movies and daydreaming as a child, to training with the army in Georgia and patrolling around in Vietnam, I knew that sometimes soldiers got shot and wounded or even killed. All the while, I had labored under the foolproof assumption that though this might happen, it was always the other guy who got hurt. Now I was that other guy. This couldn't be good.

My yell, "Gilbert, I'm hit," was more out of surprise than any expectation that he could do anything about it. Of course, he couldn't hear me over the cacophony of gunfire surrounding us and leaned over toward me for a repeat of the message. As he did, a ricochet bounced up and hit him in the chest. It didn't pierce his skin but knocked the wind out of him. He fell over, landing on his face. I jumped over his back to get to the machine gun and keep it firing.

There was shooting going on everywhere. However, there seemed to be more fire coming at us from out front and to our left a little. Perhaps this was because of a small mound or rudimentary anthill about fifteen meters out there on that side. We had to shoot around it. There were enemy, not immediately behind the anthill, but somewhat farther back, that were afforded some measure of protection by its presence. Earlier I had tried to get rid of the anthill by sawing it in half with a long, sustained burst of machine-gun fire. I was wasting my ammo. The damn thing was so tough that all my bullets did was knock off the outer layer of dust.

My solution was to stand up and fire over the mound and down behind it. The first burst rocked me back on my heels and almost off my feet. Pushing my center of gravity forward, I raked the area past the anthill with an entire hundred-round belt, then dropped back down. Firing the gun like that, upright without any support, was about as bone-rattling as drilling with a jackhammer. I was lucky it didn't loosen any of the fillings in my teeth.

By the time I had finished firing from the upright position, Gilbert had regained his composure and wanted to reclaim the machine gun. He appeared a little pale and slightly anxious, as if he had been shaken up by having had an almost spent bullet bounce off of his chest. After rotating his left arm in a circle a few times to check how his shoulder was working, he took control of the gun and resumed firing.

A little way off to my right, the 2nd Platoon gunner who was by himself turned and called out loudly, "Ammo, ammo!" I watched as a soldier behind us leaped forward carrying a large wad of several balled-up belts of ammunition, stopped, and was blown over by a stream of bullets that hit him right in the solar plexus. One that struck him looked like a tracer to me. I wondered if it would continue to smolder and burn inside him. The gunner crawled back to survey his fallen friend. Then, standing fully upright, he punched both fists into the air over his head and cursed out loud, "Oh Goddamn it." Returning to his gun with the ammo, he shot up another storm.

While this was going on, the first group of wounded was being dragged away from the fight. Some of their bandages got tangled and hooked on plants, which pulled at their wounds, making them cry out. Their weak cries were not as loud, though, as the shouts and yells of those evacuating the wounded, trying to communicate so that they could unsnag everyone and move them out of the kill zone. Once they got back a bit where it was a little safer, they could stop dragging and try to carry the casualties.

McClosky was approaching from behind with more ammo. He looked over at me when I yelled for some of his M-60 belts. Before he could throw anything to me, a bullet broke his left arm and knocked him down. Actually the force of the gunshot made him pirouette 360 degrees in the air then land on his back, crying out in pain.

Our gun jammed. Gilbert left with it, moving back to where he could work on it for a moment in a more sheltered environment. Soon my M-16 jammed. Rather than waste time with repairs, I threw it away and picked up another one. When it also jammed, I did the same thing again. There were weapons everywhere. The center part of our line near me was getting thin in terms of manpower because of the number of wounded, many of whom had not taken their weapons or other gear with them.

Rummaging around for weapons, my focus was momentarily drawn to Sergeant Sharp somewhere behind me. He had been down on his right knee firing his rifle with his left elbow resting on his left thigh. As I looked his way, he put his rifle down and lit up a cigarette with shiny chrome lighter, then gazed up toward the heavens appreciatively as he exhaled the first stream of gray-blue smoke. He did this calmly, as unhurried and unafraid as if he were having his first smoke of the day with his morning coffee. This struck me as exceedingly odd at the moment, that Americans could smoke under any circumstances, but there wasn't really time to dwell on it.

Farther back, Lopez was screaming and waving me over. He and the lieutenant had changed positions and were now about fifteen or twenty meters behind my spot. A quick sprint and headfirst dive put me nose to nose with him and Anderson so that we could communicate with our faces at movie-star distance. Fortunately, the piece of bullet in my left foot was no longer causing pain, not even when I ran on it. It was either that or I was too busy to notice anymore.

Lieutenant Anderson was issuing orders, which Lopez relayed on the radio. Between orders, Anderson fired his M-16. Lopez had called me over to get my smoke grenade. As we talked, the lieutenant lifted up his helmet to wipe his brow. WHAMMO! A bullet snapped past my left ear and hit him in the head. It splattered bloody red slop on me and Lopez, in our faces and on our hands. The lieutenant, who was prone, said nothing. His face fell forward onto his hands and he lay still.

"Medic, medic, the lieutenant's been hit," yelled Lopez before covering the wound with one of those bulky first-aid gauze packs each of us carried. In his excitement, Lopez broke procedure and used his own bandage instead of the lieutenant's, which he had been taught not to do. You were always supposed to use the wounded guy's bandage on himself so that everyone would still have one. Later, after the lieutenant got evacuated, Lopez wouldn't be able to use the lieutenant's bandage to stop his own bleeding if he got shot.

Lopez was still hollering for a medic because "the lieutenant" had been hit. It seemed to me like he was really saying that the lieutenant was worth more than me or the rest of us and that any medic around should drop whomever he was working on and rush to the lieutenant's aid. It irritated me. I put my yellow smoke grenade in front of him and crawled away on my belly like a reptile for a few feet before standing up and walking with a crouch.

What luck! On my way back to the line I stumbled across a machine gun just lying there by itself with no apparent owner. How perfect. Now it was mine. Actually it was better than perfect, because there was a hundred-round belt of ammo in the breech and no blood on the gun.

Off to my right, as I traveled back toward the line, was Cordova. He was bent over talking to some soldier that I didn't know. Cordova had a pistol in one hand and a rifle in the other. Both his arms were outstretched as he gesticulated in an attempt to help convey his thoughts to the other GI. The guy he was talking to looked as if he was coming apart at the seams. He was sitting down with his legs underneath him.

His hips were on his heels. Tears were streaming down his face and snot poured out of his nose. Wiping away the snot and tears had left his face streaked with dirt. He was a mess, blubbering like a baby. There was no blood visible or obvious injury to explain what was going on with him. Maybe he had simply reached his limit and was having a nervous breakdown. There wasn't time for me to decipher the dynamics so I ejected the scene from my worry bank and continued on my way back to where I had been firing from before Lopez had called me.

Back on the line, the VC were still tearing up the area with heavy amounts of automatic weapons fire. Smithers was gone. I never saw him again. My most constant companion during the battle, the 2nd Platoon gunner, was momentarily leaving to find ammo and had crossed my path, going in the opposite direction, as I returned. Shortly after that, my one remaining belt of M-60 ammunition was used up and I was again relegated to using M-16s. After one or two minutes the 2nd Platoon gunner returned, walking upright like he was Superman or just plain bulletproof.

"Here, use these," he said, dropping four hundred rounds next to me and carrying off at least as much for himself.

Suddenly a 100-watt bulb went on in my head. Why wasn't I throwing hand grenades at those people? There were four on my belt and five more in my backpack. I felt like Isaac Newton after the apple fell on his head. The idea was so simple it was brilliant and I couldn't understand why it hadn't dawned on me earlier. It also occurred to me that I hadn't seen a single guy with a grenade launcher since the battle had started. Probably it was just this day's manifestation of the fog of war, with all of the grenadiers from our platoon ending up in the wrong place, somewhere else.

The first one I threw made me nervous. It worried me that I might accidentally drop it, or have it blocked by an overhead tree branch. There was also some trepidation that I simply might not be able to heave it far enough away. Not to worry. When the pin was pulled, my adrenaline surged out of simple fear and that sucker flew out of my hand like a Johnny

Unitas pass. The explosion was comforting; with luck it would have some effect. The other eight grenades quickly followed as I mentally divided the area into grids and sprinkled the blasts around so that I could share the misery with everyone out there.

The effect was palpable. Although there was still enemy fire, it was diminished and seemed to be farther back. It wasn't possible to relax yet, but I could at least take a deep breath or two. Then somebody behind me started pitching grenades. Working the M-60, I saw one sail out, over my head and off to the right, where it exploded. Turning to see who it was, I saw another one going overhead. The look of horror on my face conveyed the message and the grenades stopped. Watching grenades fly out over your head is kind of hairy. I was thankful that there were only two of them and that I didn't develop a nervous tic or some type of stuttering problem while they were being thrown.

Searching the area for more grenades, I spotted McClosky still lying where he had fallen earlier. That was hard for me to figure out. His arm was certainly badly mangled but his legs were alright. Maybe he was he waiting for Doc to make a house call. That was the dumbest thing that I had seen all day. It was also very risky as there was still a swarm of bullets flying around in all directions. He should have gotten off of his ass with alacrity and raced out to where the other wounded were being evacuated before the VC shot a few more holes in him just for fun.

It looked like he had bled more than anyone else that I'd seen that day. Maybe the bullet had sliced through an artery. He seemed to be defying the medical axiom that all bleeding eventually stops, one way or another. The leaves around him were soaked. Running back, then going down on my knees, I actually skidded on the slick, bloody vegetation and banged into his fractured arm. After considerable groaning he cursed me out, which made me mad. I was already having a rough day at the office and didn't need him bitching at me. Still, it was my fault, so I apologized profusely then stripped him of two ammo belts and a grenade. He had only the one grenade, which was disappointing.

The 2nd Platoon gunner was gone when I got back to my machine gun. Now I was the one person farthest away from the main body of our troops, the tip of our formation. By myself, the place seemed a lot more frightening.

Sharp hollered for me to throw back all of the extra weapons. We were going to pull out soon and let the air force napalm the shit out of the area. I pitched back half a dozen rifles. There wasn't time to check if any of them had live rounds in their chambers or were cocked with the safety off. It was dangerous activity so I tried to lob them in such a way that they landed with their barrels not pointing directly at Sharp. There was no way that I was going to throw them back with barrels pointing in my direction. Sharp then pitched them farther back to someone else. Meanwhile, guys were dragging off McClosky. When the weapons were back and we all rose to leave, Sharp yelled that somebody had to stay behind and provide covering fire. His words made my stomach ball up in a knot.

"Well, I guess that means me," I said. It was logical because I was the only machine gunner left in the area and had the one weapon capable of putting out more firepower than anyone else to cover the men as they withdrew.

As everyone pulled back, I returned to the place where I had been firing before and laid down a slow, methodical blanket of M-60 fire from left to right, from shallow to deep and back again. My goal was to spread the shots around everywhere, make them think that there were still lots of us shooting, and not run out of ammo too soon. Sharp didn't leave with the others, but stayed about ten meters back and covered me with his M-16. When my last bullet vanished, I rummaged through the military detritus around me for a few seconds in one last futile search for ammo. There wasn't any. There was nothing left for me to use but my pistol, which I started to pull out of its holster. It worried me a little that the slow, distinct sound of a pistol being fired would signal the enemy that I was scraping the bottom of the barrel as far as my defenses were concerned.

WHAMMO! A bullet hit the right side of my jaw, tore through my tongue, and blew out on the left side of my face. The force of the blast moved me, making me spin halfway around to my left. My mouth went numb, my ears went deaf, and my mind went black. Not just blank but actually black like a television when the plug is pulled. The darkness came in from all sides and left only a little, round, fading light in the center of the screen inside my head as I pitched forward toward the ground. My right arm went out to block the fall as my mind took off to the races. An early sense of joy enveloped me while I was falling over. I was certain that my wound was severe enough to get me a ticket on the freedom bird back to the World. I had it all figured out before I hit the dirt. It was a great setup for me, a good thing. Now all I had to do was survive the rest of the day.

However, there would be no mercy for me out there, as they continued shooting in my direction. There was still time to die, so like a good Catholic boy I made the sign of the cross and then launched into the Act of Contrition. I reeled off the first part, "Oh my God, I am heartily sorry for having offended thee and detest all of my sins" by humming it loudly with my throat because my lips and tongue no longer worked. After a couple of lines, I gave up and quit praying. Prayers weren't necessary. God wasn't going to reject me on the basis of my failing to perform a last-minute incantation. That's the way it was and I felt comfortable with that.

"God helps those who help themselves." I needed to get up and get going. Moving back toward where the others had gone, I was now thinking more about myself and less about the big picture and so just left the machine gun behind for the enemy. That was a really dumb mistake. With luck someone else retrieved it.

Soon I bumped into Doc Baldwin. He seemed apologetic as he told me that he was out of medical supplies. My best bet, he said, was for me to try to hoof it out to the LZ. He then pointed me in the right direction. While walking toward the helicopter I could hear my jaw, which was broken on both sides, bouncing up and down so that my teeth made clip-clop noises like a horse's hooves on a city street. The sound was visceral and sickening. Wrapping my bloody shirt under my chin and over my head like a scarf splinted the jaw somewhat and stopped the horse noises, which made me feel better. There was numbness in my face, not pain, because the shock wave produced by such a high-velocity bullet had stunned the nerves in my face.

On my way to find the LZ, I crossed paths with a couple of other guys from the platoon. Hasbrouck was the first to see me. He was nicknamed Dum-Dum or Dumb-Dumb, I wasn't sure which. He was noted for filing off the tips of his bullets to create flat heads or dum-dums, which were outlawed by the Geneva Convention. Maybe that's where he got the nickname. But it could have been Dumb-Dumb, because he wasn't really known as a paragon of mental firepower. He also looked a bit odd. His teeth seemed smaller than normal so that when he smiled you could see a distinct space between each of them, like the teeth on a bicycle sprocket.

Looking my face up and down at very close range, he simply said, "Yeah, that looks real bad," and walked away.

At the moment his comment didn't bother me in the slightest. This was probably because I was light-headed and only heard the words without processing them. Spangler, who was behind him, slowed down and shouted, "Ronnau, grab my pack, follow me," which I did without hesitation. It was ironic to actually hear those words spoken by someone in the infantry during combat. "Follow me" was the infantry motto. The marines had *Semper Fidelis*, "always faithful." We had "follow me." The infantry soldier was supposed to lead in battle.

Hanging on to Spangler worked for a few minutes. Clutching his web gear, I put my brain on cruise control and followed him blindly, like a robot. Weary of worry, it was refreshing to tune out the world around me, even if only for a very brief time. It was also perilous. When my mind flittered back to reality I found myself alone again, not knowing how I had lost the others or where they were. No memory would ever surface to tell me how I had become separated from Spangler and the others or how they had come to leave me by myself in the jungle that day. Once again I was lost. Undoubtedly the others didn't know my whereabouts. I was now MIA, missing in action. At the moment, there were no helicopter sounds audible to help guide me. If there was any shooting going on, I couldn't hear it. The ringing in my ears was too loud. I decided to walk in the direction I had found myself facing when I realized that nobody was with me. Maybe I had been going in that direction for some reason I no longer remembered.

Fortunately, the concussion produced by being punched in the face with a chunk of lead traveling at two thousand miles an hour had left me temporarily cross-eyed stupid and an emotional dullard. It was a wonderful blessing. Being lost in enemy territory, shot up, bleeding, unable to talk or yell for help, with no food, water, weapon, or means of communication should have precipitated enough shell shock to land me on a funny farm somewhere. I should have been terrified, near panic. My brain wasn't working real well, though, and I wasn't. I simply plodded along, slowly and methodically, like a farm donkey on a familiar trail. There was some anxiety about being found. It did worry me a little. Happily, though, my mind was too foggy to connect all the dots and realize that if the VC found me they would kill me, I might bleed to death, my wounds were going to be infected soon and what the hell was I going to do if my face suddenly started to hurt. My mind was simply skipping what should have been the most terrifying moments of my life. What a fabulous break that was!

There was no telling how long I had been walking around alone. After becoming somewhat more alert and deciding which way to go, it still wasn't clear to me how long I traveled. Eventually, the jungle ahead became less dark and soon I was at the edge of a large clearing made up of farmland.

POP! A bullet snapped by my head. Immediately I realized that somebody not far behind me and a little to my left was trying to finish me off. That was fair. Even though I was wounded, I wasn't totally incapacitated. We were taught to "pop until they drop." Apparently they were taught the same thing. I turned around to see who was shooting at me and heard the very loud bang of another AK-47 shot being fired at me. It came from an area of jungle about thirty-five meters away. The bullet crackled as it sailed past me. Maybe a VC had followed my blood trail.

That second shot at me really got my attention. I felt a sudden energy surge and took off running like a track star. My swiftness surprised me. I sprinted forward about forty or fifty meters, then hurdled a three-foot berm, and landed awkwardly on my right side, half submerged in paddy water teeming with human feces and water buffalo excrement. It slopped into my mouth and ran out of the bullet holes in my face.

Crawling along my side of the berm for a few minutes brought me to drier land and several of our guys. Willis was there, still receiving medical attention. Sanguineous fluid was leaking out of the exit wounds on his back where bullets or shrapnel had gone right through him. It had turned the gauze bandages wrapped around him from white to pink. Everyone was crouching so that they were lower than the top of the berm. My hearing was beginning to return. Inside of the jungle off to my right, I could hear intermittent rifle shots and sometimes a burst of machine-gun fire. It wasn't a continuous thing like the battle earlier but more of a sporadic thing, the two sides still engaged but with less intensity. Occasional M-79 grenade explosions were also audible. Behind us a helicopter was coming in to land.

My throat seemed clogged and I began to experience air hunger and anxiety. My attempts to speak yielded only incomprehensible gurgling sounds in the back of my throat so I tried to communicate my needs by printing the word "spoon" in the soft mud in front of me. Kirkpatrick read it out loud like a question, looked at me for a second, then gave me a white plastic C ration spoon, which conveniently he had sticking out of his left front shirt pocket like a ballpoint pen.

I used it to root around inside my mouth to scoop out a bunch of pulpy stuff and purplish globs that looked like giant clots of blood. They fell to the ground, turning into nourishment for the current rice crop. After this, I was able to breathe better.

Kirkpatrick had been helping Doc Baldwin work on Willis, who was now being carried off on a stretcher that a dust-off had brought in earlier. Fred then started wrapping up my face with bandages. Suddenly a guy dived in among us with a tearful voice crying out, "Where's Willis, man, where's Willis?"

When someone else replied, "He's dead, man," the guy burst into tears.

The air force had arrived and could be seen flying around over the battle site. From the air, the pilots tried to spot the likely paths that the enemy would use to flee, and then showered them with napalm. Doc tugged my arm and then pointed toward a chopper touching down in the rice paddy behind us, about half a football field away. I walked swiftly toward it, then hopped on and took a seat.

As they lifted Willis onto the helicopter, a bunch of letters he had written home blew out of his clothes. Cordova was grabbing for the letters when the pilot yelled something about leaving and gunned the engine. Cordova responded by pointing a pistol right in the guy's face and screaming at him. He then hurriedly collected all the letters while the astonished chopper pilot waited and stared in utter disbelief. The mail was hurriedly jammed in Willis's left thigh pocket and we took off. It was a crazy scene.

The chopper turned out to be a slick from the Robin Hood Squadron, not a medevac. There was an enlisted man crew chief riding in back with us, but he didn't have any medical supplies and made no attempt at first aid. There were no attempts at conversation. We lifted off and I felt relief that my plans for survival were taking quantum leaps forward. The cool helicopter breeze and comfortable canvas jump seat were rejuvenating.

Blood slowly dripped off my chin and puddled in my lap.

Cupping my left hand to collect it allowed me to finger paint FTA in six-inch block letters on the side window. In military circles this was a well-known acronym widely used by low-ranking enlisted men. FUCK THE ARMY.

It was simply a prank on my part and not really meant to signify contempt for the army. I was being childish. Maybe it was an attempt to communicate. The day had been the most exciting and important day of my life, yet because of my injury I couldn't talk about it or discuss the events with anyone. It was frustrating.

During the flight, the discussion in my mind included more than a little concern over what I would look like after all the dust had settled. It was probably best that there weren't any vanity mirrors in the helicopter. However, despite anxiety about my eventual appearance, my mood wasn't all that bad. At five thousand feet up I wasn't as afraid of getting killed as I had been earlier. Also, though it surely wasn't official yet, I was thinking more and more that they would have to send my carcass to a repair shop back in the States. This buoyed my mood. If it were up to me the pilot would skip the army hospital and fly this chopper straight to Long Beach, California.

At Bien Hoa, a wooden sign over the entrance to the 93rd Medevac Hospital proclaimed: "Through these doors pass the bravest men in the world."

The sentiment was nice but didn't make me feel any better. Maybe it was a crude psychological attempt to set the tone, to get a bunch of confused, freaked-out, shot-up young men to think about being calm and acting as if this were just another day at the office. God only knows how many hysterical outbursts, temper tantrums, crying spells, and threats of violence went on in this place every day.

As I would eventually figure out, the sign should have been for the doctors, nurses, and ancillary staff working in the hospital. For them, the potential for psychological injury far exceeded the risk to life and limb the average serviceman in Vietnam experienced. The final rankings on my personal list of the worst jobs available in the army during the Vietnam War had hospital staff members in second place behind only the combat medics. The medics took first place because they had to work alone without other medical professionals to share the psychological burden and often did so under enemy fire. The armored cavalry was in third place, just ahead of the helicopter crews. Armor got the third spot because they were always potentially just one second away from the next mine or rocket. At least the helicopter crews got to spend some time flying so high that nothing could knock them out of the sky. My group, the 11-Bravo, foot soldiers, had slid down the list to fifth place.

Inside, the hospital was a zoo. Besides sixteen of us from C Company, there were nine guys from a 4th Division battle up the street somewhere. Twenty-five guys with gunshot and shrapnel wounds at one time is a load and a half. Initially we were all triaged, had our blood pressures checked, and our wounds inspected. I think a decision was made to let Willis die or maybe just see if he would survive until they got to him. To me the tip-off was that there was no flurry of activity to insert tubes or start a blood transfusion or wheel him to surgery. Someone took his blood pressure. Later, a rolled-up blanket was put under his head for a pillow. Still later, someone put a blanket over him for warmth. Eventually, the blanket was pulled over his face and some enlisted men carried off his stretcher.

The nurse who took my vital signs eyeballed my wounds and wrote on a clipboard. She asked if I wanted my family notified. I couldn't do that to my parents and declined. My plan was to tell them later, after the picture had clarified itself and was less worrisome with unknowns. The nurse handed me a newspaper, the *Star and Stripes*, of course, pointed toward some cots and told me to sit over there and wait my turn.

As usual, I read the front section of the paper first and saved the best part, the sports page, for last. Unfortunately, the paper was printed in tabloid magazine form. As I read along, blood and other drippings and secretions from my face turned the paper into a soggy crimson mess. Soon the pages were sloughing apart as I tried to turn them. So much for the Dodgers.

Thank God the lower half of my face was still numb. It was like I had gotten a massive overdose of novocaine at the dentist's office. So far there hadn't been an iota of pain from my wounds. My jaw was shattered on the right and an inch-and-a-half-long section on the left had been blown off. Eight teeth were gone and four more had been sheared in half. There were lacerations through my tongue and the floor of my mouth. There was a gaping, jagged, exit wound on my left cheek about two inches in diameter.

I couldn't feel any of it. If the feeling in my face had returned earlier I might have perished. Had the stunned nerves in my face recovered while I was alone and lost in the jungle the pain might have been unendurable. I might have had to curl up in a fetal position and try to fall asleep while hoping to bleed to death. Simply roll up in a ball like a sow bug and die. The numbness was another gift to be appreciated.

A few cots over was McClosky, with a clear plastic inflatable splint on his arm. At first, he was just resting quietly. Then, some unknown psychological irritant precipitated a loud diatribe, which he unleashed at no one in particular but everyone in general.

"What kind of world are we living in," he shouted, "where people go around shooting little holes in each other?"

It didn't take long until a couple of uniformed male orderlies moved toward him, pointing their fingers and outshouting him with their point of view that he needed to calm down and shut up. We had too many problems going on in that room without him adding another one. They were so quick and forceful, you could tell they had dealt with this type of theatrics many times before.

An X-ray tech waved at me to follow him. As I stood up, something in my right thigh pocket banged against my leg. When I pulled out a hand grenade, the two orderlies jumped to grab me from both sides and took it away. I guess they thought that I was madder than McClosky and was about to give them a demonstration of really acting out.

An X-ray film of my jaw and face was taken. My left shoulder had a shrapnel wound in front, probably from pieces of blown-off jaw or teeth, but possibly from bullet fragments. When they laid me on my back to shoot an X-ray I started to suffocate as my swollen and broken jaw sagged and mushed back into my airway. The shoulder X-ray was canceled. No one noticed the bullet wound in my left foot because my boots were still on and were caked with mud and blood. I'd forgotten about it myself.

Next came an IV line and some type of sedative or anesthetic. It rapidly made me groggy. I was almost asleep when I felt someone putting a plastic tube down my nose into my stomach. What a treat! It looked to be about the size of a garden hose and felt like a fire hose. Hysterically, I starting fighting with the guy and managed to slug him in the face once before passing out from the medication.

Morning found me in a Quonset hut with beds perpendicular to the walls up one side and down the other. The place was a sea of misery. Four beds just across from me were occupied by Vietnamese children. Their school bus had hit a mine. Among the visible wounds was at least one amputation per child. Two of them were double amputees. Two had their eyes bandaged. I hoped they weren't blind. All the other beds were occupied by American servicemen.

In all probability, I looked as odd to the kids, the ones that could see me, as they looked to me. The lower half of my face was swollen and much thicker than normal. Fortunately, again, there were no mirrors available. In my mind's eye, after feeling my face like a blind man, it seemed as if I should now look like Richard Nixon, with his prominent puffy jowls. The thought sort of frightened me. It was comforting to note that all of the other essential landmarks including chin, lips, and nose were still there and in the right places. I wasn't going to look like an escaped circus freak. A metal tracheotomy tube protruded from the front of my neck.

Every wound imaginable was somewhere to be seen. Collectivizing the carnage this way was probably therapeutic. We could all spot someone else whose wounds looked more shocking than our own and feel good about it, because we had escaped their fate. I wouldn't have wanted to trade places with any of those children or most of the soldiers that I could see.

Over the past four months, I'd heard more than one grunt conversation saying that they would rather die than go home with this or that type of injury. It was a common discussion. My guess was that soldiers had talked this way in all wars for perhaps thousands of years. Well, nobody was talking that way anymore in this place. We were all getting used to our individual wounds and were glad we weren't dead.

It also occurred to me that war was a young man's game because the army would rather draft an eighteen-year-old than a twenty-eight-year-old. The youngsters were more gullible and more easily led. The average age of the Americans in the Vietnam War was nineteen. At twenty, I was older than most, but not by much. I was still young enough to buy into the required myths, that of my own invincibility and that it was always the other guy who got creamed.

In World War II, the average age of the American serviceman had been a more mature twenty-six years. This made my war seem like the Children's Crusade by comparison. For every one colonel or general who was Westmoreland's age, fifty-three, it took about three squads of foot soldiers, about thirty guys, who were only eighteen, to maintain the average at nineteen. But that's what the Pentagon wanted.

You could tell youngsters to do a stand-up Pickett's Charge on a trench full of enemy soldiers, or stay behind with a machine gun to hold them off, and assure them that everything would be all right. They believed it even if the obvious facts of the situation dictated otherwise. The twenty-eight-year-olds were more skeptical and couldn't be so easily led, or misled.

Outside the window on my right was a chain-link fence and then a two-lane road about thirty meters away, which made me uncomfortable. Countless civilian vehicles were using the road, including trucks, motorcycles, and those ubiquitous three-wheeled pedicabs, each of which had too many people on board. Pedestrians by the score walked by, any one of whom was close enough to start trouble with us if they chose to do so.

My schedule seemed to call for sleeping around the clock, which is about all I had the energy to do. My mouth was wired shut so I couldn't really talk. Eating was impossible. In fact, mealtimes didn't even include a tray for me. The intravenous line in my left arm was kept running constantly.

The nurses wore standard-issue army fatigues and looked great. From my vantage point, there weren't enough of them to go around. As far as I could tell they were the ones taking care of me. My assumption was that doctors had operated on me but I couldn't recall seeing one again after that first day. They were probably overwhelmed elsewhere. The nurse who was most frequently in my area was about three years older than I and quite cute, with short auburn hair and brown bedroom eyes. She asked me to try to ignore my thirst, saying that they would be able to start me on liquids soon.

One day she surprised me with a Purple Heart medal and certificate that had been sent over to the hospital for me. She commented on how pretty it was, how proud I should be, and offered her congratulations. Surely she had done that many times before, but still she worked hard to make the presentation special for me, and it was. She deserved an Academy Award. It wasn't a very official ceremony, but I appreciated her efforts, probably more than she knew. She even offered to package the Purple Heart and mail it home for me. I had her send it to my friend Larry, because it was still too early for my parents to find out about all of this. My hopes had been to get a Purple Heart all along. My thoughts were that it was possible, maybe even probable. Being somewhat realistic at times, though, I hadn't really planned on actually getting any medals for bravery and didn't even know what it took to get one. However, in Neverland I was decorated for heroism several times and even met President Johnson there once in the White House Rose Garden during a presentation ceremony.

Going home with a Purple Heart on my chest would be

neat. Wounded in action sounded about as macho as I could get. I certainly hoped this would sufficiently impress Charlene Woolridge. She was a very pretty girl about my age who lived a couple of houses away from mine. She went to a different high school, Wilson, so I didn't know her very well. Maybe when she saw my Purple Heart ribbon she would notice me or even want to start dating me. She had been my fantasy girl for what seemed like light-years.

In Neverland, my Purple Heart had been awarded for injuries that required a pristine, white, headband-like bandage with one dab of blood about the size of a thumbprint just above my left eye, like in the movies. An alternate plan was for an injury requiring my arm to be in a sling. It would be on the left side, because I was right-handed. Also, there would be no obvious deformity. Neither of these wounds would appear hideous to Charlene. Being shot in the face and having a piece of jawbone stuck in my shoulder wasn't exactly the type of wound I had in mind.

Another platoon's lieutenant showed up for a visit. He was familiar to me by sight but not by name. They probably made him do it because my lieutenant, Anderson, had been shot in the head and wasn't available. It might have been the army's way of showing concern. Plus, they needed to find out which of us were going back to the World and would have to be replaced.

The conversation was one-sided. He asked me how I was doing and then told me how some of our other wounded were doing. He said that the company had returned to the battle site the next day to hunt down the group we had fought with but hadn't been able to find them. The brass were upset that a Starlight scope had been left behind. There was no mention of my abandoned machine gun. A Viet Cong soldier with his head blown off had been found in a spider hole out in front of my position and off to the left a bit where I had thrown several grenades. (When they found the dead VC, Kirkpatrick became temporarily deranged and began beating the stuffings out of the headless corpse and had to be restrained.) The lieutenant didn't mention whether any other bodies or blood trails had been found.

What were the chances that the decapitated Viet Cong had been the guy who had shot me in the foot? That would certainly be a case of poetic justice. Presumably the guy who had shot me in the mouth got away. Did he know that his shot had struck flesh and irreparably changed someone's life? How ironic, I'd wear the mark of his bullet on my face forever, a reminder of a man I had never met but would remember for the rest of my life.

It was too bad that I couldn't talk or I would have grilled the lieutenant a little about the possibility of other VC casualties. I wondered if any others had been found. Maybe they had been and he just didn't mention it. Maybe they had been dragged away to be buried somewhere else or been burned up by the napalm. It didn't seem possible that we could hold our ground like we did and punch it out with them all day at close range and not bag more than one. What a bitter pill that would be.

After a few minutes, the lieutenant departed. He hadn't looked directly at me during most of our visit. He had spent a lot of time massaging his forehead with one hand, as if he was trying to block out the sunlight at dusk or any sight of me at the moment. It must have been disconcerting for him to see so many of us in this chewed-up state. In fact, he looked a little green around the gills, and I had been somewhat fearful that he might throw up on the floor next to my bed.

Henry Fonda also showed up. He was by himself, going from bed to bed visiting the wounded one-on-one.

"Well, what happened to you?" he said with a big warm grin. I made a pistol with my right hand and shot myself in the face to show him what had happened. He offered me words of comfort and encouragement. His daughter Jane wasn't mentioned. Later, after he left, it bothered me that I may have given him the impression that I had shot myself. It was amazing to me that I could always conjure up something else to worry about, as if there weren't enough real problems at the moment.

Elsewhere in the hospital, for the Black Lions, the grief continued. Some number of days after the battle, Henry Fleming, the only person I had ever met in my life from the state of Delaware but fortunately did not know very well, died of his wounds. His lower abdomen, perhaps his bladder, had been perforated during the battle by some type of high-speed metal, either bullets or shrapnel, I wasn't sure which.

The doctor told Henry that the surgery had gone well and that happily he would be shipped home soon. Henry protested that something was still wrong inside and that he was going to die if they didn't fix it. The surgeon wasn't convinced and assured him that he would make a full recovery and they would all laugh about it later. It didn't work out that way.

After five days with nothing to drink, my thirst was reaching astronomical proportions, even with the IV fluids topping off my tank twenty-four hours a day. Intravenous normal saline and dextrose solution were simply a poor substitute for a plain old glass of water or can of soda pop. Around midday the same tall, fruity, black man that pushed the lunch cart every day showed up. As usual, he had a meal tray for everyone but me.

He pursed his lips and chirped that once again I was on the do-not-feed list, as if it was no big deal. Then he giggled to himself as he moved away with grub for everybody else. My gut feeling was that he didn't really mean to act callously but just wasn't thinking clearly about how he was speaking to me.

Still, it irritated me so badly that I hocked a loogie at him when his back was turned. There was no end to the secretions in my trach tube and I had learned by accident that if I closed my lips and coughed the trach became a goober mortar. It was frightening. The first gob of phlegm I fired landed in the aisle next to the meal cart. The second broke up in mid-trajectory and landed between the beds across from me. Part of it hit him in the back. Sensing something, but not really comprehending what was occurring, he gave me a short quizzical glance over his left shoulder. My only defense was to droop my right upper eyelid about halfway down and cock my head to the side like dogs do when you blow one of those high-frequency whistles that they hear but humans can't. I hoped this maneuver would make me look like a sledge-stunned cow in a slaughterhouse that wasn't capable of willful intent and thus was undeserving of any retaliation.

When the meal ended, all of the trays were returned to the cart, which was pushed to the far end of the hut and temporarily abandoned. Out of bed and dragging my IV pole along like a drunken dance partner, I shuffled my way toward the cart. There was half a glass of iced tea on one tray and half a glass of lemonade on another. After combining the two in one glass, I guzzled away with unbridled glee. It was truly ambrosia, nectar of the gods. The wonderful qualities of that drink defy any attempt at description, and could never in my lifetime be replicated. This was in spite of the fact that a significant portion of the liquid gushed out of various holes in my face and soaked my pajama top.

Over at the nurses' station the head nurse, Major Helen Mackey, watched me out of the corner of her eye. She supervised the other nurses in the area and always seemed to work harder and longer than any of her charges. When the iced tea and lemonade slopped out of my face she smiled and kept on doing what she was doing. This made me think that it was okay to be up and that I didn't have to scurry back to bed before being caught.

Emboldened, I lingered by the cart before heading back at a leisurely pace. It was enjoyable to be in an upright position for a change. The only patient I recognized was the mangled white guy from the claymore blast. His skin wasn't so green and he looked healthier than he had looked on the battlefield, which made me glad. I mumbled a "hi" at him even though he was asleep. All four of his limbs were in long white casts with swirls of pink where his blood had soaked through the plaster of paris. He looked like a giant barber pole.

The drink changed everything. My IV was removed, liquid meals started arriving, and orders came for me to be sent to a hospital in Japan. Soon my gurney was being pushed down the aisle toward the door. The always busy Major Mackey was working at the nurses' desk.

"And, Ronnau, have a good time in Japan," she said cheerfully as I passed by. She was a neat lady. Despite her workload, she knew my name. That personal touch made me feel special.

Outside, the gurney service ended and I walked to a helicopter and climbed in. It would fly me to Tan Son Nhut Air Base, where a giant C-141 aerial ambulance would shuttle us to Japan. I was the only patient in the chopper. It was a helicopter ride for one, which made me feel important. There was a cute Red Cross girl with short blond hair sent along for the ride. She carried a portable suction machine, ostensibly in case secretions plugged my trach tube. It didn't seem necessary, because I could cough hard and blow almost anything out of there.

At Tan Son Nhut, I went into a Quonset hut with three times as many patients as there had been in my hospital Quonset hut, even though it was the same size. There were just as many beds plus an equal number of chairs. There were guys standing or walking who wouldn't sit down or lie down or shut up. The atmosphere was festive. The noise level was high from conversations and laughter. It was party time. After congregating there until we had enough wounded to fill the plane, we were leaving. In a few hours for us the war would be over, at least temporarily. The doctors in Japan would determine whether we were sufficiently maimed to be sent back to the States, or could be repaired and returned to battle.

My mood was jovial even though I couldn't fully participate in the conversations. Believe me, beaucoup good stories were being told in that room. One GI on crutches had a newspaper clipping that said that Junction City had gone on for a little over a month but was over now. It said that the American casualties on that one operation had been more than three hundred killed and fifteen hundred wounded. Of course, the number of enemy reported as killed, wounded, missing, or captured was so high that you would need a slide rule to figure out the total. Whether the numbers were accurate was another story. Some friendly soldier I didn't know offered me a smoke. When I demurred because of my physical limitations, he was delighted to explain how to put a cigarette in the trach and inhale through closed lips. It worked and after a week without a smoke it was great, even though the cigarette, a Kool, was a menthol brand and I didn't normally smoke those.

For the first time, I began to think of the trach as useful rather than a nuisance. It was also slightly worrisome. If the plane went down in the water between Vietnam and Japan, I would drown. The thought didn't dominate my day or make me want to turn back, but it was there. Having grown up on the seashore, I could swim like a seal but not with water pouring in through a hole in my neck. Why couldn't they give me a little cork or rubber stopper?

The plane was massive. There were about seventy litters plus half again as many passenger seats. An air force enlisted man showed me to an assigned litter. This brought a protest on my part. I didn't want to go home on a stretcher. I wanted to walk over to a seat and fly off like a regular passenger, like they hadn't beaten me. It was completely symbolic, but that's what I wanted. The aircrew was very understanding and switched me to a seat without any hesitation. About two hours into the flight I was exhausted and literally did not have the energy to sit up straight. Sheepishly, I asked the crew if I could lie down. Again they switched me without any criticisms or snide comments. They were really nice about the situation.

Our flight to the Land of the Rising Sun was otherwise pleasant and uneventful. To me, it was also incredible. After being wounded, I had been swept off of the battlefield before the sun went down. Now after a few days in a war zone hospital, they were sweeping me off of the continent and sending me to a neutral country that was safe. The whole setup was wondrous.

It was things like this that had caused me a while back to try to convince Tynes, Ortiz, and some others in the squad that all things considered, Vietnam was a wimpy war compared to Korea and World War II. In fact, it seemed that all of our major wars had one or more distinct advantages for the guy actually out in the field getting his ass shot off that made his war much more tolerable than the preceding one. From the Revolution to the Civil War to the world wars to Korea and then Vietnam, there were always advancements in areas like communications, transportation, and medicine that improved the lot of the average combatant. Who could have put up with being in a war with no regular mail from mom, no horse-drawn ambulances, no general anesthesia, a war in which amputations and no antibiotics for the inevitable wound infections were routine? It was inconceivable.

In Vietnam we knew ahead of time that if we were wounded we would probably be in a hospital within an hour and out of the combat zone in days. We didn't have to survive brutal, freezing winters. We always had plenty of food and cigarettes. We had to fight for only twelve months, then we could call it quits and go home. Some of our predecessors didn't go home for years at a time. To top it all off, one time or maybe even twice during our tour of duty, if we felt too stressed-out or afraid we could call a Kings X, a time-out, stop the war, and take a week off. The week was spent on R & R at centers in Australia, Japan, Malaysia, Thailand, Taiwan, or our newest state, Hawaii. How sweet a deal was that?

Nobody agreed. Just being in Vietnam was a painful burden. Because they were in the Nam they were miserable and wouldn't buy into my happy song and dance routine that our war was the easy war. They didn't give me a chance to mention that the enemy didn't have an air force or even artillery. That was certainly another fabulous break for us.

Our flight landed at an American air force base on Honshu, the main island of Japan. Mount Fuji, Japan's sacred mountain, was there to welcome us with its majestic, snow-capped peak visible in the distance. Seeing it was an unexpected treat. It inspired me to feel more positive about the way things were going at the moment. I was sure that being in its shadow was a good omen.

A short bus ride took us to Kishine Barracks at the American military hospital in Yokohama. There my assigned room was on the fourth floor. My roommate, Rudy Richter, was a sergeant from the 173rd Airborne Brigade. He said that he had previously been with the French Foreign Legion in Indochina. He was a German citizen and, after serving with the French, had joined our army to help him gain American citizenship. The idea of noncitizens joining our army had never even crossed my mind.

Rudy was smart and friendly, which made him a nice roommate. Like me, he had been shot in the mouth and had a variety of jagged telltale scars on his face. One of his eyes had been knocked out and his uvula, that thing that hangs down in the back of your throat, had been blown off by the bullet that had struck him. Apparently it was now lying out there in the jungle somewhere. I didn't even know what the uvula did, but the story of it being shot off made me cringe.

Besides Rudy, a number of interesting characters were in the hospital with us. The saddest was Willie-Peter, that's what we called him. He accepted the nickname with good humor. Most of his body had burns from a white phosphorus grenade that had accidentally gone off inside his hootch. His body was wrapped from head to toe in white bandages that made him look a lot like Boris Karloff in *The Mummy*. Without enough skin to keep all of his fluids in, he leaked. His bedding was regularly soaked. The nursing staff would sit him in a chair while they changed his blanket and sheets. By the time they were done, there was always a small puddle underneath the chair.

Willie-Peter was fighting off serial infections. One day, in a moment of unusual candor, a nurse confided in me that they all expected Willie-Peter to die. Eventually, they thought, he would pick up an infection that he couldn't beat and that would be the end of him. I was greatly saddened to know this and wondered why they didn't bring his family to Japan to say good-bye or attempt to send him stateside on a more urgent basis. I didn't want to never see Mom and Dad again and was glad that I wasn't him.

The most oddly injured patient I met was a black soldier who had been hit in the face with several pieces of glowing white phosphorus in an event totally unrelated to Willie-Peter's injuries. The pieces had continued to burn as they pierced his skin and seared their way into the meat of his face.

We had all been taught that the way to deal with smoldering white phosphorus on someone was to either smother it with sand or water or to dig it out which in this case is what someone did. Another GI had taken his bayonet and peeled the black soldier's face like a carrot. This had successfully removed the burning metal and saved the soldier from further damage. Unfortunately, the black soldier's face had been left with multiple strawberry-red, half-inch-wide, depigmented stripes. His face didn't look so much frightening or hideous as it did strange. Just plain weird as hell.

The most unsettling character was a white kid, about my age, whose ankle had been broken in more than one place. I wasn't sure how it happened. The sawbones had operated on his ankle and put in a few nuts and bolts to hold it all together. Afterward, they had him ride around in a wheelchair for a few weeks. When I got to Japan, he was up on crutches and just about ready to give them up and be sent back to the war.

Understandably, he was as nervous as a cat about his future prospects. For weeks he had been living among the blind, the burned, and others who had been maimed in every hideous way conceivable. His idle time was spent talking with guys like me who had coffee leak out of holes in their faces when they took a drink. He watched the puddle grow underneath Willie-Peter's chair. For this poor fellow, the myth of invincibility hadn't just been tarnished, it had been obliterated. He had seen enough to know that these wounds were real and that any of them were possible. Slowly, he had been transformed into a mental basket case. His half of our conversations had become so rattled and agitated that he often seemed to be babbling. Sometimes it worried me that he was going to mentally implode right in front of me. Sending him back to the action was truly a cruel and unusual punishment. Once again I analyzed the situation at hand and was glad that it was somebody else and not me. That seemed to be happening a lot to me lately.

To my mind, I had never been as nervous in Vietnam as that guy was going to be when he went back. But you couldn't tell that by looking at my hands. Not long after arriving in Japan, my fingernails would start returning to normal in appearance. At the moment, though, they were still a mess. I had been an inveterate nervous nail-biter since high school. With all of the things there were to be anxious about in Vietnam, I had been chewing my nails almost down to the first knuckle for the last few months. Now, with my jaw wired shut this wasn't possible, so they were getting better.

Late in the afternoon of my first day at the hospital, I noticed from the doorway of my fourth-floor room that most of the patients and staff were looking out of the windows at the streets below. Young Japanese protesters, about four hundred in number, were marching around and around the medical complex outside of the closed gates, circling us like a school of barracuda. It was fascinating. I hadn't yet witnessed an antiwar demonstration. Down below, protest songs by Joan Baez were blared at us on a loudspeaker. As they marched, they chanted various well-known antiwar slogans. The most benign one was "One, two, three, four, we don't want your lousy war." A more melodious one they sort of sang rather than just chanted: "One, two, three, four, what are we fighting for? Five, six, seven, eight, we don't give a damn, we ain't going to Vietnam." The most hateful was "Hey, hey, LBJ, how many babies did you kill today?" Anti-American, antiwar protests and riots were common here and there all around the world in 1967, not just in America. This was one of them.

What the protestors couldn't see was the two hundred or so

Japanese riot police waiting in a walled-off courtyard. They wore shiny black helmets and were practicing karate kicks and judo flips. Some were twirling four- to five-foot-long wooden dowels about as thick as an American cop's billy club. They practiced whacking and thumping each other.

Each time the group of protesters passed by the main gate, they swarmed forward and tried to push it open but couldn't. After the police tolerated this activity for some time, an hour or two, the gates were opened and the protesters poured in, running wildly in all directions. Simultaneously, the riot police raced out to confront them. What a spectacle—six hundred people brawling in front of the hospital, and we had ringside seats. The black helmets won the day. They quickly kicked ass and had the protesters running back out the gates. We all clapped and cheered. Everyone was laughing and having a good time.

After I got settled in, the first order of business was a medical exam. Two oral surgeons checked me over, using words that I didn't understand, such as "necrotic" and "aphasia," to discuss my condition. Then they spoke to me in English about good news and bad news.

The good news was that my face couldn't be repaired quickly, so my tour of duty in Vietnam was over. HALLE-LUJAH! I had survived. They would soon forward me to Letterman Army Hospital in San Francisco. The picture was now clarified to the point where I could write home to tell my parents what had happened to me. The bad news was that my mandible, or lower jaw, was infected and I had to have another surgery right away to remove some dead tissue and bone chips.

The next morning found me on a gurney in the pre-op area with an IV in my arm. The room had a set of swinging doors at each end, but no windows. There was another gurney present, occupied by an overly muscled black man who was growling, sweating profusely, and struggling to free himself from the leather restraints that confined him. His right elbow knocked over a nearby bed stand and sent a container of ice chips dancing across the terrazzo floor in all directions. The bright overhead lights made them sparkle like diamonds. The guy appeared to be a raving lunatic.

A tall, svelte female in plain green scrubs and a mask came in to announce that she had a shot to relax me. Her eyes were also green, iridescent green, and just visible above the mask. She had on too much makeup, considering the situation, but still was exceedingly pretty. After checking the name on my wristband, she shot a syringe full of clear liquid into my IV tubing. Then she instructed me to take a nap. When I asked about the guy in the other bed, she said he had rabies. That didn't seem right to me. Before I could question her further, she departed without even telling me her name.

Soon after she left, I started getting high from the opiates she had injected into my arm and began to nod off. After the long mental torment of trying to survive in a combat zone, the sensation of being stoned and feeling relaxed was so wonderful that the last thing I wanted to do was fall asleep. It had been a while since I had felt this secure and comfortable. Across the room on a small table, there was a paperback book, which I retrieved to help me stay awake. It was *Go Tell It on the Mountain* by James Baldwin. I read the first line.

"Everyone had always said that John would be a preacher when he grew up, just like his father."

The sentence was slow and time-consuming, but enjoyable. It didn't bother me that the psycho in the other bed was now chewing through his restraints. He stared intently at his work. Occasionally, I became a momentary distraction from his bondage and he would look up trying to pierce me with his eyes while growling out loud. It was the best of times and I was going to enjoy myself. I read on.

"Everyone had always said that John would be a preacher when he grew up, just like his father."

By now it didn't matter what my face looked like or where the rest of the platoon was at the moment. All was right with the world. It was easy to understand why kids in the ghetto used this stuff.

Later Green Eyes reappeared and my gurney took flight toward the operating room. She chided me for not trying to snooze a little. I didn't care. Everything was swell, like in Neverland. My war was over, I had lived, my wounds were a small price to pay, the rabies guy hadn't gotten me, and I was going home. It couldn't get much better than this. I read on.

"Everyone had always said that John would be a preacher when he grew up, just like his father."

POSTSCRIPT

ED BURKE retired from the military as a colonel. I sometimes still call him captain when we meet because that was the most important rank he ever held as far as I was concerned. He is employed as the executive director of the Society of the First Infantry Division and manages a wide variety of services and activities for the 1st Infantry Division veterans.

ART CORDOVA works for the Department of Disability Services in Albuquerque. Ironically, some of his clients are Vietnam veterans. Art is active in the community and has been quite successful coaching Pop Warner football. We see each other at reunions and keep in touch by phone between gatherings.

MANCIL FAIRMAN finished his career in the military and retired in Tennessee. When I first heard that he was at one of our reunions, fear struck my heart. I was afraid that he would either slug me or make me do push-ups in front of everyone. He turned out to be the most pleasant person imaginable. He claimed that he hadn't disliked me more than any of the others and that his memories of me were, in fact, those of an "okay" soldier. From him, that was high praise. He's about as close to being a real American hero as anyone I'll ever meet.

STANLEY GILBERT was shot and killed on October 17, 1967, during a battle near a place called Ong Thanh. Some years later, I managed to make contact with his family in Minnesota and sent them several enlarged photographs of Stan, including the one of the two of us on the back of that tank, Barfly, that we helped save from the snipers. To this day, Stan's family remains deeply saddened by his death. His brother tells me that they still get gloomy around the anniversary as well as over Memorial Day weekend.

DAN HUISH was severely disabled in the crash of a helicopter that was shot down. He now lives in Huntington Beach, California, and seems to be friendly and in good spirits at the reunions he attends.

LIEUTENANT JUDSON hasn't been at any reunion I've attended. Others tell me that when the army was downsized after Vietnam he was forced to take a reduction in rank from officer to enlisted man to stay in the service. Later he became a preacher man in Alabama.

FRED KIRKPATRICK lives in Ohio, where he has been married for more than twenty years and has two daughters. After finishing one career as a purchasing agent, Fred has changed directions and is launching a second as a private investigator. He is the driving force behind all the battalion reunions and does an outstanding job of it. He also designed and runs the battalion website. I always enjoy his company and our long conversations when we get together.

RONALD MENENDEZ and I crossed paths once in the St. Louis airport. He told me that he wanted to learn more about what happened when he was in Vietnam. He said that he has almost no memories of his time with the Black Lions. He didn't say if he was still using drugs and I was afraid to ask.

BILLY MURPHY completed a career with the army and now lives in Missouri. After his tour of duty as a foot soldier with the Black Lions, he attended flight school and returned to Vietnam as a helicopter pilot. He told me that he got shot at much more as a pilot than he ever did as a foot soldier.

BOB REEVES almost bought the farm a couple times during the rocket attacks at Lai Khe after I left. In one close call, when the rockets started falling, he had to dive into a ditch from a moving jeep to survive. He and I are still close friends and see each other often. He lives in Phoenix, has been married for thirty-some years, and works as an executive in the banking industry.

CHRIS RONNAU, the author, was sent to Letterman Army Hospital in San Francisco. There I received excellent medical care, which included half a dozen surgeries. The left side of my jaw was rebuilt using one of my ribs. After being discharged, I went back to college, then to medical school, and have practiced emergency medicine for many years. I'm divorced with three wonderful children in their twenties. A few years ago, the middle child asked, "Dad, why don't you write a book about your experiences in Vietnam for us to read someday so we'll know what you did over there?"

JOHN SIEVERING also lives in Ohio where he works as an executive for a motorcycle company. He comes to some of the reunions, the ones that are close enough that he can ride his motorcycle to get there.

MARK SMITH received a battlefield commission and became an officer. He stayed in the army and eventually returned for more duty in Vietnam. During a battle at Loc Ninh in 1972, he was shot several times and taken prisoner. After being held captive in a hole in the ground for almost a year at a POW camp inside Cambodia, he was released when the war ended and the American prisoners were freed. He now works as a military advisor for the government of Thailand and always has a lot of good stories to tell at our meetings.

I don't know much else about the others mentioned in this book except that none of their names are etched on the wall of the Vietnam Memorial in Washington, D.C. They made it home alive.

Gashed with honorable scars
Low in glory's lap they lie
Though they fell, they fell like stars
Streaming splendor through the sky

CIVIL WAR MEMORIAL
Edenton, N.C.

Acknowledgments

Many thanks are owed to my dear friend Margaret Sheppard. The former *St. Louis Globe Democrat* reporter kindly helped edit this text. She did not quit in disgust when she discovered that I had referred to a German shepherd in the canine corps as a German Sheppard. Her work helped transformed this book from a sloppy mess to a passable effort. I am truly grateful for her assistance.

Ches Schnieder also deserves my gratitude. He has already published a book about his own tour of duty in Vietnam entitled *From Classrooms to Claymores*, so he knows how much work a book requires. His encouragement was appreciated, as were his skills at editing and formatting, which he freely shared with me.

Last, thanks go to Larry Poitevin, an English teacher and lifelong friend. I needed his advice and counsel. He spent countless hours helping me with all aspects of the text. His assistance was invaluable in helping me mold and polish this manuscript into its final form.